WATCH THE
THRONE

First published by Pitch Publishing, 2021

Pitch Publishing
A2 Yeoman Gate
Yeoman Way
Worthing
Sussex
BN13 3QZ
www.pitchpublishing.co.uk
info@pitchpublishing.co.uk

A CIP catalogue record is available for this book from the British Library.

ISBN 978 1 78531 770 5

Typesetting and origination by Pitch Publishing

Printed and bound in India by Replika Press Pvt. Ltd.

LUKE WILLIAMS

WATCH THE THRONE

THE TACTICS BEHIND THE PREMIER LEAGUE'S EUROPEAN CHAMPIONS

pitch

Contents

Part 5: Liverpool 2018/19

Acknowledgements

I know that it is a cliché, but this book would not have come into fruition without the help and dedication of some very important people.

Firstly, thank you to my family. Thank you to my father, Ben, for sharing all of football's highs and lows with me (and giving me my first 'coaching' role as his assistant manager when I was ten!) and for his proofreading, but also for being an inspirational role model every single day. Thank you to my mother, Nia, for her undying love and support and of course for her underrated levels of football wisdom! She is the strongest person that I know. Thank you to my brother, Josh, for being the person who I learned to love playing football with, and with whom I have also shared some wonderful match-going experiences.

Thank you to my girlfriend, Gemma, who also helped proofread this book. But more than that, she is a daily source of inspiration for me and I will always cherish her support. My thanks also go to Carole and Steve Brough for their support and for letting me spend hours on end analysing these matches in their study!

Of course, I am extremely grateful to Paul Camillin, Jane Camillin and Graham Hales from Pitch Publishing for their roles in bringing this book to life. Also, thank you to Duncan Olner from Olner Design for his brilliant work on the cover design.

Introduction

The UEFA Champions League is the most prestigious club competition in the world's most popular sport. Even during an era when the Beautiful Game has sometimes felt impurified by hyper-commercialisation and corporate interests, the Champions League has still blessed us with some of the greatest matches that we have ever seen – nights that have changed lives, inspired millions and granted legendary status to those on the winning side of history. Personally, I feel extremely privileged to be able to say that the Champions League has given me some of the best times of my life, visiting new places and sharing priceless experiences with those who share my unadulterated passion for football.

There are many people who excellently recall their European adventures, describing famous nights from the perspectives of those on the pitch or in the stands. I do not claim to be one of them. Instead, this book focusses on those who guided their teams to glory – those who formulated the game plans that gave us mere mortals the experiences that we will never forget. This book will analyse the matches that took Premier League teams and their managers to their Holy Grail, from Manchester United in 1998/99 to Liverpool in

2018/19, discussing the tactics that helped these teams to become the champions of Europe.

Some theoretical elements will be provided, but the beauty of talking tactics is that everything is open to individual interpretation. This is my take on how Ferguson, Benítez, Di Matteo and Klopp won European football's biggest prize and I simply hope that it inspires you to consider your own view from a tactical perspective too. I hope to add tactical context to the fixtures that made these managers legends of the continental game, celebrating the incredible level of detail required to win matches at the highest level.

The games took place across a 20-year period that saw notable changes to the sport we love, many of which these managers had to adapt to and embrace in order to achieve success. I sincerely hope that the tactics that took these managers to victory provide you with the same fascination that they do myself, and I hope that you will feel inspired to continue seeing a game through a more tactical lens in the future.

Part 1

Manchester United 1998/99

Manchester United dominated English football in the 1990s, winning four Premier League titles in six seasons. However, at the start of the 1998/99 campaign their position as England's standout side was under threat. While Blackburn Rovers' journey to the title in 1994/95 was anomalous, in 1997/98 Arsène Wenger guided Arsenal to a spectacular double that saw them beat United to the title by a single point before winning the FA Cup. It was a mightily impressive performance from the London outfit in Wenger's first full term in the job and the Frenchman was determined to sustain this success.

Alex Ferguson, manager of Manchester United since 1986, was under pressure to deliver a response and re-establish his team's domestic superiority. While this would be his initial priority, United supporters also hoped to see more from their side in European competition. After winning the UEFA Cup Winners' Cup in 1991, United had hoped to consistently challenge for honours on the continental stage but had so far fallen short in every season since. Between the 1991/92 and 1995/96 seasons they failed to survive in Europe beyond Christmas. In 1996/97 they harboured hopes of glory until they were beaten home and away by Borussia Dortmund in the semi-final stage of the Champions League, and in 1997/98 they fell to Monaco on away goals in the quarter-final.

In the summer of 1998 United spent over £27m on three major signings: defender Jaap Stam, midfielder Jesper Blomqvist and forward Dwight Yorke. The team received another boost as captain Roy Keane returned for the new season after spending the best part of a year out with a cruciate ligament injury. United's squad looked fresh and ready to pursue new heights in the 1998/99 campaign.

With the Champions League's expansion now requiring England's runners-up to navigate a qualifying round before entering the group stage, Ferguson's side defeated ŁKS Łódź 2-0 at Old Trafford before playing out a goalless draw in Poland a fortnight later. They then came through that season's 'Group of Death' unbeaten by drawing home and away with both Bayern Munich and Barcelona and brushing aside Brøndby of Denmark. In that season's format, the six group winners were joined in the quarter-final by the two best runners-up. United were the second-best runner-up. In contrast, Arsenal failed to make it through a group consisting of Dynamo Kyiv, Lens and Panathinaikos.

By March 1999 United were flying, unbeaten in all competitions for almost three months despite losing assistant manager Brian Kidd to Blackburn Rovers (he was initially replaced by Jimmy Ryan, then Steve McClaren). Every time they looked beaten in a match, they somehow survived – week after week. Hope was growing among supporters that a historic treble of the league, FA Cup and the Champions League was actually possible, something that would require ending United's 31-year wait for European club football's biggest prize.

Chapter 1

Quarter-final – Manchester United 3 Inter Milan 1 (aggregate)

First leg: Manchester United 2 Inter Milan 0, 3 March 1999

To progress beyond the quarter-final stage, Manchester United would have to do what so many teams across the continent struggled to do throughout the 1990s – defeat Italian opposition. Serie A was indisputably Europe's best league for the duration of this decade, emphasised by the fact that it had provided a finalist for every single European Cup/Champions League Final between 1992 and 1998. Furthermore, every UEFA Cup Final between 1990 and 1998 featured at least one Italian side. United's 1999 quarter-final opponents, Inter Milan, had won the UEFA Cup in 1998 with a brilliant 3-0 victory over compatriots Lazio. Although 1998/99 was proving to be a tough season for them domestically, their European form had not faltered and they attained the joint-highest points total in the group stage despite facing holders Real Madrid (who finished second and qualified as the best runner-up). For United, this was a huge test.

Not only was this quarter-final a meeting between two giant clubs aiming for European glory, it was also the first meeting between David Beckham and Diego Simeone since the latter feigned injury to get the former sent off during a round-of-16 clash between England and Argentina at the 1998 FIFA World Cup. Beckham had spent the season receiving abuse at away grounds across England and United were keen to avoid discussing the issue before their encounter with Inter, but Simeone revelled in the controversy and spent the day before the first leg speaking freely about how he had cheated to get Beckham red-carded. In response, Ferguson calmly stated that United would do their talking on the pitch because 'the referee is there to sort out Simeone on the field'. This was good management from Ferguson, whose words put pressure on the game's chief official (Hellmut Krug of Germany) to be wary of Simeone and not get sucked into making a rash decision that could harm the Mancunian outfit.

The team selections, shown by *Figure 1*, were as follows:

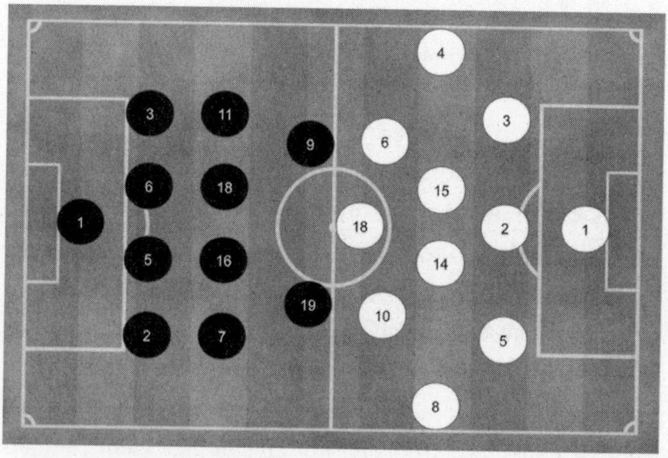

FIGURE 1

Manchester United (1-4-4-2): 1. Schmeichel; 2. G. Neville, 5. Johnsen, 6. Stam, 3. Irwin; 7. Beckham, 16. Keane (captain), 18. Scholes, 11. Giggs; 19. Yorke, 9. Cole.

Substitutes: 17. van der Gouw, 8. Butt, 12. P. Neville, 15. Blomqvist, 20. Solskjær, 21. Berg, 30. Brown.

Head coach: Alex Ferguson CBE.

Inter Milan (1-3-4-2-1): 1. Pagliuca; 3. Colonnese, 2. Bergomi (captain), 5. Galante; 4. Zanetti, 15. Cauet, 14. Simeone, 8. Winter; 6. Djorkaeff, 10. Baggio; 18. Zamorano.

Substitutes: 22. Frey, 11. Ventola, 13. Zé Elias, 16. West, 21. Pirlo, 20. Gilberto, 25. Milanese.

Head coach: Mircea Lucescu.

United lined up in their usual style – a well-balanced 1-4-4-2 with solidity at the back, energy in midfield, quality on the wings and an excellent strike partnership leading the line. Goalkeeper Peter Schmeichel, in his last season for the club, was an excellent shot-stopper thanks to techniques that he had developed by playing handball in his youth. Right-back Gary Neville – one of several homegrown graduates from the United academy's famed Class of '92 – was a mature, reliable player who combined his defensive ability with simple ball-playing decisions that helped his side retain possession. Jaap Stam was a magnificent centre-back who would step out of the back line to intercept passes and engage with opponents while his partner, Ronny Johnsen at the start of this match, would cover behind to protect the space that Stam vacated. Left-back Denis Irwin was a versatile and hard-working defender who earned plaudits for his understated levels of consistency. In central midfield, Roy Keane and Paul Scholes complemented each other wonderfully to supply both industry and quality in equal measure. On the right wing, David Beckham possessed an immense crossing and passing ability, and on the left Ryan Giggs was the side's key dribbler. Last but by no means least, the forward line of Dwight Yorke and Andy Cole had everything – power, intelligence, technique and, most importantly, goals.

Despite being managed by a Romanian, Inter Milan's setup was quintessentially Italian. In goal, Gianluca Pagliuca was a fantastic shot-stopper, although he was sometimes susceptible to crosses and operated best behind centre-backs who could dominate in the air. The right and left centre-backs were strict man-markers tasked with sticking tight to opposition strikers, with the third central defender sweeping up behind them. This would change if a striker moved deep and central though – if this happened then the central defender, Bergomi, would follow the relevant striker so that the side centre-backs could retain a solid shape in anticipation of through balls. In this match, Francesco Colonnese was Andy Cole's primary man-marker and Fabio Galante was Dwight Yorke's.

The wing-backs Javier Zanetti and Aaron Winter were technically gifted, but only encouraged to venture high up the pitch if Inter needed goals (Winter was a midfielder playing out wide here in the absence of injured defenders). The central midfielders, Benoît Cauet and Diego Simeone, were hard-working players in functional roles, prioritising discipline over individual expression. In the absence of superstar forward Ronaldo, Inter employed two *trequartisti* – the extremely talented pairing of Youri Djorkaeff and Roberto Baggio – with ex-Real Madrid star Iván Zamorano leading the line. A key feature of Italian football in the 1990s, a *trequartista* operated between the lines of midfield and attack with the freedom to explore and exploit space across the pitch as their side's primary creative force. There was little onus on them to contribute defensively; hence it was important for the defensive and midfield lines to play with vitality and discipline.

The Old Trafford pitch was in poor condition after several days of persistent rain in Manchester, although the atmosphere inside the ground remained fiery and expectant. There was a real hope that this United team was finally capable of going a step further on the continent than it had done in recent years.

United had developed an unhealthy habit of conceding early goals in European matches and Inter tried to start the game with a high tempo, hoping to seek out and then capitalise on any early Mancunian nerves. There were extremely loud boos for Simeone every time he touched the ball – they would persist all night.

Inter took a calculated risk by looking to start quickly away from home and it backfired. It was a struggle for them to keep hold of the ball in the opening stages. They took two long goal kicks in the first few minutes that only reached the midfield area, where United won the initial aerial challenge, with either Yorke and Cole in the centre or Beckham and Giggs on the wings able to aggressively challenge for the second balls and ensure the easy regaining of possession. By battling for first and second balls at a high intensity, United were being asked to do nothing different to what was expected of them in the opening exchanges of a typical domestic match.

It was from a goal kick that United punished Inter's risk and opened the scoring in the sixth minute. Pagliuca booted his clearance into midfield, where United won the first challenge and Giggs dribbled the loose ball away and into space down the left, before being closed down and winning a throw-in. Irwin threw short to Scholes, who passed short to his midfielder partner Keane. As this was happening, Yorke moved deeper to create a passing option between Inter's midfield and defensive lines and Bergomi stepped out to follow him through the middle. Keane tried a through pass to Yorke but Bergomi got a toe on it, looping the ball up into the air, which encouraged Winter to inexplicably charge inwards to try and make a clearance. Despite Winter's challenge, Yorke won the ball in the air and headed it onwards for Beckham to meet it on the right-hand side of the Inter penalty area. Galante moved out to try and press Beckham in Winter's absence but had too much ground to cover. The English winger produced a chipped cross to the centre of the six-yard box for Yorke to run on to and head United in front.

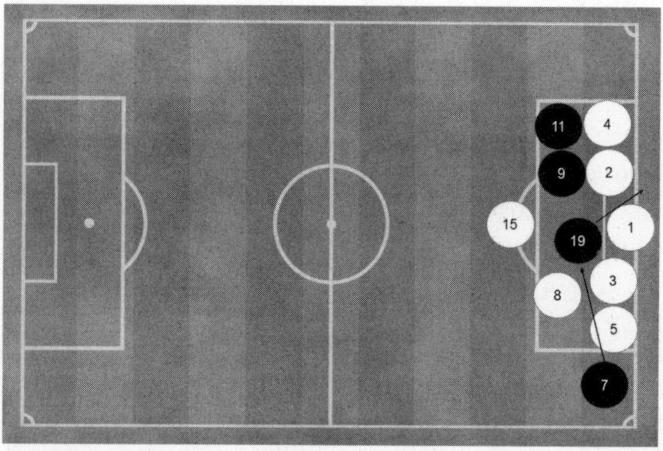

FIGURE 2

Colonnese, who had been marking Andy Cole, had left him alone to cover Galante and zonally mark the ball-side area of the box ready for Beckham's cross, so Bergomi rushed back to try and mark Cole instead. Showing his intelligence, Cole then drifted to the back post and took the recovering Bergomi with him, leaving Yorke free to attack the ball in the centre. *Figure 2* shows Beckham's cross and Yorke's header, with the arrows illustrating the path of the ball. Notice how outnumbered United were in the penalty area, Beckham's superb cross took maths out of the equation by landing right on Yorke's head.

Despite the poor defending from the visitors that aided the goal, it was an example of several factors that made United such an effective team. Ryan Giggs used his dribbling ability to force the opposing team backwards after the initial battle for the ball in midfield. Scholes and Keane showed their ability to attract opposition midfielders closer (done here via Scholes's short pass) before looking to accelerate proceedings and progress the ball forward (via Keane's through ball). Yorke used his power to pull defenders around and beat them in the air before bursting forward to meet a perfect Beckham delivery in space created by Cole's clever movement.

This was a dream start for Ferguson's men, who instead of conceding an early goal in a European tie had scored one themselves. There was ecstasy in the stands, and even the stewards behind the goal in the East Stand celebrated Yorke's header wildly.

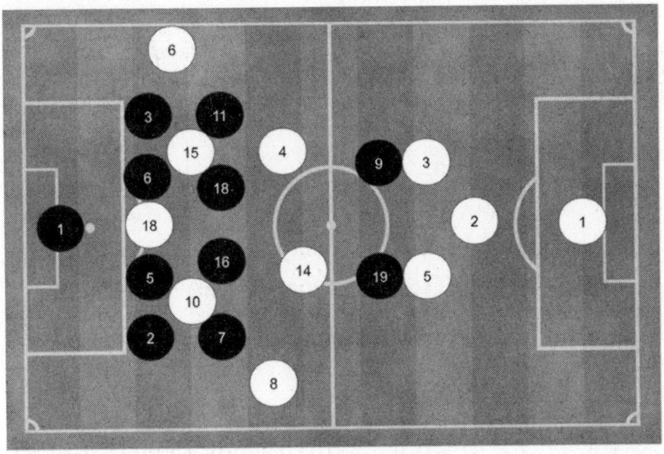

FIGURE 3

As Inter found their feet in the aftermath of conceding, their system became clearer. *Figure 3* illustrates their standard formation when establishing possession in United's half. Zanetti looked to move inside from the right and assumed a more central position in front of United's midfield line alongside Simeone, with Cauet looking for space either between or behind United's midfielders. In response to this, Djorkaeff would move to the right and look for space in wide areas. If he received the ball out wide, he would try to dribble inside towards United's defence, looking to take men on or find clever through passes. If Inter moved the ball across to the left side, Baggio would occasionally move wider to assist Winter who, as previously mentioned, would refrain from venturing too far forward unless Baggio needed someone to make a run in front of him.

The main purpose of the movements shown in *Figure 3* was to try and create a central overload – simply, when Inter had the ball they wanted more players in central areas than United had. Inter sought to overload Keane and Scholes with a central four v two (Zanetti and Simeone in front of them, Cauet and Baggio behind them).

To defend against this attempted overload, United were happy to sit deep and retain two solid lines of four in front of Schmeichel. Wingers Beckham and Giggs made sure to track back and form a narrow midfield line either side of Keane and Scholes, so the hypothetical four v two became a four v four. Staying horizontally compact meant that the midfield could limit the space for passes into Cauet and Baggio from Zanetti and Simeone. This meant that the home side conceded space in wide areas, but they were able to cope with this too.

If Djorkaeff dribbled inwards from the right, he dribbled towards left-back Irwin, who was naturally right-footed and was therefore content to see his opponent attack his stronger side rather than go outside him and make him defend with his left foot. If Baggio dribbled inwards from the left, he did so towards United's compact shape, with the home side knowing that Baggio lacked the pace to run wide and try to isolate Gary Neville.

The problem for United came on transition when they won possession because the gap between their midfield and their strikers was too large, a risk teams run when defending deep. This made it difficult to adequately perform quick forward passes to Yorke and Cole once United won the ball back because Zanetti and Simeone were able to sweep up in front of them. If the ball did reach its intended target, it often took too long for the home midfield to advance forward and support their strikers, who were outnumbered themselves by Inter's three centre-backs.

Theoretically, Inter's system was far more sophisticated than the tactics that Ferguson was used to facing at domestic level. Unwavering defensive discipline was needed from his players, something that he did not always get with his 1998/99 side despite the success that was to come. With regards to United's tactics when in possession of the ball, simplicity was key. The full-backs would play simple balls either inside to Keane and Scholes or wide to Beckham and Giggs, who would use their creative abilities to accelerate and progress play. Irwin was capable of supporting attacks but would rarely overlap, leaving the wide left area to the left-footed Giggs and giving him room to isolate and dribble against opponents. Alternatively, he could play long channel balls down the left for a striker to chase with Giggs in support. On the right, Neville would often stay deep but was capable of overlapping Beckham if necessary. When a match was in the balance, one central midfielder would push forward and the other would sit back behind the ball to provide cover. The strikers were tasked with both holding the ball up with their back to goal and running to chase long passes into wider areas, depending on specific match situations.

Inter began to establish more periods of possession than United and had largely been in control of the tempo and direction of the game since going behind, as the hosts continued to struggle to create anything meaningful from transitions. The crowd kept on encouraging the home team, but there was a growing sense of tension, illustrated on the pitch by Schmeichel kicking two passes out of play when only under a small amount of pressure. For all their possession, Inter were still struggling to create clear-cut chances and the United back four was defending well. Stam was having a very good half, reading play and timing tackles expertly. So much of a team's success in elite European football rests on its ability to survive the opponent's periods of positive momentum, and the solidity of United's defence gave them an ability to safely negotiate these periods of Inter possession in a way that lesser teams would have found difficult to do. No team, however great they are, dominates the entirety of a Champions League knockout tie. Ferguson now had a team capable of sufficiently limiting an opponent's strengths at this level, giving the attacking players a platform to build from once chances arose. It was not in United's nature to defend first and attack second – they had conceded 11 goals in the group stage – but it was a necessary approach for long spells in this match.

As the tension increased, so did the levels of aggression being shown on the pitch. Keane and Zamorano both received yellow cards after a confrontation with each other – cheap bookings to receive in such an enormous fixture.

Beckham began to drop deeper when his team had possession and instead of looking central for Yorke, he tried to play long crosses to Cole – one of which resulted in a significant chance. Despite finding it difficult to dominate the game, Beckham's extensive passing and crossing range made him dangerous from anywhere and, by coming deeper, he gave himself more space to showcase his talent. These deeper movements also brought Winter further forward from his slot as Inter's left wing-back so that he could try and close Beckham down, which opened space down this side of Inter's three centre-backs. Beckham could then play wide passes for Yorke, who could engage in a wide one v one battle, which proved more effective for United than simply knocking the ball into central areas where Inter enjoyed their overload.

This led to United's second goal, as they transitioned with a direct channel ball to Yorke, who received it and switched play to Irwin, successfully establishing possession in Inter's half. Irwin played the ball back inside with a short pass to Scholes, who received on the back foot, opened out and fed the now inward-moving Yorke centrally with his back to goal. Yorke laid the ball back to Keane and the Irishman passed square to Neville. Neville shifted the ball on to Beckham, wide on the touchline, who crossed brilliantly to the centre of the six-yard box again for Yorke to double the Red Devils' lead. As the cross came over towards Yorke, he checked his run slightly so that he created some space between himself and Galante and earned the freedom to jump up unopposed and meet the ball. Pagliuca showed his vulnerability to crosses with what was a rather half-hearted attempt in trying to deal with Beckham's delivery. Beckham, under so much media scrutiny, let his football do the talking via two superb assists.

After struggling to impose themselves on large periods of the half, United took ownership of the key moments and scored two quality goals to give themselves firm control of the tie. Old Trafford was in dreamland and suddenly it was difficult to envision Inter getting back into the quarter-final, but not improbable. United had raced into a 2-0 first-half lead against Barcelona in September 1998 only to concede three times and draw 3-3. Protecting the existing lead and keeping a clean sheet against Inter would signify that progress had been made at this level, even in comparison to just a few months beforehand.

Half-time – Manchester United 2 Inter Milan 0

United made a substitution at the interval, replacing Ronny Johnsen with Henning Berg in a like-for-like swap. They started the second half positively, buoyed by their second goal. This momentum was halted briefly when Scholes received a yellow card for an accumulation of fouls. Both central midfielders were now on a booking and were unable to defend with the same bite and tenacity shown in the first half. Inter then offered a reminder of their danger when Schmeichel was forced into making a brilliant save to deny a close-range header from Zamorano, who was free at the back post after Djorkaeff had made an inward run to drag Irwin inside. This was an example of how the Dane used handball as inspiration for his goalkeeping techniques, as he made a starfish shape to become as imposing as possible and block the goal-bound header.

In addition to his two first-half assists, Beckham was contributing well defensively – tasked with both tracking left wing-back Winter and moving inside to press Simeone, who was looking to receive the ball with space between himself and United's midfield line in the hope that he could pull Keane or Scholes out of position to engage with him. While Beckham and Giggs are rightfully remembered as being very gifted on the ball, their willingness to work hard off it was also an important factor in their team's success. They worked hard to track back and retain a compact defensive shape to block off passes into wide areas, while also being able to move inside and defend against central overloads like Beckham was doing here. There was some added tenacity in Beckham's tackling on this occasion, with Simeone feeling the force of one or two feisty challenges that were met with delight from the Old Trafford crowd.

Zanetti continued to be more effective than Winter when Inter had possession, but the Argentine's involvement was leaving space for United to attack behind him with a combination of Giggs's dribbling and leftward movement from Cole and Yorke – one striker would drift wide to receive a pass while the other remained central to make a run into the box and Giggs would burst forward on the underlap. While United got some joy breaking into the space, they lacked end product and failed to create many meaningful opportunities to further increase their lead. By understanding Inter's use of Zanetti and how they could exploit it, United showed how they could tactically adapt in-game in a manner that they were rarely given credit for.

Baggio played more centrally in the second half, looking to receive in front of United's yellow-carded central midfield pairing and dribble at them in the hope of enticing them into committing more fouls. He was now more involved in proceedings and Inter improved. They thought they had scored a crucial away goal when Simeone, of all people, headed in from a corner, but the referee blew his whistle, citing a foul in the centre of the box. In truth, it was a very soft disallowance – but as you will discover in this book, there is little point in pretending that luck is not a factor in European success.

The visitors made their first substitution in the 68th minute, replacing the ineffective Zamorano with Nicola Ventola. Ventola was an exciting young striker, fast and energetic and always willing to make threatening runs into the space behind the opposition defence. He was tasked with doing exactly that, threatening the space behind United's centre-backs so that Inter could force them deeper and unsettle what had so far proven to be a compact and disciplined defensive shape. Without space between United's defence and midfield lines for them to operate in, it was difficult for the *trequartisti* to impact the match in dangerous areas.

A minute later, United introduced Nicky Butt in place of Scholes, so that they now had a central midfielder on the pitch who could defend without the restrictions of a yellow card hanging over his head. This was especially important considering that United were sitting deep against persistent Inter pressure, with the back four often in line with the semi-circle on the edge of the penalty area. When a team defends this deep, they must ensure that it is difficult to penetrate their lines centrally and Butt's introduction as a ball-winning midfielder helped in this regard.

Baggio had begun to lose effectiveness and was replaced by the young Andrea Pirlo in the 79th minute. Pirlo was deployed centrally, with Djorkaeff moving to both the left and the right to try and find space in which to operate. The Frenchman appeared to focus more on moving to his left, from where he could look to receive the ball and dribble inwards.

United restricted the visitors to precious few open opportunities, yet they almost lost their clean sheet when Ventola got down the side of Stam and used his pace to beat the Dutchman to a through pass. Schmeichel rushed out of his goal to meet Ventola but could only palm his shot into the path of the onrushing Colonnese, who had gambled and run forward to support the attack. Colonnese looked certain to score, but Henning Berg made a fantastic goal-line clearance to retain United's two-goal advantage. Whereas United had scored at both ends of the first half, Inter should have scored at both ends of the second period but were denied by two moments of individual defensive heroism. United won the big moments and, combined with better defending than they had previously produced in Europe, it won them the match.

After surviving this late scare, Ferguson's charges were content to keep possession until full time and see the game out, using Giggs to protect the ball by the corner flag. A lead of 2-0 was a perfectly acceptable one to take to Italy. Shutting out Inter was a milestone night in United's defensive development – it was their first clean sheet in a Champions League knockout match at home since March 1997. It should be noted that Ferguson had given the exhausted Schmeichel some time off in January to get some winter sun in Barbados, a masterstroke that saw the Dane come back fresh and ready for the challenges ahead. Schmeichel's starfish save against Zamorano was not just a brilliant stop, it was one of the most important of his career. Giving tired players winter holidays does not guarantee a return to form, but Ferguson showed his ability to manage big players to help them return to playing at the required level, even within such busy schedules. He had an awareness of the needs of his players – an important quality for any manager. In return, they delivered for him when it mattered most.

Full time – Manchester United 2 Inter Milan 0

United absorbed pressure brilliantly against an Inter Milan side that saw plenty of the ball but was rather blunt in attack. The scoreline could be explained easily; United managed to score with their two best chances, Inter failed to with theirs. Inter hoped to have Ronaldo fit for the return leg in a fortnight's time, a man who was capable of single-handedly turning the tie on its head. However, if the Red Devils could reproduce the good level of defending from the first leg then they were perfectly suited to playing on the counter-attack. Preventing an Inter away goal had put them in firm control of the tie and they fancied their chances of progression.

Second leg: Inter Milan 1 Manchester United 1
17 March 1999

Dreaming of a treble, United followed up their first-leg victory with a 2-0 FA Cup quarter-final replay triumph against Chelsea after the original match was drawn 0-0. Remarkably, they had kept three clean sheets in three knockout matches in the space of seven days. As has been previously mentioned, it was not always in their nature to defend first and attack second, but in a make-or-break week for their pursuit of a treble they had kept clean sheets when the pressure was on. Newcastle United were then beaten 2-1 in the league to keep the Red Devils at the top of the table. In stark contrast, Inter dropped league points against Bari and AC Milan in addition to being knocked out of the Coppa Italia by Parma. Struggling in the league and out of the cup, Inter only had Europe to focus on and the pressure was on for them to salvage something from an otherwise disappointing campaign.

Both sides made changes for the second leg, as shown by *Figure 4*.

Manchester United (1-4-4-2): 1. Schmeichel; 2. G. Neville, 21. Berg, 6. Stam, 3. Irwin; 7. Beckham, 16. Keane (captain), 5. Johnsen, 11. Giggs; 19. Yorke, 9. Cole.

Substitutes: 17. van der Gouw, 10. Sheringham, 12. P. Neville, 15. Blomqvist, 18. Scholes, 20. Solskjær, 30. Brown.

Head coach: Alex Ferguson CBE.

Inter Milan (1-3-4-1-2): 1. Pagliuca; 3. Colonnese, 2. Bergomi (captain), 16. West; 4. Zanetti, 15. Cauet, 14. Simeone,

24. Silvestre; 10. Baggio; 18. Zamorano, 9. Ronaldo.

Substitutes: 22. Frey, 5. Galante, 6. Djorkaeff, 8. Winter, 11. Ventola, 13. Zé Elias, 17. Moriero.

Head coach: Mircea Lucescu.

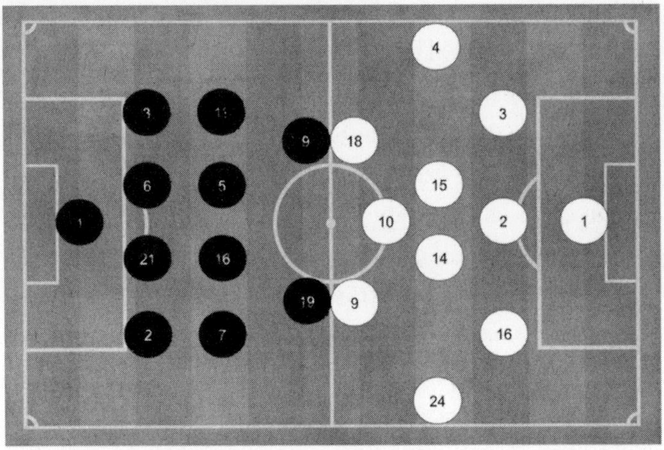

FIGURE 4

Mircea Lucescu's contract at Inter was a short-term deal that expired at the end of the season. This was his one chance to win the Champions League with the club and, with that in mind, he brought Brazilian superstar Ronaldo back for the second leg. Ronaldo, the FIFA World Player of the Year in 1996 and 1997, was being plagued by injuries and there were serious doubts over his fitness levels going into this match. Even with a lack of sharpness, he still carried a threat that United needed to be very wary of. At left wing-back, Mikaël Silvestre replaced Winter. Silvestre was fast and energetic, but most importantly he was naturally left-footed and would provide more balance than Winter had done at Old Trafford. Nigerian international Taribo West came into the side at centre-back in place of Galante.

Anticipating the return of Ronaldo, Ferguson opted for a more defensive-minded central midfield partnership. Johnsen took Scholes's place and Berg came in from the start as the right-sided centre-back. Scholes and Keane were both one yellow card away from a suspension, so bringing in somebody without that jeopardy hanging over them made sense for a game that would undoubtedly require a lot of defending in central areas.

The visitors were met with an intense atmosphere inside the Giuseppe Meazza Stadium, beginning in the warm-up when oranges were thrown down from the stands in the direction of the bemused players. Not in the mood for niceties, Roy Keane conducted the pre-match handshakes like a man possessed, storming straight past Ronaldo and Simeone without acknowledging them as the pair bent down to adjust their socks.

As had been the case at Old Trafford, Inter Milan wasted some early goal kicks by kicking into midfield, where United easily won possession. This time, the Inter players were more compact in anticipation for the kicks, but they just did not challenge for them with the same desire as their opponents. Ryan Giggs won two headers in the opening minutes of the match while Zanetti stood and watched him unchallenged. It was quite absurd viewing, but it showed that tactics can always be undone by a lack of application if players do not win their necessary individual battles.

The personnel changes saw Inter change their in-possession approach from the first match. Ronaldo and Baggio rotated the responsibility of partnering Zamorano, with the other moving wide to the left. Silvestre had the energy to overlap on occasion, but he often stayed deep to leave space ahead of him for the Ronaldo/Baggio rotation to take place. Zanetti still tucked inside, but was not quite as central as he had been in the first leg. This allowed space for both Cauet and Simeone to operate in front of United's midfield line, rather than having Cauet push forward. Keeping Cauet deeper left room, in theory, between United's defence and midfield for Baggio and Ronaldo to try and exploit, with Zamorano looking to attack Stam's side to occupy the big Dutchman.

The Milanese used the 'third man' concept to try and get Ronaldo or Baggio on the ball in threatening positions. In football, the third player is simply an unmarked player who is free and able to receive a ball. They are the third player because the original ball-carrier passes to another team-mate for them to give the ball to the third player, instead of just playing one direct pass. A basic example of this is available in *Figure 5*, which shows the following:

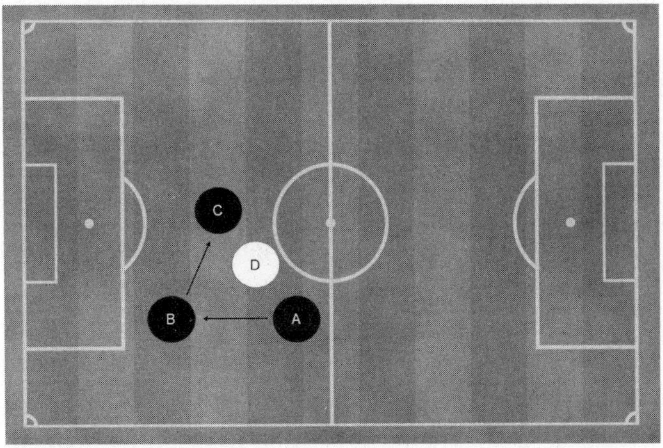

FIGURE 5

Player A has the ball and wants to pass to Player C, but a defender – Player D – is blocking the pass. Therefore, Player A passes to Player B, who in turn then passes to Player C. It is a simple concept, but it can be extremely effective if performed well.

Figure 6 is an example of Inter implementing the 'third man' idea, with Ronaldo acting as the third player in this

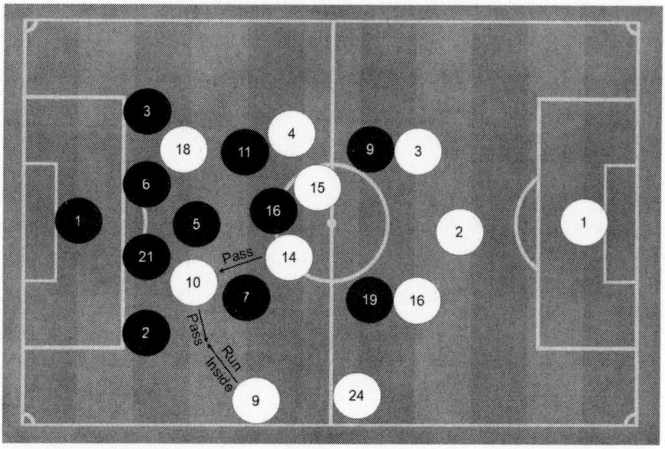

FIGURE 6

instance. As Simeone begins to perform the action of passing forward to Baggio, Ronaldo bursts infield. Baggio, with his back to goal, lays the ball off into the path of Ronaldo, who is now moving inwards at speed against the United defensive line. Third-man combinations rely on good timing, something that quality players are of course capable of producing. If Ronaldo was to come inside too early, he would have less space in which to run at United's defence. If he arrived too late, Baggio would have to hold on to the ball until it was an appropriate time to pass, which would slow the move down. The passes performed by Simeone and Baggio needed to be timed so that Ronaldo received the ball at the right moment in relation to his run. When the combination was performed well, as it was done here, it could threaten a United defence that could not afford any lapses in concentration.

Of course, it was important for United to once again be compact when defending. They remained vertically compact by reducing the space between their defence and midfield lines, and horizontally compact by limiting the space between

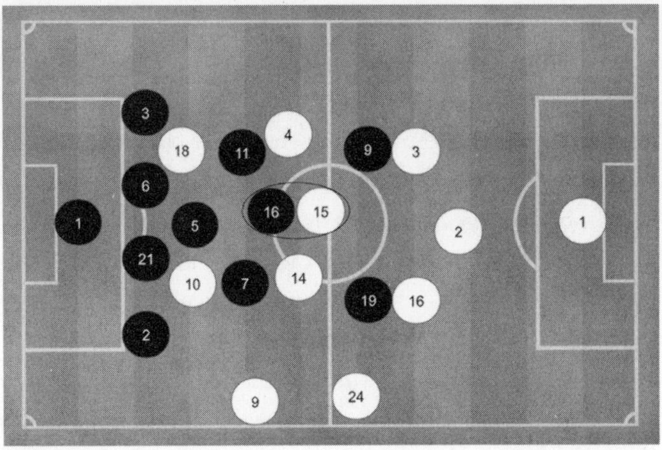

FIGURE 7

individual members of those lines. *Figure 7* shows both their vertical and horizontal compactness in action. Not only is the gap between their defence and midfield lines minimal, but the members of those two lines are close together, often no more than ten yards apart. *Figure 7* also shows how United tended to adopt a diamond shape in midfield when they initially conceded possession to Inter in central areas. The nearest central midfielder to the ball would close down the Inter ball-carrier (circled), with the other central midfielder staying behind to cover. Beckham and Giggs would tuck inside to ensure that the pressing central midfielder left no space behind them that could be exploited – retaining the midfield's horizontal compactness. This made it extremely difficult for Inter to attack centrally. If United's midfield line was broken, they would retreat deeper into a standard line of four. They were clearly disciplined and well-drilled.

The hosts had a strong penalty appeal turned down in the 16th minute when Schmeichel took down Zamorano when the pair were one v one in the penalty area. The referee waved the claims away, perhaps because of Ferguson's pre-match comments regarding Inter's reputation for diving and looking for fouls. Regardless, it was a stroke of good fortune for United, who had another scare when Henning Berg produced a superb hook off the line to clear a dangerous cross from Zanetti. The Argentine wing-back then crashed a shot from the edge of the area against the post after the away team had failed to sufficiently clear a corner kick. These three incidences were Inter's standout moments of the half as they struggled to play through United.

Finding it difficult to trouble their opponents, Ronaldo and Baggio changed their attacking movements. Ronaldo began to drop deeper and more central, which United reacted to by bringing Beckham in even narrower when out of possession. This created a central three v three. Ronaldo would then look to receive and then lay the ball off to a central midfielder before moving out to his left, and taking Beckham wider with him to try and create space for Baggio to move into. Berg would move out of the back line to follow Baggio and vacate space that Ronaldo could look to attack. However, Ferguson's men remained diligent and disciplined and retained their vertical and horizontal compactness. When Berg stepped out with Baggio, Neville made sure to move narrower to cover the space and Beckham kept pace with an admittedly half-fit Ronaldo. Keane and Johnsen did not get overly attracted to the ball and prioritised blocking central passes rather than pressing too high.

Giggs was looking threatening, but in a different way to in the first leg. When Zanetti was defending against him, he was reluctant to get too tight in one v one situations in case he was dribbled past. This often prevented Giggs from dribbling beyond his rival, but it gave him room to get his head up and play early crosses that Zanetti could do nothing about. Inter were able to address this situation, though – Taribo West was doing a better of job of marking Yorke than Galante managed in Manchester and United's front pair was nullified well in the first half.

Much to the delight of the away end, Diego Simeone was substituted off in the 32nd minute after failing to recover from an ankle injury that he picked up early in the game. His replacement, Zé Elias, was an energetic left-sided central midfielder. There was still time for Inter to turn the tie around, but in contrast to the previous summer it was Beckham's turn to see Simeone exit proceedings prematurely.

Both Bergomi and Johnsen picked up yellow cards as United comfortably navigated their way to half-time. They were lucky not to concede a penalty, but they had successfully limited Inter to only two shots on target and that deserved credit. Ronaldo had offered little more than the occasional quality touch and it remained to be seen how long he would stay on the pitch.

Half-time – Inter Milan 0 Manchester United 0

With only 45 minutes left to save the tie, Inter started the second half with a high tempo and committed both wing-backs higher than they had done in the first period. This left space for United to play long channel balls on transition, where Beckham and Giggs would look to receive and play a cross into Yorke and Cole. Whereas one central midfielder often broke forward and supported attacks in the first half, Keane and Johnsen were now more cautious and stayed behind the ball. These counter-attacks were not amounting to anything due to an uncharacteristic lack of quality on the crosses, but as long as United counter-attacks were happening it meant that Inter were not scoring and that was what mattered now.

Baggio was now Inter's sole *trequartista*, with Ronaldo up front alongside Zamorano, focussing on being an option for through balls rather than dropping deep to receive himself. He latched on to one brilliant through ball from Baggio, breaking free of Berg after making a run across the box while Zamorano sprinted in the opposite direction to confuse the United defence, but he shot straight at Schmeichel. It was a chance that should have been converted and it was becoming increasingly apparent that this was not going to be Ronaldo's night.

Just before the hour mark Lucescu replaced Ronaldo with Ventola, who had looked promising in his cameo two weeks before. He was much more suited to the task of running down the sides of centre-backs on to through passes than a half-fit Ronaldo was.

To his manager's delight, Ventola scored just four minutes after his introduction when United failed to properly defend the second phase of an Inter corner. As his team pushed out following the initial clearance, Keane was unaware of Ventola's presence on his outside and was caught flat-footed as Cauet lobbed a pass over his head for Ventola to volley over Schmeichel. Suddenly, Inter were back in the tie and had plenty of time to go searching for an equaliser.

Inter made their third and final substitution in the 69th minute, replacing centre-back Bergomi with right-winger Francesco Moriero. They were now going all out for that equalising goal, changing to a 1-4-2-4, shown by *Figure 8*. Baggio was now deployed as a left-winger, but regularly moved inwards. Zanetti moved further infield when Inter had the ball, like in the first leg, which allowed Cauet or Zé Elias to push forward centrally or move wide and support Moriero wide on the right-hand side.

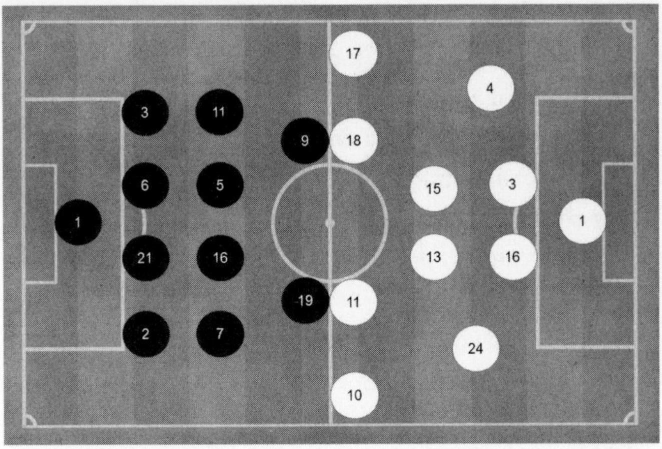

Figure 8

Inter began to attack more down their right, so United were forced to defend strongly on their left before looking to counter on their right, where there was more space.

Ferguson made his first substitution of the night in the 76th minute, taking off the yellow-carded Johnsen for Scholes. As he had done in the home leg, Ferguson made a change so that his team could defend deep without the precariousness of having both central midfielders on a booking. Six minutes later, Phil Neville, the versatile younger brother of Gary, came on for Giggs on the left side of midfield. This gave United an extra defensive-minded player on the side that Inter were attacking down the most. He could support Irwin in wide areas if necessary, but most importantly he could follow Zanetti inside and prevent him from finding space in central areas. This further reinforced United's idea of stemming the flow of attacks down their left side and countering down their right.

The atmosphere remained raucous, but frustration was growing among the *Nerazzurri* players. With little more than a couple of minutes of normal time left, Colonnese received a booking for throwing the ball at Beckham to try and force the winger into taking a quick throw-in, which he of course had no interest in doing, given the circumstances. Yorke moved out towards the corner flag on the right-hand side to receive the throw-in and Colonnese, still visibly wound up, rushed out to try and slide-tackle him. Yorke passed back to Gary Neville, who crossed deep to Andy Cole on the far side of the Inter penalty area. Aware that Colonnese was stranded out wide, Scholes made a run into the centre of the box and was not followed by an Inter midfielder. Cole produced a fantastic knock-down to lay the ball into Scholes's path for a simple finish. *Figure 9* shows how the goal transpired, with the arrows showing the path of the ball, beginning with Neville's cross.

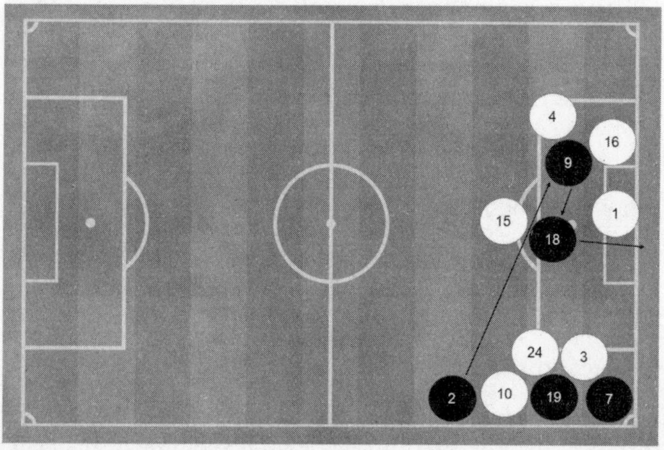

FIGURE 9

Scholes's goal took all hope and energy out of the hosts, both on the pitch and in the stands. United saw out the final few minutes with ease as their fans lit flares and sung songs of joy and admiration.

Full time – Inter Milan 1 Manchester United 1; Manchester United win 3-1 on aggregate

United had been victorious in the quarter-final two seasons earlier against an inferior Porto side, but defeating a star-studded Inter Milan team that had won three UEFA Cups in eight years was a big statement. By starting Johnsen over Scholes and then swapping the pair to such great effect, Ferguson proved beyond reasonable doubt that he was a tactician capable of operating at this level – he was more than just a strong figurehead in charge of great players. Beginning with two ball-winning midfielders helped United restrict Inter's star players to limited opportunities. Introducing Scholes for the final quarter of an hour then gave United a player intelligent enough to exploit space centrally as Inter became more desperate for an equaliser. Ferguson gave his players a platform on which they could perform to their strengths, and that they did.

Elsewhere in the quarter-final stage, holders Real Madrid were knocked out by Dynamo Kyiv thanks to three goals from rising star Andriy Shevchenko. The competition had been blown wide open.

Chapter 2

Semi-final – Manchester United 4 Juventus 3 (aggregate)

First leg: Manchester United 1 Juventus 1, 7 April 1999

Four points in their next two league matches saw United stay top of the table ahead of Arsenal and Chelsea. In Europe, the Red Devils were once again drawn to play at home in the first leg and would host Juventus just four days before their FA Cup semi-final meeting with Arsenal. Whereas the Mancunians had never played Inter in competitive fixtures before this season, Juventus were familiar foes. United lost home and away to them in the 1996/97 group stage before beating them 3-2 at home and losing 1-0 away at the same stage one season later.

Between 1996 and 1999, Juventus were the dominant side in Europe's dominant league. Not only had they won two *Scudetti* (Serie A titles) in a row, they had been Champions League finalists in three consecutive seasons, beating Ajax in the 1996 final before falling to surprise defeats against Borussia Dortmund and Real Madrid in 1997 and 1998 respectively. However, they were having a dire season in comparison to their recent high standards and were already out of the Serie A title race by the time of the first leg.

Legendary manager Marcello Lippi had left and been replaced by 39-year-old Carlo Ancelotti, who had enjoyed a stellar playing career throughout the 1980s but was still finding his feet as a manager after serving as an assistant for the Italian national team between 1992 and 1995. Zinédine Zidane had won both the FIFA World Player of the Year and the Ballon d'Or in 1998 thanks to his heroics for France at that year's World Cup, but found consistency difficult to come by at club level throughout 1998/99. He had been nursing a knee problem and had also been operating without the injured Alessandro Del Piero since November. It would never be straightforward facing this Juventus team in a European semi-final, but they were the most vulnerable they had been for several years. When Juventus qualified out of the group stage in December, Gary Neville's disappointed reaction was caught live on television. They were the team to avoid, regardless of form, but their run of final appearances had to end at some point.

The team selections, shown by *Figure 10*, were as follows:

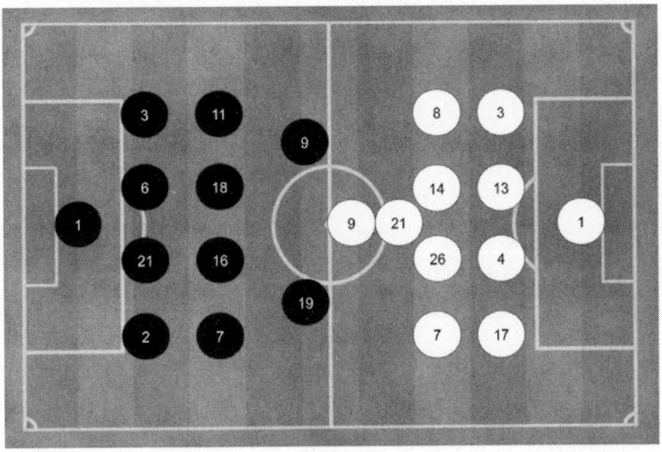

FIGURE 10

Manchester United (1-4-4-2): 1. Schmeichel; 2. G. Neville, 21. Berg, 6. Stam, 3. Irwin; 7. Beckham, 16. Keane (captain), 18. Scholes, 11. Giggs; 19. Yorke, 9. Cole.

Substitutes: 17. van der Gouw, 5. Johnsen, 8. Butt, 10. Sheringham, 12. P. Neville, 15. Blomqvist, 20. Solskjær,.

Head coach: Alex Ferguson CBE.

Juventus (1-4-4-1-1): 1. Peruzzi; 3. Mirković, 13. Iuliano, 4. Montero, 17. Pessotto; 8. Conte (captain), 14. Deschamps, 26. Davids, 7. Di Livio; 21. Zidane; 9. Inzaghi.

Substitutes: 12. Rampulla, 2. Ferrara, 15. Birindelli, 16. Amoruso, 19. Tudor, 20. Tacchinardi, 34. Esnáider.

Head coach: Carlo Ancelotti.

Ferguson reverted to the central midfield partnership that played the first leg against Inter Milan – the Keane-Scholes combination was clearly his preferred pairing in matches where United were expected to impose themselves on proceedings. Henning Berg started at the back alongside Stam, as had been the case in Milan.

Carlo Ancelotti was a loyal disciple of the legendary Italian coach Arrigo Sacchi, who championed a compact 1-4-4-2 system. Ancelotti had keenly stuck to this ideology as Parma manager between 1996 and 1998, where he rejected the chance to sign Roberto Baggio and sold Gianfranco Zola to Chelsea because he wanted to play with two strikers rather than with a *trequartista*. By the time he got the chance to manage Zidane at Juventus, he had become more flexible and adopted a 1-4-4-1-1 system instead, looking to maintain two strict lines of four while allowing Zidane the freedom to explore space and showcase his talents. Behind him in central midfield, Juventus boasted French captain Didier Deschamps and Dutch star Edgar Davids.

Another loud atmosphere greeted the players as they took to a pitch greatly improved from the sorry state that it had been in for the visit of Inter. The game started fast – Juventus were evidently comfortable on the ball, apart from Peruzzi who kicked it out of play unopposed, to the delight of the Old Trafford faithful. Whereas Inter looked to start fast and faltered, Juventus were clearly a level above. They started fast because they were capable of taking charge of the match and that is exactly what they did.

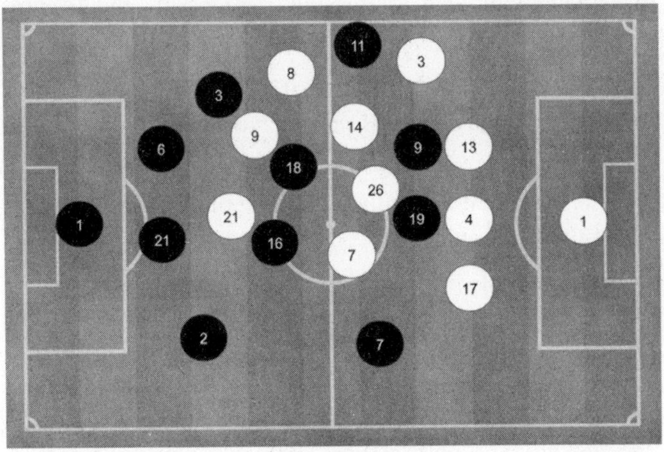

FIGURE 11

Figure 11 shows Juventus's defensive shape – Irwin is in possession for United at left-back. Juve's ball-side winger, Conte, presses Irwin from out to in, ensuring that he blocks off the potential passing lane to Giggs. This significantly limited the Welsh winger's impact in the first half. Inside Conte, Deschamps would look to block the passing lane from Irwin to the ball-side United striker, often Cole, although Irwin managed to find his striker occasionally. Zidane and Inzaghi worked as a pair so that Juventus's defensive shape was still the 1-4-4-2 that Ancelotti preferred; Zidane just had the freedom to drop deeper when his team had possession. By working as a pair defensively, they were able to prevent passes from United's full-backs in to Keane and Scholes. If United had the ball on their right-hand side, Di Livio would press Neville and block passes to Beckham, with Davids trying to block the passing lane to Yorke.

Ancelotti's men stayed vertically compact and the back four expertly performed an offside trap that snared the home side on several occasions. Yorke began to drop deeper to help his team in possession, but if he managed to receive with space to turn and look for an early through pass for Cole, the Juventus back line stepped forward together as the pass was made and caught Cole offside. The offside trap was straight out of the Arrigo Sacchi playbook and showed how man-marking teams like Inter Milan were in danger of being left behind as their opponents evolved tactically. Bypassing the Juve press was not at all straightforward either – Montero was very strong in the air and beat Cole in several aerial duels when United looked long. Scoring here was going to be much more difficult for United than it had been in the first leg of the quarter-final.

Not only were the Mancunians struggling when they had the ball, they were having a hard time defending as well. Inzaghi was a nightmare for Berg to defend; he would drop deep to pull Berg out of position and leave space that Zidane could burst into. When this happened, Keane would track the Frenchman and sacrifice space in midfield. This would prompt Davids to move forward and Conte to tuck inside from the right, with the latter making diagonal runs in front of or on to United's defensive line. If Inzaghi stayed high when his team had the ball, Zidane would look to combine with Deschamps and Davids to form a central three v two overload against Keane and Scholes, while Di Livio stayed wide on the left to maintain width and deter Beckham from covering inside.

Inzaghi nearly opened the scoring when he peeled off the back of Berg, who misjudged an aerial ball, and forced

Schmeichel into a good save. Just as United began to get to grips with the away team's system, Juve made some slight alterations. Conte began to stay wider and deeper, which pulled Irwin away to mark him and isolated Stam one v one against the lively Inzaghi. However, Inzaghi often tried to make contact with Stam so that he could go down and look for cheap fouls rather than engage in a race with the Dutchman. This saved Stam from a lot of trouble – the referee stood firm and did not buy into Inzaghi's theatrics. Juventus's repertoire of rotations did not end there, as Inzaghi began to drift further to the right, with Conte bursting inside in his place.

Beckham thought that he had opened the scoring when he went close with a free kick and within the blink of an eye Juventus shocked the home crowd with an away goal at the Stretford End. Zidane pulled out to the left to receive a long ball and took Berg with him. He passed inside to Davids, who was free to receive because Keane had retreated into the back line to try and cover for Berg, as an overlapping run from Di Livio had kept Neville out wide. As Zidane played his pass, Inzaghi drifted out to the right and was duly followed by Stam – leaving a large space between Keane and Stam for Conte to move into. Davids flicked the ball cleverly between the legs of the recovering Scholes for Conte to receive and fire past Schmeichel to the delight of the travelling fans. Juventus's attacking movements were paying dividends for Ancelotti and the Turinese were on course for a fourth Champions League Final in as many years. This goal is illustrated by *Figure 12*, with the arrows once again signalling the ball's travel.

Juventus's positive start was deserving of a goal and they continued to play at a pace that United found difficult to match. The hosts regularly struggled on transition after losing

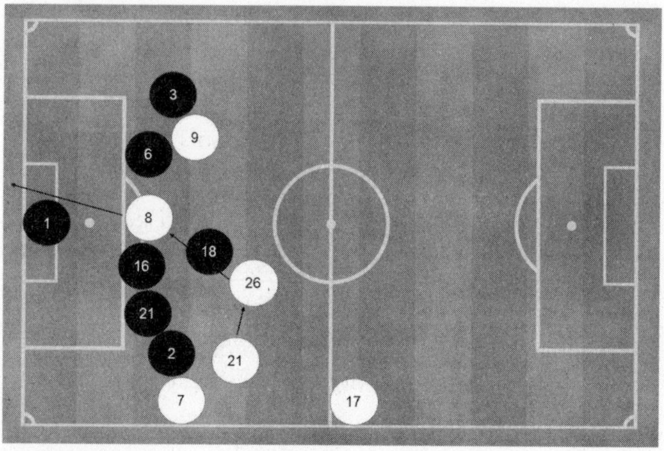

Figure 12

the ball, rarely managing to get back into their defensive shape before Juve quickly played through midfield and built another attack. Davids was having a good half, covering a lot of ground and retaining possession well. He was finding a lot of space because Keane was trying to man-mark Zidane, who would drift away from the ball and pull Keane out of position, leaving space for his Dutch team-mate to exploit.

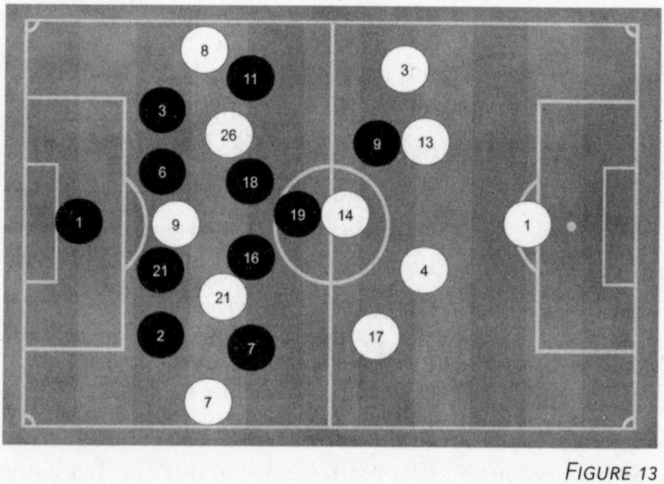

Figure 13

Yorke moved deeper out of possession too, so that when Zidane tried to help create a three v two overload against Keane and Scholes, it was now a three v three with Yorke up against Deschamps, shown by *Figure 13*. Unfortunately for Ferguson's men, the Juventus midfield were all extremely intelligent and adept at performing double movements – threatening to move in one direction before quickly going in the other to either receive the ball or create space for a team-mate. This intelligence was hard for United to cope with. When the Red Devils did win the ball and looked to attack themselves, Yorke and Cole continued to have trouble against the efficient Juventus back line.

Half-time – Manchester United 0 Juventus 1

As they had done in the first leg against Inter, United swapped one Norwegian centre-back for another at half-time as Johnsen replaced Berg. Berg had picked up an injury and would miss the rest of the season.

In the second half, Beckham came narrower when United had possession to try and help his team establish some control. This was important because the visitors had effectively been preventing Neville passing down United's right. Beckham created an initial three v three alongside Keane and Scholes, while Yorke still looked to try and receive the ball behind Juventus's midfield. The Trinidad & Tobago international was not having his best night, though, as the visiting back four continued to catch Cole offside on Yorke's attempted through balls.

Montero had a splendid game and led Juve's defensive line superbly, but he was forced to withdraw through injury in the 68th minute and was replaced by Ciro Ferrara. Although Ferrara had a reputation as a top-class defender in his own right, losing such an in-form centre-back was a blow for

Ancelotti's men. At 32 years of age, Ferrara was lacking pace and was soon beaten to a long channel ball from Irwin to Cole. This appeared to give United a lift, as playing direct passes from deep had a higher chance of being successful now that Montero was not on the pitch to deal with them.

Juventus were soaking up pressure well, yet they were no longer offering much of an attacking threat themselves. Inzaghi found it tough in the second half; he kept making runs into space behind the United defence, but when Zidane and Davids received the ball in midfield they tried to dribble forward with it themselves instead of passing. The home side found this easier to deal with thanks to the aggressive tackling of Keane in midfield and the strong individual defending of Johnsen and Stam in defence.

The home crowd continued to will their team forward. As the ball got to Cole more often, an equaliser felt closer. Juventus responded to the growing pressure by subbing off Di Livio in the 77th minute and bringing on Alessio Tacchinardi – a central midfielder by trade. Tacchinardi, known for his excellent defensive ability, was deployed on the left side of midfield as Ancelotti sought to settle for a one-goal lead ahead of the return leg in Turin. Tacchinardi's fresh legs were used to try and counter Beckham's energy, who continued to come narrow for the ball while also running out wide to perform crosses.

Yorke was taken off two minutes later, with Teddy Sheringham coming on in his place. It had not been Yorke's best game and Sheringham was a capable replacement, able to move between lines to receive the ball and reliably finish chances.

Mirković shackled Giggs expertly for 80 minutes until he was given a yellow card for a terrible foul and could no longer mark the Welshman as tight and aggressively. Concentration is crucial in tight European matches and temporarily losing his cost Mirković dearly – he was now suspended for the return leg. The booking made Mirković more hesitant and Giggs grew in effectiveness. Rather than make dangerous forward movements, Conte now had to focus on tracking back and helping his full-back.

The home side were on top and had a goal disallowed when a Keane strike from outside the penalty area took a deflection off the offside Sheringham. Juventus brought on fresh legs up front by swapping Inzaghi for Juan Esnáider, whose introduction to this match was largely redundant as United kept the ball at the opposite end of the pitch. Juventus surrendered territory and United's push for an equaliser was simply a race against the clock. Scholes was gambling more, making runs into the box from midfield, and this brought him two chances that he probably should have put away. First, he missed a header from the edge of the six-yard box after Cole had headed a Giggs cross back across goal. Seconds later he made a run into the penalty area to meet another Giggs cross, but his shot was blocked. Ferguson's men needed to make their good second-half performance count for something and avoid going to Turin a goal behind. It was hard to foresee them dominating long periods of the second leg like that they had done in this half.

Finally, the breakthrough came in stoppage time. Gary Neville launched a long throw into the Juventus penalty area and the Italians only half cleared it. The ball fell to Beckham on the right side of the area and he hooked it over his head and back inside. Sheringham beat Peruzzi to the first ball outside the front post before Scholes and Cole jumped for a second ball that they both lost to Ferrara, but his header was not clean enough and the ball landed at the left foot of Giggs, who brilliantly half-volleyed the ball above two players on the goal line and into the roof of the net. The scruffy build-up should take nothing away from the quality of the finish. The Old Trafford crowd went crazy and implored their team to push for a second goal, but Juventus held out to take an equal scoreline back to northern Italy. A 1-1 draw was a fair result – Juventus had the best of the first half and United had the best of the second. One positive for Ferguson was the fact that Keane and Scholes avoided bookings at Old Trafford, so they were both available for the return leg. Juventus had proven to be much tougher opposition than Inter Milan, but it was still all to play for in Turin.

Full time – Manchester United 1 Juventus 1

Second leg: Juventus 2 Manchester United 3, 21 April 1999

The fortnight between the two meetings with Inter had been a dramatic one for United, but the two weeks between the two Juventus matches took their season to a whole new level as the treble progressed from being a dream to a genuine possibility. Four days after the first leg, United met Arsenal in the semi-final of the FA Cup at Villa Park, with both teams still in with a chance of a domestic double. The match ended goalless after extra time and was replayed three days later. An additional 30 minutes was needed again to separate the sides after Arsenal missed a late penalty, with the tie eventually decided by Ryan Giggs scoring one of the greatest solo goals in the history of the competition. It was yet another crazy twist in United's season, further fuel to their belief that nothing was beyond them. A rotated side then put Sheffield Wednesday to the sword at Old Trafford in a 3-0 win.

Meanwhile, Juventus only had two matches to negotiate between the semi-final legs, drawing 2-2 at home to Bologna before beating Lazio 3-1. Their minds were solely on the

Champions League – a luxury that they could afford, unlike their Mancunian opponents. But if anybody could end Serie A's run of Champions League finalists it was this United team, who never knew when they were beaten and were brimming with self-belief. The starting teams for the second leg are shown by *Figure 14*.

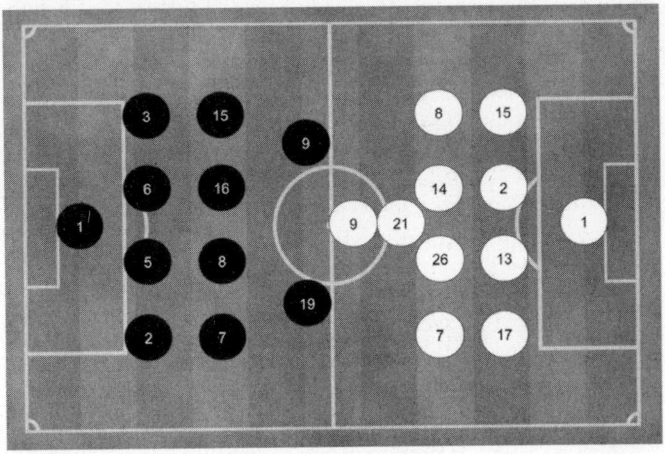

FIGURE 14

Manchester United (1-4-4-2): 1. Schmeichel; 2. G. Neville, 5. Johnsen, 6. Stam, 3. Irwin; 7. Beckham, 8. Butt, 16. Keane (captain), 15. Blomqvist; 19. Yorke, 9. Cole.

Substitutes: 17. van der Gouw, 4. May, 10. Sheringham, 12. P. Neville, 18. Scholes, 20. Solskjær, 30. Brown.

Head coach: Alex Ferguson CBE.

Juventus (1-4-4-1-1): 1. Peruzzi; 15. Birindelli, 2. Ferrara, 13. Iuliano, 17. Pessotto; 8. Conte (captain), 14. Deschamps, 26. Davids, 7. Di Livio; 21. Zidane; 9. Inzaghi.

Substitutes: 12. Rampulla, 4. Montero, 11. Fonseca, 16. Amoruso, 19. Tudor, 20. Tacchinardi, 34. Esnáider.

Head coach: Carlo Ancelotti.

Once again, Ferguson dropped Scholes to the bench in place of a more defensive-minded midfielder for the away leg, with

Nicky Butt starting alongside Keane on this occasion. Yorke and Cole started together again – they were rotated in the league to ensure that they were fit and ready to compete in these big European ties. Giggs was injured and replaced by Jesper Blomqvist. Juventus replaced the suspended Mirković with Alessandro Birindelli and Ferrara started in place of Montero, who was only fit enough for the substitutes' bench.

The United players were greeted with another hostile Italian atmosphere at the Stadio delle Alpi. It was a night for Ferguson's men to stand up and be counted.

In the opening five minutes, United looked good. As he had often done at Old Trafford, Yorke came deeper than Cole to try and get on the ball in front of Juventus's midfield. Stam was also able to assist the midfield in possession, as they kept the ball well and looked settled. Then came the concession of an extremely cheap goal. After conceding from the second phase of a corner in Milan, United would have been determined to keep their concentration when defending Juve set pieces, and conceding from another corner would have been very upsetting. Zidane took the corner from United's right-hand side and played a short one-two with Di Livio, which dragged Yorke and Johnsen out of the penalty area. Neither of them could stop Zidane's cross, which travelled across the six-yard line for Inzaghi to get to in front of Neville and tap the ball home at the back post. After starting comfortably, United had gifted Juventus an early boost. The goal did not change the complexion of the tie that much – United knew that they needed to score at least once anyway – however that task would surely be more difficult after allowing Juventus to get their tails up with an early goal.

The Mancunian outfit picked themselves up and initially responded well to going a goal behind. They created a good chance as Neville underlapped Beckham and crossed well to find Cole, whose overhead kick went straight to Peruzzi. There was no need to panic, they were still very much in the tie. Then, in the 11th minute, disaster. As Juventus built possession down their left-hand side, Johnsen stepped out into no-man's-land to try and press Davids and left Stam isolated one v one against the onrushing Inzaghi. Davids played wide to the supporting Pessotto who, as a naturally right-footed player, was able to play a quick pass to Inzaghi through the space vacated by Johnsen. Stam managed to guide Inzaghi wide of the goal, but the Italian's shot looped off Stam's foot, over the hapless Schmeichel and into the net. Juventus now led 3-1 on aggregate and they had hardly got out of first gear.

As had been the case in the first half at Old Trafford, United were struggling to cope with Edgar Davids, who was dictating a lot of Juventus's play. As shown by *Figure 15*, he often came deep to act as a short passing option behind and inside Pessotto and Di Livio so that he received the ball in front of United's midfield. If someone pressed Davids, they forfeited space behind them. If nobody pressed him, he

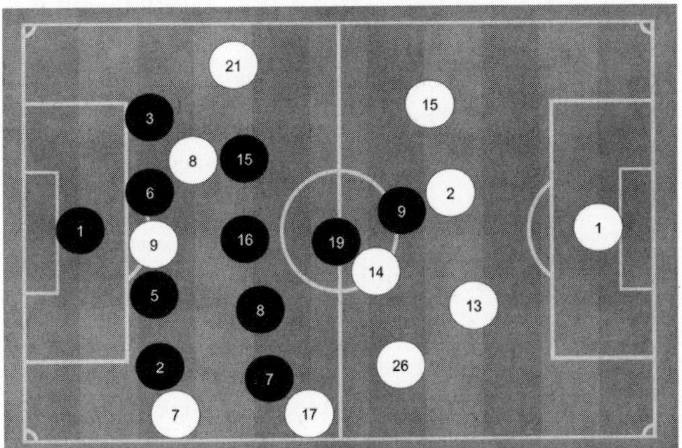

FIGURE 15

was able to showcase his unquestionable ability unopposed. Zidane and Conte were also rotating regularly, which often left Zidane free in space in wider areas while Conte looked to threaten like he did for his goal in the first leg. Zidane was up for the fight and was covering Conte on transition when Juventus lost the ball, which then also made him an option to receive and expertly retain possession once his side won it back.

Meanwhile, when United got the ball to Yorke they encountered the same problem as before – the Juventus offside trap was brilliantly timing its movement to step forward and catch Cole offside. While Yorke could receive in front of the opposition defence and look for passes, he was not the type of player who would turn and dribble at the back line to force somebody to press him and leave a gap. So, Yorke and Cole reverted to playing as a more standard pair and they rotated more often, with Yorke now playing on the side of Ferrara. At 32 years of age, this was the last thing that Ferrara wanted. United looked capable of threatening but the issue was that there was no margin for error at all from a defensive point of view. Two instances of bad play had been ruthlessly punished.

The visitors had a strong penalty appeal turned down in the 22nd minute. Schmeichel booted a long goal kick down the middle of the pitch and Juventus, seemingly lacking Montero's leadership and aerial ability, failed to deal with it. Yorke ran on to the loose ball and was pulled down by Ferrara on the edge of the penalty area. The experienced defender then rushed to his feet and blocked a Beckham strike with his right hand. Although nothing was given, it was a reminder that United were indeed capable of troubling the home side.

Within two minutes of the penalty appeal United had their lifeline. They established a good period of possession inside the Juve half, with Stam once again pushing into midfield to assist with the safe and secure progression of the ball from United's right-hand side to their left. Irwin played a one-two with Blomqvist, bringing the Swedish winger deep and leaving space wide left for Cole to drift wide and chase a through pass, winning a corner against Ferrara. Beckham hit an in-swinger towards the edge of the six-yard box where captain Keane, who had burst free of his marker, Pessotto, headed superbly across the goal and into the net. The away end came to life – the game was back on. Keane pumped his fist and sprinted back to his half, demanding that his team go again. It was unlikely that United would enjoy good periods of possession throughout the match, so getting a goal back while they were doing so was vital.

The events that then take place during the rest of this match can arguably be explained by one statement: this was a contest between two teams – one that was scared by the prospect of failure and one that was excited by the possibility of success. Juventus had everything to lose – not only were they a team of superstars, they had twice experienced failure in the final, were failing domestically and did not want to round off a difficult season by failing in Europe again, especially not from a winning position. There were question marks hanging over both the manager (he was inexperienced and had replaced a legend) and several players (people wondered if they had peaked). Where would failure against United leave their careers? After falling short of European glory in the last two seasons, how would they cope with losing this semi-final, knowing that they would be more experienced than both potential final opponents, Bayern Munich and Dynamo Kyiv?

On the other hand, yes, United had experienced disappointment at this level, but they had only really been viewed as genuine contenders for this season's competition after making it out of the group stage instead of Barcelona. As much as past failures, such as in 1997, ate away at Ferguson, his team was an exciting side that believed that this season was their time. Why fear needing two more goals away in Turin after just beating Arsenal in such dramatic fashion? After scoring twice in two minutes to come from behind to beat Liverpool? After scoring three away at the Camp Nou?

Manchester United was a football club bathing in positive momentum. Instead of sitting back and settling for a one-goal disadvantage at half-time, Ferguson continued with the same tactics so that his players could march on in search of glory, rather than playing with fear. Playing with fear would mean being passive and allowing the game to drift, which would be incredibly dangerous considering Juventus had already scored with two half-chances. This is not to say that there was no pressure on United to win, of course there was. They were just so well placed to deal with it by this point in the season. After the first 27 minutes, United had enjoyed 62 per cent of possession away in a Champions League semi-final.

Zidane produced some magic to dig out a left-footed cross to Inzaghi in the 30th minute, which Schmeichel failed to deal with. Fortunately for the Danish keeper, Stam was on hand to clear the ball off the line and away from danger – the fourth big moment of the half and the second to go United's way.

Yorke and Cole were causing Ferrara and Iuliano problems, while Neville and Irwin were pushing further forward, buoyed by their side's domination of the ball. A fifth major moment of the half then tested United's mental strength and desire, as Keane mis-controlled a Blomqvist pass and purposefully fouled Zidane to avoid a counter-attack. He was booked, meaning that he was suspended from the final if his side were to make it through. As much as this was a poor mistake from Keane, it also highlighted the reduction in threat on United's left without Giggs on the pitch. Blomqvist turned and passed back to Keane instead of dribbling forward – he did not take opponents on with the same directness and verve as Giggs. He spent the first half of this match passing sideways and backwards rather than attacking himself.

Undeterred by the booking of their captain, the Red Devils equalised in the 34th minute and now led the tie for the first time due to the away goals rule. Gary Neville looked long down the right for Beckham and found him. Beckham nodded the ball down to Cole, who had peeled off to the right in anticipation of Neville's direct pass. Iuliano had come out to follow Cole, so only Yorke and Ferrara were left in the Juventus penalty area. Cole crossed over the flat-footed Ferrara for Yorke to head past the despairing Peruzzi. From two goals down and with a yellow-carded captain, United had received the ultimate reward for their good spells of possession. They had now scored 14 away goals in the 1998/99 Champions League and still had one half of football left to play. The onus was now on the dejected hosts to respond.

Ferguson's side kept looking to play long balls because it was working. Yorke hit the post in the 39th minute when Juve failed to deal with another direct pass in the air. The hosts began to play longer but with much less success – they were bypassing their midfield, which was their strongest area of the pitch.

Half-time – Juventus 2 Manchester United 2

After an enthralling half of football, the team that had maintained the best spells of possession had the advantage in the tie, albeit a slender one. Juventus were showing why they had struggled for consistency all season and United had capitalised on their passiveness. The absence of Montero was a significant factor; the Turinese defence was noticeably weaker than it had been at Old Trafford.

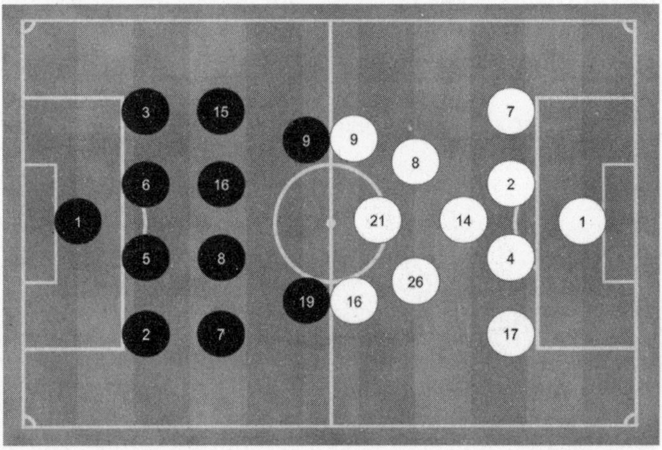

FIGURE 16

Ancelotti responded and changed to a 1-4-3-1-2 at half-time, as shown by *Figure 16*. Birindelli and Iuliano were replaced by Amoruso and Montero. Di Livio moved from the left side of midfield to right-back, with Montero directly replacing Iuliano as the left-sided centre-back. Deschamps was the holding midfielder, with Conte to the right and Davids to the left. Zidane stayed in a central attacking role, now behind two strikers – Inzaghi and Amoruso.

Now faced with two men, Stam refrained from pushing into midfield when his side had the ball. Instead, Beckham moved narrower so that Keane and Butt still had extra help in retaining possession in central areas.

Zidane began drifting left of centre, where he was receiving the ball and looking to thread passes through United's lines for Inzaghi and Amoruso to chase. Zidane found himself in space on the left because Davids would come narrow to prevent a United central midfielder from engaging with Zidane, while Pessotto overlapped high to occupy Beckham. Therefore, when Montero had the ball he had an open passing lane straight to Zidane, as shown by *Figure 17*. United stood firm at the start of the half though and did not concede early goals like they had done in the first period.

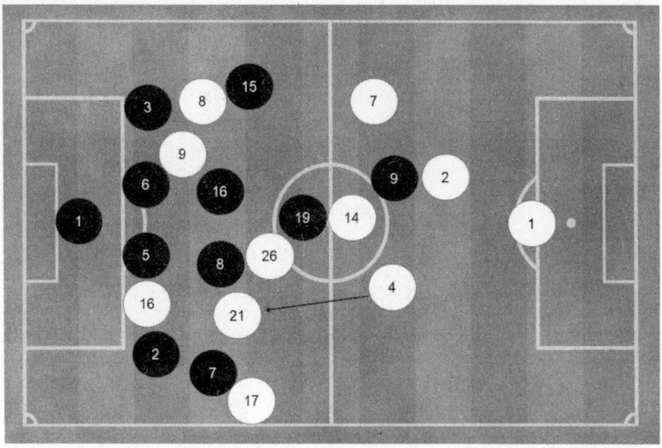

FIGURE 17

In the 53rd minute Davids took a swipe at Beckham, who went down holding his ankle with one hand and signalling for a yellow card to be shown with the other. Unsportsmanlike? Yes, but it showed a cynicism that Beckham had most probably learned thanks to his experience against Simeone in France the previous summer. It was a moment that summed up United's journey in elite European competition – even though they did not keep a lot of clean sheets, they were far more streetwise than they had been previously. Here, Beckham was merely playing Juventus at their own game. With that booking, Davids would now miss the final if Juventus qualified, putting him in the same situation as Keane.

Although he was less threatening than Giggs on the ball, Blomqvist played an important role for his team defensively. With natural winger Di Livio moving to right-back, Blomqvist had to defend well in one v one situations, to avoid getting dribbled past and to shut off Di Livio's attempts to pass inside to Deschamps, Davids and Zidane. Instead, Blomqvist allowed Di Livio to pass wide to Conte, who moved wide when Juve had possession and could be pinned to the touchline by Irwin. As Conte received the ball, Blomqvist would make sure that he still blocked off passes into central areas, encouraging Conte to try and take Irwin on, cross early, or pass back to Di Livio. United could cope with all three of those situations.

Inzaghi had a goal disallowed for offside in the 62nd minute, refocusing United minds on the task at hand. In response to Blomqvist's solid defensive work, Conte positioned himself narrower in possession, leaving the wide space for Di Livio to overlap into. This was tiring Blomqvist, who began to waste the ball on transition as he became more fatigued. Ferguson acknowledged this and made his first change of the evening in the 68th minute, with Scholes replacing the exhausted Swede. Nicky Butt moved to the left of midfield, with Scholes in the centre alongside Keane. This change made United's midfield line even more compact when out of possession. Butt tracked Conte centrally then used his exceptional energy levels to move out and press Di Livio when necessary, with Scholes and Keane moving across to the left to cover. Beckham on the right and Yorke behind the Juve were midfield were United's key outlets on the counter-attack – particularly Beckham as Pessotto continued to push high and support attacks.

Tactics are an important aspect of elite football, but a manager's job can be made much easier by outstanding individual performances. On a night when Ferguson needed his players to deliver, Keane most certainly did. In addition to scoring the goal that started the comeback, he won countless duels in midfield, most notably in the 74th minute when he beat Davids in a challenge for a loose ball and then beat Deschamps to the seconds before getting fouled by the Frenchman. Zidane had given up drifting towards the left because Keane was tracking him relentlessly as the right-sided central midfielder with Scholes to his left. When a footballer plays like Keane did in this match, it seems inconceivable to even consider the possibility of them ending up on the losing side.

In the 76th minute, Scholes committed a terrible tackle on Deschamps and received a booking, meaning that he was now suspended for the final too. Both of United's central midfielders now had the difficult task of guiding their team to a final that they were banned from featuring in. Brought on for his on-the-ball qualities, just as in Milan, this was a poor mistake from Scholes. Not only were Keane and Scholes out of the final but they were both one more bad challenge away from being sent off and leaving United with ten men.

Changing to 1-4-3-1-2 did not have the desired effect for Juventus, who made their final substitution on 80 minutes, replacing Di Livio with forward Daniel Fonseca and changing to a lopsided 1-3-3-1-3 formation. Fonseca was deployed as a third striker in support of the tiring Inzaghi and the ineffectual Amoruso. Ferrara, Montero and Pessotto formed a back three, although Pessotto pushed forward to support attacks. Conte moved to wing-back on the right and, while there was no fixed wing-back on the left, there was space free for Davids to move out and occupy if needed. Deschamps remained the anchor man in the middle, with Zidane behind the front three. Juventus needed one goal to win the tie and go through; Ancelotti was looking for an attacking onslaught from his team in search of it.

There was to be another goal in the tie, but it was a United one. Pessotto had moved forward, leaving Ferrara and Montero two v two against Yorke and Cole. Davids overhit a pass aimed for Inzaghi and it was collected by Schmeichel, who quickly kicked the ball long towards his two strikers. Montero met the ball but made an uncharacteristic mistake with his rushed clearance and inadvertently gifted possession to Yorke. Both centre-backs dived in desperately to try and stop Yorke, allowing him to skip through the middle of them and advance into the penalty area. Peruzzi came out and tripped him, but Cole was first to the loose ball, scoring from an acute angle to give United a 4-3 aggregate lead – their first outright advantage in the entire tie. The away end descended into carnage and the home fans were stunned into silence. In a season of incredible comebacks, this goal rounded off United's best one yet.

Like Scholes's in Milan, Cole's strike took the sting out of the tie and United were able to see out the final minutes with ease.

Full time – Juventus 2 Manchester United 3; Manchester United win 4-3 on aggregate

This result was a magnificent feat for several reasons. Juventus had not lost a two-legged European tie since the 1995 UEFA Cup Final and were unbeaten at home in the Champions League since November of the same year. For United, it was a night on which their squad of continental underachievers came of age. While the quality that Stam brought to the defence was clear, solid performances by the likes of Gary Neville should not be overlooked either. In midfield, Roy Keane gave the defining performance of his career; it was just a shame that he and Scholes would miss the final after contributing so much to their side's journey. Up top, the Yorke-Cole strike partnership continued to deliver.

It was a huge achievement for Ferguson to take United to their first European Cup/Champions League Final for over three decades, especially after a semi-final where things threatened to go horribly wrong in the first half of both legs. At no point did his side panic, even when 3-1 down on aggregate. He had successfully created a culture of undying self-belief at the club that ensured there was never a need to rush into changes on the pitch – the players knew that they were always capable of achieving a positive result, regardless of circumstances. This belief would now be tested further as United's pursuit of a treble entered its final stretch, but it would be brave to bet against them. For now, they could celebrate knocking out the mighty Juventus. It was the night of their club careers. Well, for four weeks.

Chapter 3

Final – Manchester United 2 Bayern Munich 1, 26 May 1999

With the treble now firmly in sight, United completed the first phase of their pursuit by winning the Premier League on the final day of the season, coming from a goal behind to beat Tottenham Hotspur 2-1. It was Ferguson's fifth top-flight English title, bringing him level with United legend Sir Matt Busby. Six days later they beat Newcastle United 2-0 at Wembley to win the FA Cup and secure a domestic double. They had equalled Arsenal's achievement from the previous season; now it was all about going one better.

United's opponents in the final, Bayern Munich, were chasing their first treble as well. Their league season had not quite finished by the time of the final, but they already had an unassailable lead at the top. They had also reached the final of the German Cup, where they would face Werder Bremen in June.

In the Champions League, they beat fellow German side 1. FC Kaiserslautern 6-0 on aggregate in the quarter-final and saw off the brave challenge of Dynamo Kyiv in the semi-final, winning the tie 4-3.

Of course, the two finalists had already played each other twice in the group stages, drawing 2-2 in Munich and 1-1 in Manchester. The key thing for United to take from the group-stage encounters was that they were clearly capable of competing with Bayern. In fact, they should have won the away fixture and conceded a late equaliser due to an error from Schmeichel. Bayern's manager, Ottmar Hitzfeld, had been in charge of Borussia Dortmund when they beat United and went on to win the 1996/97 Champions League; now he was out to do it again. As an interesting side note, this was the second season in which the runners-up of Europe's eight strongest domestic leagues had been granted qualification for the Champions League, and both finalists had qualified for the competition by virtue of this new rule. As recently as the 1996/97 season, these two teams would have been contesting for the UEFA Cup instead. The impact of the tournament's expansion was clear.

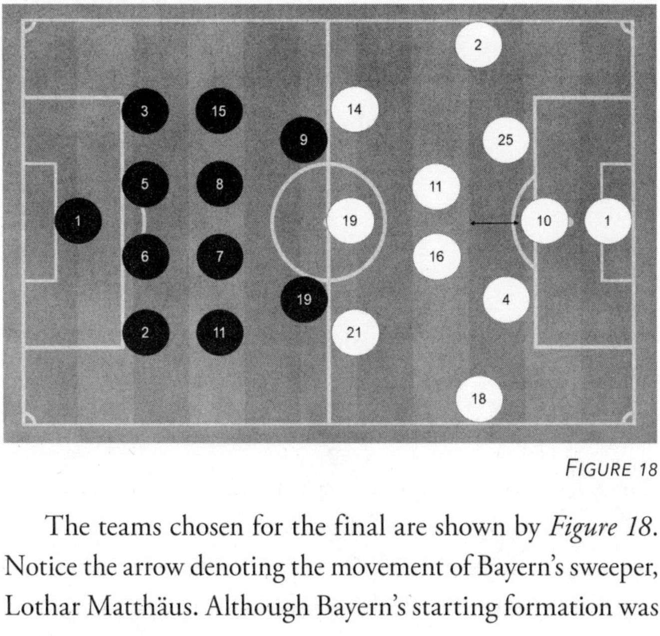

FIGURE 18

The teams chosen for the final are shown by *Figure 18*. Notice the arrow denoting the movement of Bayern's sweeper, Lothar Matthäus. Although Bayern's starting formation was essentially a back five with him sweeping behind centre-backs Linke and Kuffour, he also had licence to sweep in front of the defensive line, which would see Bayern adopt more of a 1-4-1-4-1 shape, with Basler and Zickler dropping deeper so that Bayern had two banks of four either side of Matthäus. Operating with a sweeper was deeply entrenched in German football culture and there was no one better at performing the role than the legendary Bayern man. Ferguson had chosen Keane and Scholes as his central midfield partnership for both group-stage matches against Bayern. In their absence, Beckham and Butt started in central midfield, with Giggs moving to the right and Jesper Blomqvist lining up on the left. Whereas Stam played as the left-sided centre-back against Inter Milan and Juventus, he started on the right here. This meant that he would be closer to Bayern's dangerous forward, Carsten Jancker. Schmeichel took the captain's armband in his final game for United.

Manchester United (1-4-4-2): 1. Schmeichel (captain); 2. G. Neville, 6. Stam, 5. Johnsen, 3. Irwin; 11. Giggs, 7. Beckham, 8. Butt , 15. Blomqvist; 19. Yorke, 9. Cole.

Substitutes: 17. van der Gouw, 4. May, 10. Sheringham, 12. P. Neville, 20. Solskjær, 30. Brown, 34. Greening.

Head coach: Alex Ferguson CBE.

Bayern Munich (1-1-4-2-3): 1. Kahn (captain); 10. Matthäus; 2. Babbel, 25. Linke, 4. Kuffour, 18. Tarnat; 11. Effenberg, 16. Jeremies; 14. Basler, 19. Jancker, 21. Zickler.

Substitutes: 22. Dreher, 5. Helmer, 7. Scholl, 8. Strunz, 17. Fink, 20. Salihamidžić, 24. Daei.

Head coach: Ottmar Hitzfeld.

The Camp Nou in Barcelona was the venue for the final and it was packed to the rafters with over 90,000 people in attendance. Willed on by the energy in the crowd, the game began at a fast pace. Both teams looked to play direct and aerial, rather than build possession patiently from deeper positions. There were no early nerves on show in either back line, though, so neither side created a chance in the opening stages.

Bayern's system was typically German and relied heavily on man-marking. Wing-backs Babbel and Tarnat were tasked with defending Blomqvist and Giggs respectively, with Linke and Kuffour tracking Cole and Yorke. Effenberg and Jeremies had a two v two in midfield against Beckham and Butt, while Basler and Zinckler could track back against Irwin and Neville if required. This left Matthäus as the spare player, operating as a sweeper with experience and guile. If he swept behind Linke and Kuffour, he created a three v two against Yorke and Cole. If he stepped in front of his centre-backs, he could look to intercept through passes aimed at United's strikers and stop Yorke from receiving in front of the Bavarian back line.

Giggs was the first United player to look positive on the ball, dribbling inwards from the right and winning a throw-in in a good position for his team, allowing them to push up the pitch. Neville took the throw and went long into the Bayern penalty area for Yorke and Cole to battle against Linke, Kuffour and Matthäus. Although the two United strikers won the initial challenge, Tarnat retreated to help his team-mates and booted the ball away from danger. Beckham positioned himself underneath the ball as it returned from orbit, but he got his control horribly wrong. The loose ball rolled towards Jancker, who got in front of Stam and played the ball back to Jeremies, who in turn passed forward to Zickler on Bayern's left.

This was a nightmare scenario for United – Stam had been pulled out of the back line to challenge Jancker for the loose ball and was now out of position as Bayern entered the

United half. Johnsen was isolated on his own in the centre of defence, stuck between moving across to press Zickler and staying central to try and prevent a through pass. Zickler lofted a first-time pass over Johnsen into the path of Jancker, who had outpaced Stam and left him stranded. The desperately retreating Johnsen had little choice but to push Jancker to the ground to prevent him advancing into the penalty area. Referee Pierluigi Collina signalled for a Bayern free kick about 20 yards from goal and about ten yards left of centre. United had been caught on transition, with Jancker winning his first one v one battle against Stam.

Schmeichel selected a five-man wall to stand between himself and the free kick, with Neville covering the near post. With little over five minutes played, this was the first promising opportunity for either side. Babbel stood in front of Butt, who was the most leftward player in the wall. Jancker moved next to Babbel and Butt, bringing marker Stam with him. As Basler ran forward to strike the free kick, Jancker ran away from the wall and took Stam with him. At the same time, Babbel stood side-on to Butt so that the Englishman could not move to the side, then the German ducked to avoid blocking Basler's strike as it flew through the gap created by Babbel and Jancker and into the bottom corner. It was 1-0 Bayern and once again, United were going to have to do things the hard way if it was to be their night.

As much as the free kick was well worked by the Bavarians, it was an extremely disappointing goal to concede due to the way United had been exposed by one counter-attack. The Red Devils were shellshocked and a mix-up between Schmeichel and Johnsen a minute later added to the Mancunian tension. Schmeichel was able to boot the ball out of play to escape punishment, but improvement was needed quickly.

Like against Juventus, Yorke began to drop away from the Bayern back line to try and receive the ball in front of them. He and Cole had a poor start to the match though – they were not retaining the ball well enough to allow their team-mates to push up in support. When Yorke and Cole started a match slowly it impacted the whole side. Kuffour was winning his individual battle against Yorke, and Linke was winning his against Cole. Matthäus was not being troubled at all.

Beckham and Giggs began to operate well together, despite being in different positions to normal. In the absence of Scholes, Beckham was the United midfielder looking to receive the ball from the back four to try and dictate possession for his side. Bayern's midfield was not pressing high up the pitch, so Beckham was able to receive, turn forwards and pass to his right to Giggs. From there, Giggs could take the ball from a wide starting position and dribble infield on his favoured left foot, with Beckham using his energy to overlap him. Giggs could either continue to dribble inwards before passing, crossing, or shooting himself, or he could pass out wide for Beckham to cross. This is shown by *Figure 19*, with

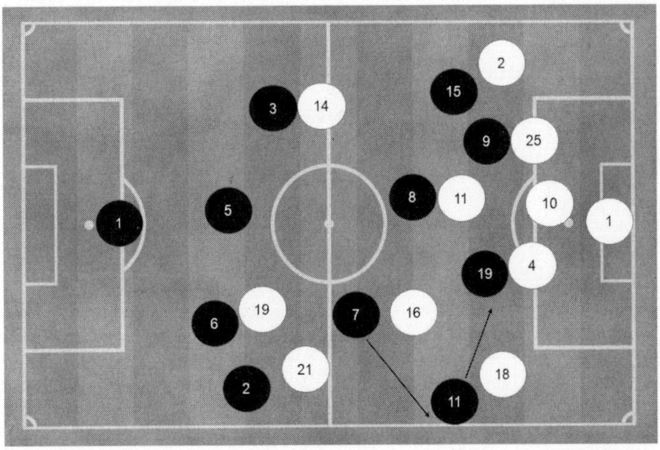

FIGURE 19

the arrows showing the movement of Beckham and Giggs. With Blomqvist struggling to trouble Babbel and with Yorke and Cole starting slowly, Beckham and Giggs were United's most important combination in the first half. Butt was playing in a box-to-box role and would push forward when Beckham dropped deep to receive, relying on his stamina to recover if possession was lost.

This prompted Matthäus to spend more time in front of Bayern's back line. Initially, this meant that Bayern reverted to 1-4-1-4-1. Matthäus closed off the space that Yorke wanted to move into, hoping that it would keep United's strikers isolated from their midfield. It also meant that the veteran could cover in midfield if Jeremies needed to move wider to keep up with Beckham. By 43 minutes, United had managed 57 per cent of possession and it was no wonder that Bayern were the side making tactical adjustments. The adjustments were working, though, as United found it hard to create clear-cut opportunities.

Half-time – Manchester United 0 Bayern Munich 1

The first half was typical of an elite-level cup final. Neither side overcommitted or created a significant number of quality chances; the half-time score had simply been decided by one team capitalising on the half's key moment. Note the importance of set pieces – attention to detail allowed Bayern to grasp the moment and score the free kick. The game was certainly not settled, though. Giggs looked dangerous and was sure to create a big chance at some point. Beckham was playing well too and although Ferguson would have hoped for more from Yorke and Cole in the second half, he had capable replacements on the bench if he needed them. Sheringham scored and assisted in the FA Cup Final, while Ole Gunnar Solskjær had a reputation for delivering big goals in big moments, so the options were there.

Bayern retained their 1-4-1-4-1 for the second half, with Basler and Zickler dropping deeper when out of possession. They allowed Neville and Irwin to have the ball and prioritised limiting their ability to pass forward to United's wingers. Hard work was particularly demanded of Zickler, who was tasked with preventing Neville (and Beckham if he dropped deep) from passing to Giggs. Matthäus could look to take control of the game by operating between the lines.

Bayern still could not stop Giggs getting on the ball and dribbling dangerously. In the 56th minute he provided the quality chance that he had been threatening to create for most of the match, crossing left-footed for Blomqvist, who was making an inward run from the left. The Swede got in front of Babbel but put the ball over the bar from the edge of the six-yard box. It was United's best chance of the night so far and it was completely unsurprising that Giggs was responsible for it.

Both teams had endured long, difficult seasons and they began to tire early. With the technical standard of the match reducing, United were in danger of the game drifting away from them. Therefore, Ferguson acted and made the first substitution of the evening, bringing on FA Cup hero Sheringham in place of Blomqvist. United were now playing more of a 1-4-3-1-2 shape, with Butt holding in midfield, Yorke behind Cole and Sheringham, Beckham on the right and Giggs on the left. As shown by *Figure 20*, Beckham and Giggs started narrow and would then move wide when appropriate. Beckham came narrower than Giggs, sometimes receiving the ball centrally off a defender, passing it on and sprinting out to the right to become an option out wide. Yorke was not playing as a standard attacking midfielder; he

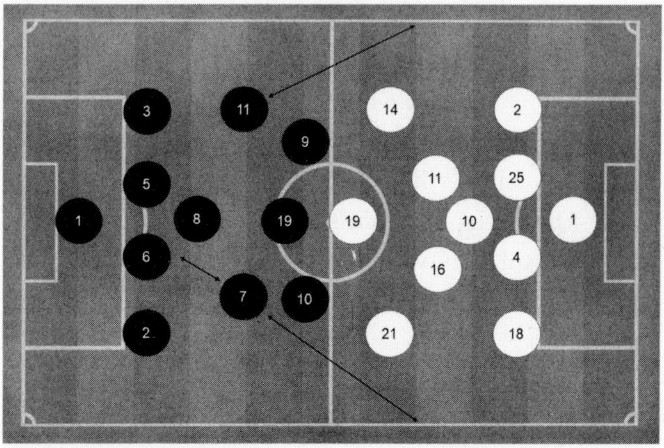

FIGURE 20

was a link player between the midfield and the front two. As time ticked by, Neville and Irwin pushed further forward to support attacks.

Bayern were happy to defend deep, but this was leaving Jancker isolated up front on his own. Stam and Johnsen were able to deal with the German forward, regain possession and play it forward again for their team. Needing more of a threat on the counter-attack, Hitzfeld made his first substitution, replacing Zickler with Scholl. A naturally right-footed attacking midfielder, Scholl was able to drive inwards with intelligence when Bayern had the ball.

Occasionally, United would mix things up by having Yorke move wide when Beckham was narrow. This gave Bayern's man-marking system a problem. Who could keep up with the relentless Beckham? Would somebody follow Yorke out wide and potentially leave Kuffour and Linke two v two against Cole and Sheringham? Overall, though, Beckham was the biggest issue for Munich. Maintaining a high level of passing at such an intensity, deep into an exhausting season off the back of a controversial World Cup campaign, was truly incredible. Matthäus and Jeremies swapped positions in the hope that Matthäus could use his experience to marshal Beckham more effectively.

Introducing Scholl was a good move by Hitzfeld and it gave fresh impetus to Bayern. Within two minutes of coming on, Scholl threaded a lovely pass through United's defence for Jancker, who laid the ball into the path of Effenberg in the United penalty area. Schmeichel kept his side in the game by tipping Effenberg's shot over the bar. Effenberg's run was not tracked by anyone, with United now a man less in midfield when caught in transition. Bayern counter-attacked again in the 79th minute and Scholl dinked the ball over Schmeichel, only for his effort to hit the post and bounce into the hands of the grateful Danish keeper. The Bavarians squandered two big chances to put the game to bed. If either of those had resulted in a goal, Hitzfeld would have been lauded for the excellent timing of his substitution. Instead, his second substitution would end up being much more memorable. Matthäus was exhausted and not prepared to chase Beckham any longer, so he was replaced by Thorsten Fink in the 80th minute. A minute later, Andy Cole made way for notorious super-sub Solskjær. It had not been Cole's night, but he deserved commendation for his wonderful season.

Another big Bayern chance was wasted in the 84th minute, this time by Jancker. United switched off on the second phase of a corner, like they had done when they conceded against Inter. Jancker was left free on the edge of the six-yard box but his overhead kick crashed against the crossbar. Bayern capitalised on their one big moment in the first half. In the second, they had three come their way and they failed to score with any of them.

Without Matthäus on the pitch, Bayern began to lose their shape and United were able to build some pressure again. Solskjær had a good headed chance that he failed to convert. United were in a race against the clock to create one final quality opportunity and they had no more attacking options on the bench. In their first group-stage match of the season Bayern threw away a 1-0 lead with three minutes to go against Brøndby – it had happened before and it could happen again. To try and force the Mancunians back towards their own goal, Bayern replaced Basler with Hasan Salihamidžić, swapping right-winger for right-winger in search of new counter-attacking energy.

With 90 minutes almost up and three minutes of added time to come, Babbel misplaced a pass aimed for Finke, who was forced to clear the ball out of play under pressure from Solksjær. United had a throw-in on their left-hand side, deep in Bayern's half. Neville came across from the right to take a long throw, which Bayern cleared to the edge of their penalty area, where Beckham collected the ball, dribbled past Scholl and passed wide to Neville. His first-time cross was blocked by Effenberg – corner for United. Beckham to take. Schmeichel sprinted forward for the corner – it was now or never. Beckham crossed towards the centre of the box and Bayern, under pressure from Schmeichel, failed to clear the initial cross. The ball came to Giggs on the edge of the area, who hit a tame volley. As the ball trickled towards the goal, Sheringham reacted first – side-on so that he could quickly swivel and strike low into the bottom corner. After a frustrating season on a personal level, he had now scored two cup-final goals in the space of four days.

United changed back to their usual 1-4-4-2 shape, with Yorke on the right and Beckham back in central midfield, but with a minute or so left there was little emphasis on formations – Bayern were shellshocked and booted possession straight back to United from the restart. Irwin knocked a channel ball long down the left-hand side for Solksjær to chase as United looked to test Bayern once more before the end of regulation time. Solksjær beat Kuffour to the ball and blasted it against the Ghanaian defender to win another corner.

Beckham delivered another cross towards the middle of the penalty area – the plan appeared to be to simply put the ball into an area where his team-mates could challenge for it and try to make something happen, rather than conducting any specific set piece routines. Of course, Schmeichel stayed back for this corner now that the scores were level. Sheringham got to the cross first but he had jumped a split second too early, limiting the amount of contact that he could get on his header. So, instead of trying to head powerfully downwards towards the near post, he flicked the ball on in the hope that a United player would win the second ball. Kuffour, who had been marking Solskjær, got attracted towards the ball and was caught the wrong side of his man, leaving the Norwegian to reach out and poke home. United had turned the game around in the greatest 134 seconds in the club's history. There was absolute bedlam in the stands and on the pitch, where the United substitutes had all sprinted across to mob the scorer. A team that had spent an entire season redefining the meaning of 'impossible' left its greatest comeback until last.

Bayern hopefully punted the ball long with seconds left on the clock, but Stam won the aerial challenge for the ball and Butt hooked it back over the halfway line as the final whistle blew. United had to wait an awfully long time for their two big moments, but they took them both and were European champions as a result. With regards to Bayern, they did not take their chances in the second half and failed to effectively defend two corners in stoppage time – fatal errors in elite football. You must earn the right to be champions of big competitions and Bayern did not do enough. It is nonsensical to suggest that Bayern deserved to win simply because they had some big chances; they would have deserved to win if they had scored them. After the journey that they had endured throughout the competition, United were worthy victors.

Full time – Manchester United 2 Bayern Munich 1

His domestic legacy was already secure but guiding Manchester United to their first European Cup/Champions League triumph in 31 years took Alex Ferguson to a whole new level. He had reached the pinnacle and won the one trophy that had always eluded him. Winning it on what would have been the 90th birthday of Sir Matt Busby, the United manager in 1968, made it even more special. Ferguson knew that he needed to be a European champion to achieve truly legendary status at the football club and now he had managed it. The way in which United won the competition; winning a qualifying round, surviving the Group of Death, beating Italian opposition twice and then rescuing the final in stoppage time, was deserving of its place in the history books. The last English European Cup win – Liverpool's in 1984 – also came alongside two domestic honours (the First Division and the League Cup), but no English side had ever won a First Division/Premier League, FA Cup and European Cup/Champions League treble before.

From a tactical perspective, United's victory was a fascinating one. In the quarter-final they faced an Inter side that played in the 'old' Italian way, with a sweeper and two man-markers, functional wing-backs and midfielders, *trequartisti* and athletic forwards. Then in the semi-final, they defeated a star-studded Juventus side that Ancelotti had playing the 'new', Sacchi-inspired Italian way, with two lines of four and an offside trap. Finally, Bayern Munich epitomised the German approach to football in the 1990s with a sweeper, man-marking and physically strong attacking players.

Ferguson defeated these teams with his trusted 1-4-4-2 formation – the most common formation in English football at the time – and a Plan B of a moving Yorke behind two more advanced strikers. He made far fewer in-game adjustments than his opponents, but that was because he did not need to change things as often. His game plan suited his players, all of whom believed in what he was trying to achieve. When changes were necessary, they were effective. Decisions such as bringing Phil Neville on as a left-sided midfielder in Milan displayed an ability to read a match and act accordingly. He did not waste substitutions and timed them well, not least in the final where both substitutes scored the goals that turned the game around. This also shows the importance of man-management – Sheringham and Solskjær were occasionally frustrated by their lack of game time, but Ferguson had them primed to be ready for when he needed them to deliver. There was no great tactical secret behind United's success, but the importance of having a positive team culture was clear for all to see.

Ferguson won a long list of individual honours as a reward for his incredible managerial performance. He was the European Football Coach of the Season, the Premier League Manager of the Season, the LMA Manager of the Year, the Onze d'Or Coach of the Year, and the IFFHS World's Best Club Coach. He was also knighted and given the BBC Sports Personality of the Year Best Coach Award.

United's standout players were also awarded for their performances. Beckham finished second behind Rivaldo in both the Ballon d'Or and FIFA World Player of the

Year votes – what a response to the World Cup controversy (another sign of Ferguson's man-management ability). Keane finished sixth in the Ballon d'Or vote, while Yorke, Stam, Schmeichel, Giggs and Cole also made the shortlist. In the FIFA World Player of the Year standings, Cole finished ninth and Yorke tenth.

Part 2

Liverpool 2004/05

The 1999/00 Champions League saw further expansion to the competition with the admission of four teams from each of Italy, Germany and Spain, and three each from France, the Netherlands and England. It was thanks to United's success the previous season that England ranked as the sixth best league in Europe and attained the third qualification spot. England finally reached third place in the league rankings (behind Spain and Italy) and earned a fourth qualification spot for the 2002/03 edition. These extra places were wasted, though, as England only had three semi-finalists between 2000 and 2004 – Leeds United in 2000/01, Manchester United in 2001/02 and Chelsea in 2003/04.

Liverpool had been at the forefront of English football's continental dominance in the late 1970s and early 1980s, winning the UEFA Cup in 1976 before winning the European Cup four times between 1977 and 1984. They then spent six years away from European competition in the aftermath of the Heysel disaster. The club experienced more dark times in 1989, when 96 supporters never came home from their side's FA Cup semi-final against Nottingham

Forest at Hillsborough Stadium in Sheffield. In the aftermath of such devastation and the departure of several key figures, the 1990s was a difficult decade for the club, with no league title after the advent of the Premier League and only one continental campaign of note – reaching the semi-final of the European Cup Winners' Cup in the 1996/97 season. Frenchman Gérard Houllier came in and won a cup treble in 2001 consisting of the League Cup, the FA Cup and the UEFA Cup (the latter of which saw the Reds impressively defeat Roma, Porto and Barcelona before beating Deportivo Alavés in the final), but they never kicked on to greater heights.

Houllier was replaced in the summer of 2004 by Rafael Benítez, who arrived on Merseyside off the back of winning La Liga and the UEFA Cup with Valencia. Three key elements of Houllier's side were sold – Michael Owen (who won the Ballon d'Or in 2001), Danny Murphy and Markus Babbel (he had joined from Bayern Munich in 2000). Houllier's last act as Liverpool boss was to sign forward Djibril Cissé for £14m before Benítez recruited four fellow Spaniards – José González Rey (Josemi), Antonio Núñez, Xabi Alonso and Luis García.

Benítez endured a slow start domestically and spent much of the season battling with local rivals Everton for a place in the top four, although he managed to reach the final of the League Cup (more on this later). Like United in 1998/99, Liverpool's European campaign began in the final qualifying round. They beat Grazer AK 2-1 on aggregate, with Steven Gerrard scoring both goals in a 2-0 away win before the Austrian side claimed a 1-0 win at Anfield. Liverpool only scored six goals in the group stage and three of them came in the last half of the last match. By the final matchday, Monaco had guaranteed their passage to the knockout stages and Deportivo La Coruña, semi-finalists in 2003/04, were rooted to the foot of the table. Liverpool needed to beat Greek side Olympiakos by two clear goals to progress and avoid dropping into the UEFA Cup. Olympiakos led 1-0 at half-time, but a tactical switch from 1-4-4-1-1 to 1-3-4-1-2 helped Liverpool complete the necessary comeback, with a late Gerrard thunderbolt securing a 3-1 win.

In the round of 16, Bayer Leverkusen were swept aside 3-1 in both legs. Liverpool were not expected to challenge for the 2004/05 Champions League as they continued to falter domestically, but when it comes to Liverpool and European football, anything is possible.

Chapter 4

Quarter-final – Liverpool 2 Juventus 1 (aggregate)

First leg: Liverpool 2 Juventus 1, 5 April 2005

The quarter-final draw meant Liverpool would play against Juventus, whom they had not met since the aforementioned Heysel tragedy. Fears of crowd safety dominated the narrative in the build-up to both legs, creating a difficult environment within which the two teams had to try and focus on the actual football.

After their defeat to United in 1999, Juventus failed to even reach the quarter-final of the Champions League until they went all the way to the final in 2002/03. Having won Serie A that season, they were expected to see off fellow Italians AC Milan but fell short on penalties after a goalless draw at Old Trafford.

Milan were managed by Ancelotti, who had been sacked by Juve in 2001. Although Serie A was no longer so far ahead as Europe's standout league, Juventus were still a top side on paper and were managed by the legendary Fabio Capello. Capello had a poor record against Liverpool, losing to them as Roma manager in both the 2000/01 UEFA Cup and the 2001/02 Champions League. Considering his squad's strength in comparison to Benítez's, Capello was expected to right those wrongs and emerge victorious here.

The team selections are shown by *Figure 21.*

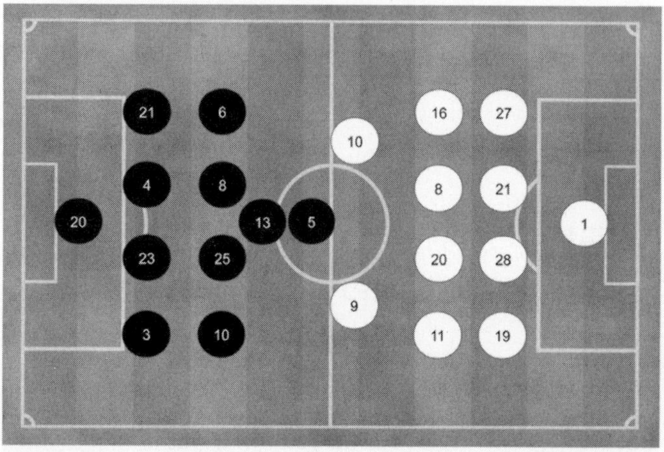

FIGURE 21

Liverpool (1-4-4-1-1): 20. Carson; 3. Finnan, 23. Carragher, 4. Hyypiä, 21. Traoré; 10. García, 25. Bišćan, 8. Gerrard (captain), 6. Riise; 13. Le Tallec; 5. Baroš.

Substitutes: 1. Dudek, 11. Šmicer, 14. Alonso, 18. Núñez, 32. Welsh, 34. Potter, 35. Warnock.

Head coach: Rafael Benítez.

Juventus (1-4-4-2): 1. Buffon; 27. Zebina, 21. Thuram, 28. Cannavaro, 19. Zambrotta; 16. Camoranesi, 8. Emerson, 20. Blasi, 11. Nedvěd; 10. Del Piero (captain), 9. Ibrahimović.

Substitutes: 33. Chimenti, 4. Montero, 7. Pessotto, 17. Trezeguet, 18. Appiah, 24. Olivera, 25. Zalayeta.

Head coach: Fabio Capello.

The players were a greeted by a raucous Anfield atmosphere, which then was silenced in memory of those who lost their lives at Heysel.

Liverpool had so many injuries going into this game that their starting 11 effectively picked itself. Xabi Alonso wasn't in from the beginning because his return from a broken ankle sustained in January was being carefully managed. Scott Carson was 19 years of age and making his European debut, with Jerzy Dudek nursing a groin problem and Chris Kirkland out with a long-term back injury. Steve Finnan was a popular and reliable right-back who, similarly to Neville in Part 1, could push forward to support attacks but preferred to make simple decisions with the ball and focus on defending. Jamie Carragher was a tough-tackling defender enjoying his first season as a centre-back after spending most of his time under Houllier as a full-back. He partnered Sami Hyypiä – a marvellous Finn who rarely got the credit that he deserved from outside the club. Djimi Traoré had endured a difficult Liverpool career so far, but Benítez's decision to move Carragher into the middle had given him a fresh opportunity to establish himself at left-back. He supported attacks less than Finnan, ensuring that his side always had at least three defenders back as cover.

Luis García had struggled to adapt to the physicality of the Premier League but had a knack of performing in Europe, scoring three goals across the two legs against Bayer Leverkusen. Igor Bišćan, like Traoré, had struggled to perform consistently in a Liverpool shirt but was getting a run in the team due to an injury to Dietmar Hamann. Alongside him, Steven Gerrard played deeper than usual in the absence of Alonso. Captain since 2003, he was rapidly developing into one of the world's most complete midfielders and was very vocal about his desire to challenge for the game's highest honours. John Arne Riise was comfortable as either a left-back or a left-winger, and was not a great dribbler but could strike a ball magnificently. Aged 20, Anthony Le Tallec was given a rare start behind lively Czech striker Milan Baroš.

Juventus played in their usual 1-4-4-2 shape and had world-class talent all over the pitch. Gianluigi Buffon had become the world's most expensive goalkeeper when he joined from Parma in 2001. The four defenders were all extremely talented – Thuram and Cannavaro enjoyed one of the best centre-back partnerships of the era. Zebina was a more defensive full-back than Zambrotta, who loved to fly forward into advanced areas. Emerson and Blasi were both functional central midfielders who offered little creativity, tasked instead with covering defensively while Mauro Camoranesi and Pavel Nedvěd attacked with the exceptional Zlatan Ibrahimović and Alessandro Del Piero.

In Part 1, both Italian visitors to Old Trafford tried starting fast in the hope of imposing themselves on proceedings, something that worked for Juve in the semi-final. They opted for a slower, more reserved beginning here, though, and it completely backfired. The tone for the first half was set at kick-off as Emerson slipped over under pressure from the onrushing Baroš. They had less individual quality than the Turinese, so Liverpool knew that they needed to start with a high intensity – the longer it took for the away side to settle, the more chance the Reds had of getting a lead before Juve found their rhythm and established superiority. Capello's side wanted to take the sting out of the match and trust that their ability would eventually shine through.

Liverpool's intensity gave them the upper hand in the opening stages. They played early, direct passes between Cannavaro and Zambrotta for Baroš to chase one v one against Cannavaro. The Italian centre-back was an extremely intelligent defender, but he was vulnerable when forced into running back to defend space behind the back line. In the ninth minute, Baroš beat him to a direct pass and won the home side a corner. Gerrard swung it out to the near post, where García beat Ibrahimović to the ball and flicked it on to the far edge of the six-yard box. There, Zebina switched off and let Hyypiä drive a lovely volley past Buffon and into the net. A good start was vital for the Reds and they had achieved one – they were 1-0 up after ten minutes. As much as it was a well-taken corner, questions must be asked about how 6ft 3in Ibrahimović allowed 5ft 7in García to beat him at the near post. Zebina's attempt at marking Hyypiä was also extremely poor. Simply, Liverpool wanted to score from that corner more than Juventus wanted to effectively defend it. The team with the most desire came out on top.

Due to their early dominance, Liverpool were comfortable playing short from Carson as well as going long to Le Tallec, who was fantastic in the air. They continued to try and play early for Baroš to run against Cannavaro, a situation that was exacerbated from a Juve perspective by the fact that Zambrotta pushed up high on his side's left wing when they had the ball and left space behind him. As balls were played forward for Baroš, García would move inside from the right to be a central passing option, with Le Tallec regularly drifting over to the right in case Baroš needed to pass backwards. On the far side, Riise would make runs outside Zebina to maintain width. Whereas Gerrard would normally play in the role being performed by Le Tallec, he was deeper here to be the side's primary passer. With no Alonso, it was Gerrard's job to play the searching, riskier passes while Biščan acted as the team's main ball-winner. This role limited Gerrard's ability to make lung-bursting forward runs, but it was necessary to maintain balance.

Carragher and Hyypiä spent the first half sticking tight to Ibrahimović and Del Piero, so Juventus's attacking plan revolved around trying to drag those two out of position and leave space for Nedvěd to move into the area highlighted in

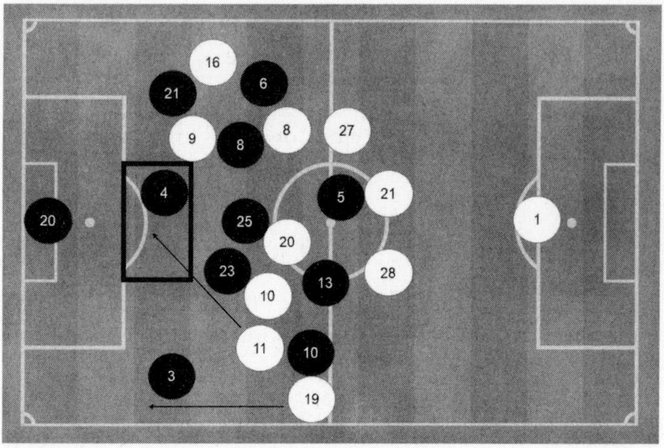

FIGURE 22

Figure 22, which is commonly referred to as 'Zone 14'. In the mid-2000s, Zone 14 was generally acknowledged as the best area on the pitch for creating goalscoring chances and it made sense for Juve to try and get someone as talented as Pavel Nedvěd into this position. Nedvěd was proven at the top level and if he could move into Zone 14 and receive the ball on his preferred right foot then he would undoubtedly create high-quality attacking situations for his team. Liverpool defended in a 1-4-4-2 shape and relied on García to track Zambrotta and, most importantly, Finnan to diligently defend against Nedvěd.

Liverpool doubled their lead in the 25th minute with one of the goals of the season. Once again, Luis García delivered a big goal on the European stage. García's goal is illustrated by *Figure 23*, with the arrows showing the ball's path as Finnan lobbed Zambrotta to find Le Tallec, who had moved to the right as García made a run inside. As Baroš made a forward burst in anticipation of another direct ball down the Liverpool right, taking Cannavaro with him, Le Tallec played a hopeful ball forward into the space vacated by the

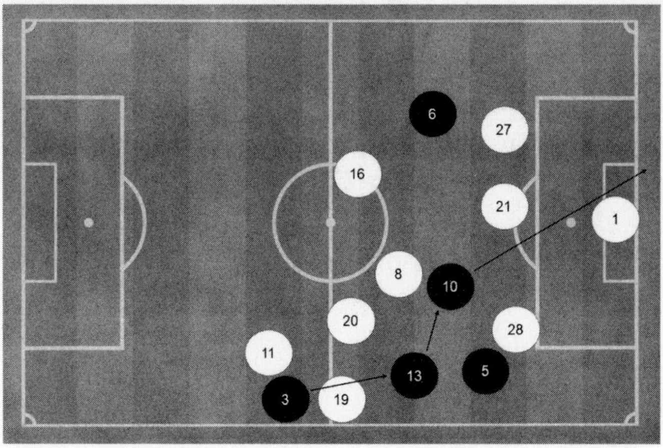

FIGURE 23

Czech forward. García, once again with more desire than his opponent, beat Emerson to the loose ball and spectacularly volleyed over Buffon for 2-0. Credit must go to Benítez, who had clearly asked Le Tallec and García to rotate, and those movements had now led to a goal.

Ibrahimović hit the post with a shot from the edge of the area straight after García's goal, warning Liverpool that the Turinese had the quality to strike back if given the opportunity. Nedvěd then successfully received the ball in Zone 14 and played a pass into space behind Carragher for Del Piero to run on to. Carson, on the biggest night of his career so far, saved the Italian's shot from short range to keep the score at 2-0. A third big Juventus chance came in the 40th minute, when Camoranesi played a direct pass over the top for Del Piero to run in behind. Del Piero headed over Carson and into the goal, but the linesman flagged incorrectly for offside. Again, no team has won the Champions League without some luck on the way.

García's goal had awoken the Juventus beast and Del Piero's offside effort prompted Liverpool to drop deep and slow the game down so that they could survive to the end of the first half without conceding a goal. Having started full of excitement and energy, they now needed to show concentration and discipline as Juve looked to get back into the tie.

Liverpool's shirt sponsor for the 2004/05 season was a certain Danish beer that, if they did first halves, would probably have done this one. The Merseysiders knew that a fast start was crucial, but a two-goal lead against one of Europe's form sides was the stuff of dreams.

Half-time – Liverpool 2 Juventus 0

Capello acted at half-time and made a substitution, replacing Blasi with Pessotto. As seen in Part 1, Pessotto usually played at full-back, but he was brought on here in central midfield. Juventus's new system is shown in *Figure 24.* They

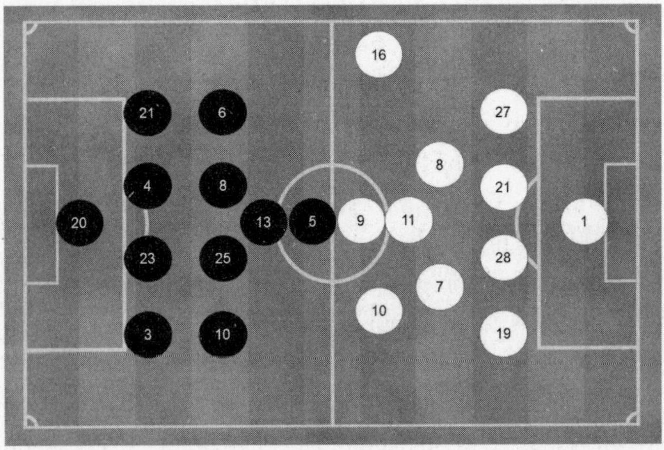

FIGURE 24

changed to a lopsided 1-4-2-3-1, with no out-and-out left-winger, though they moved back into a 1-4-4-2 when they lost possession. Del Piero started on the left side of a line of three behind Ibrahimović but made narrow forward runs while Zambrotta or Pessotto overlapped outside him. Nedvěd operated centrally instead of starting wide and moving inwards, though he retreated to the left of midfield out of possession to form the 1-4-4-2 defensive shape so that Del Piero could stay high up the pitch.

The Italians started the second half well, winning two early corners and taking them quickly as they looked to set the pace rather than suffer under it. They tried to overload their left-hand side with Zambrotta and Pessotto, while using Del Piero to make direct runs against Carragher. Theoretically, this would either force Finnan and Carragher deeper and create space in front of them, or they would push out to press and sacrifice space behind them. Finnan stood tall against the dangerous Zambrotta and Pessotto, aided by García tracking back to support him. Carragher and Hyypiä defended differently to in the first half, remaining in position rather than tracking opponents tightly. This left space in front of the Liverpool back four rather than behind it, so the midfield had to drop deeper and defend this space. The defence and midfield lines retained their vertical compactness, but Le Tallec and Baroš were left isolated further forward. Under increasing pressure, Liverpool continued to try and play direct passes early, now looking aerially for Le Tallec rather than into space behind for Baroš. Le Tallec used his height well to win initial aerial duels, but he struggled to retain possession for long enough to allow his team-mates to move high in support. It was a lot of pressure for a young player to deal with on his first Champions League start.

With an hour gone Juventus made their second substitution, introducing French star David Trezeguet in place of Del Piero. Trezeguet was deployed as the right-sided striker, with Ibrahimović to his left. This placed Trezeguet

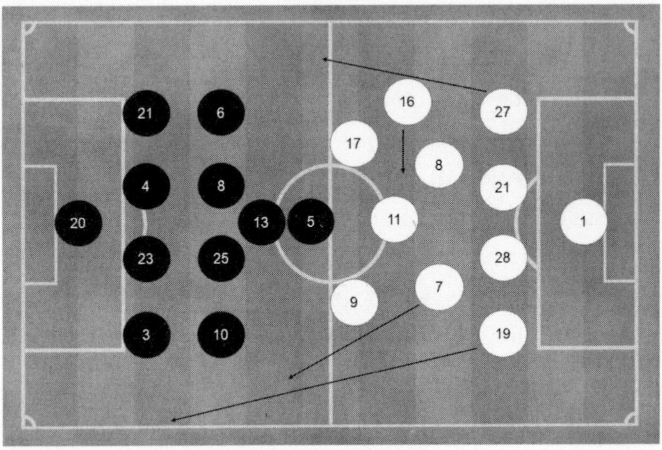

FIGURE 25

against Hyypiä, and Ibrahimović, who had been kept quiet by the big Finn, against Carragher. Nedvěd stayed central behind the pair but continued to fall back into a left-midfield position out of possession. Zambrotta kept overlapping from left-back and was now joined by right-back Zebina, who was more adventurous than before as Camoranesi tucked inside to get on the ball more. These movements are shown by the arrows on *Figure 25.*

The away goal that Juventus craved finally came in the 63rd minute. For the third time in the second half, Juventus took a short corner before crossing into the box, taking Riise and Baroš out of the penalty area. Liverpool cleared this cross thanks to Traoré at the back post, but it fell to Zambrotta wide on Juve's left with space to cross first time. He played the ball back across the penalty area to Cannavaro, who beat Finnan in the air and headed the ball down into the ground in front of Carson. The young goalkeeper, evidently nervous, dived too early and the ball bounced over him and into the goal. Liverpool now had a decision to make – try and push for a third goal or settle for a slender 2-1 lead? With several players looking exhausted and no substitute forwards on the bench, Benítez chose the latter option.

With Juventus still on top, Liverpool made their first change after 65 minutes of play. Baroš had ran himself into the ground, selflessly chasing direct passes, and was swapped for Antonio Núñez. Núñez played on the right of midfield, with García central behind Le Tallec, who was now the centre-forward. Liverpool continued to look long to Le Tallec in the hope that García's technical ability would help him to retain possession easier. The young Frenchman was lacking match fitness and was rapidly tiring though, so was replaced by Vladimír Šmicer seven minutes later. Šmicer took Le Tallec's place up front despite naturally being a winger. Benítez simply had to work with what he had at his disposal and hoped that Šmicer would run the channels well to force the Juventus back line deeper and get Liverpool up the pitch. Núñez took a while to get into the game and bemused the Anfield crowd when he ran back from an offside position to latch on to a pass aimed for Finnan, bringing to an end the first decent spell of Liverpool possession all half.

Despite his shaky start, Núñez settled down and began to combine well with Finnan down the Liverpool right. It was a good move from Benítez to introduce fresh legs on the side of the pitch where Zambrotta was bombing forward on the overlap – the Italian full-back became more cautious now that he had a new winger to deal with. Gerrard and Biščan swapped sides so that Gerrard was the right-sided central midfielder and was closer to Núñez, allowing him to combine with the Spaniard more easily. Pessotto was still occasionally moving wide to support possession, but now also had to be wary of Gerrard's ability to exploit the space that he was leaving centrally. Without a recognised striker on the pitch the Reds lacked a cutting edge, so favoured trying to establish possession in advanced, wide areas rather than looking to goal. Gerrard sometimes grew impatient and looked for killer passes through the centre of the pitch, but Emerson and Blasi used their experience to block central passing lanes and make interceptions. Behind them, Thuram and Cannavaro made light work of dealing with García and Šmicer.

Zebina suffered an injury and was forced to leave the field in the 81st minute, so Montero came on in his place. The visitors attacked with less intensity in the final ten minutes, hoping for a second goal but prepared to leave Merseyside with a one-goal deficit ahead of the return game. Deciding what to settle for in first legs is one of the most crucial elements of European football, because big chances are so few and far between and momentum can change course at any point. For Liverpool, taking a 2-1 lead to Turin would be commendable and give them something to defend out in Italy, but conceding just one goal out there would mean that they would have to find another themselves. They had been odds-on to lose the first leg and be out of the tie by this point, so any lead was better than no lead. As the seconds ticked by towards full time, it made sense to try and retain the ball out wide and slow the game down. For Juventus, Capello had to decide whether or not he trusted his players to score in both legs and, unsurprisingly, he did. They lost away to Real Madrid by a single goal in the round of 16 before turning the tie around in the second meeting; he expected the same to happen again.

Benítez also made the decision to not risk Alonso at all, even though his side were finding it difficult to keep the ball and might have benefited from the added quality. The other outfielders on the bench were young and inexperienced, so the 11 on the pitch were left to see out the final few minutes as the home fans sang their players home with a rousing version of the club's anthem, 'You'll Never Walk Alone'.

Full time – Liverpool 2 Juventus 1

In isolation, beating Juventus was a great achievement for a Liverpool side enduring a testing season. The feeling among many supporters and neutrals alike was that they deserved praise for winning the first leg and giving their fans something to cheer, but conceding the away goal gave hope to a Juventus side that would probably blow the Reds away in Turin. However, those who had paid attention to Valencia's run to UEFA Cup glory the previous season knew that if anybody could set sides up to defend away in Europe, it was Rafael Benítez.

Second leg: Juventus 0 Liverpool 0, 13 April 2005

Four days after their first-leg victory, Liverpool's domestic woes continued with a defeat away at Manchester City. Meanwhile, Juventus drew 3-3 with rivals Fiorentina in a classic encounter. Across all competitions they had scored 13 goals in their most recent seven games. Security for the second leg was extremely tight; firstly because the Liverpool fans were promised a hostile welcome from the home supporters, and secondly because the quarter-final between AC and Inter Milan had to be abandoned the night before as crowd trouble had spilled on to the pitch.

Heysel was once again remembered as part of the pre-match ceremony at the Stadio delle Alpi.

The team selections, shown by *Figure 26*, were as follows:

Liverpool (1-5-3-1-1): 1. Dudek; 3. Finnan, 23. Carragher, 4. Hyypiä (captain), 21. Traoré, 6. Riise; 18. Núñez, 14. Alonso, 25. Biščan; 10. García; 5. Baroš.

Substitutes: 20. Carson, 9. Cissé, 11. Šmicer, 13. Le Tallec, 32. Welsh, 34. Potter, 35. Warnock.

Head coach: Rafael Benítez.

Juventus (1-4-4-2): 1. Buffon; 21. Thuram, 4. Montero, 28. Cannavaro, 19. Zambrotta; 16. Camoranesi, 8. Emerson, 24. Olivera, 11. Nedvěd; 10. Del Piero (captain), 9. Z. Ibrahimović.

Substitutes: 33. Chimenti, 7. Pessotto, 15. Birindelli, 18. Appiah, 20. Blasi, 25. Zalayeta, 34. Masiello.

Head coach: Fabio Capello.

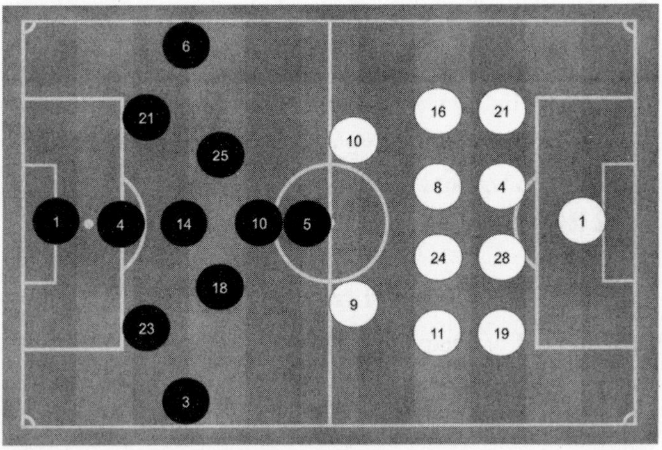

FIGURE 26

With Steven Gerrard added to Liverpool's ever-growing list of injured absentees, Xabi Alonso came in to make his first start in over two months. It would remain to be seen how long he could last, as Liverpool changed shape to protect him. Cissé was also back in the matchday squad for the first time since breaking both his tibia and fibula in October 2004 – the speed of his recovery from such a horrifying injury was incredible. Zebina had not recovered in time to return for Juventus, so Thuram moved to right-back and Montero started in the centre of defence. The attack-minded Rubén Olivera started in midfield instead of Blasi.

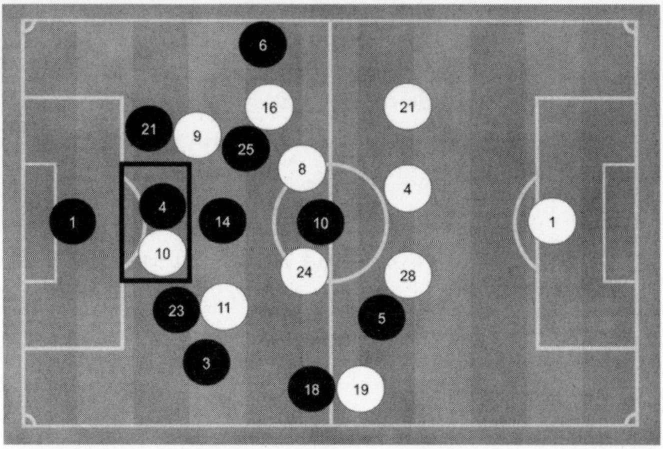

FIGURE 27

Figure 27 shows how the two systems matched up against each other. Liverpool's back five was asymmetrical, with Finnan staying deep while Riise ventured high and wide when the Reds had possession. When Liverpool regained possession and could transition forward, Núñez would move wide into the space vacated by Finnan and sacrificed by Nedvěd, who attacked centrally like in the first leg. This was clever from Benítez – Finnan stayed deep to limit the space for Zambrotta, who also had to track back against Núñez's forward runs. Zambrotta's attacking threat was effectively removed from the match. Finnan's proximity to his centre-backs also closed off the space wanted by Nedvěd.

Baroš was once again tasked with running the channels against Cannavaro, with García offering for the ball in front of the Juve back line. Alonso and Biščan stayed deep to provide central cover, with Liverpool's back line pushed up close behind them to operate an offside trap and shut off access to Zone 14 as much as possible. Unable to play through the visitors, Juventus played long and early. Thuram stayed deep, hoping to entice Riise forward before clipping aerial passes for Ibrahimović to battle for against Traoré. Carragher and Hyypiä stepped forward well to execute their respective roles in the offside trap, but Traoré sometimes found himself too deep and allowed Ibrahimović to latch on to passes that he should have been offside for.

Still nursing a groin problem, Dudek refrained from kicking long when possible and played short to his centre-backs. Alonso dropped deep to assist the centre-backs in creating a safe four v two against Del Piero and Ibrahimović in deep possession. The Basque midfielder recycled possession masterfully with a variety of short and long passes while hardly moving at all. The way in which he managed himself through this match was a true masterclass in the art of 'letting the ball do the work'.

Once safe possession had been established, Liverpool looked long to Baroš and García.

Juventus started slowly, making it clear that they would rather go through on away goals via a boring 1-0 win than push forward and risk competing in an entertaining match. For as long as it was 0-0, they were one moment of quality away from the semi-finals. This approach had worked for them against top-quality opposition in the past, but against a Liverpool team so thin on the ground it seemed unnecessarily cautious. The Reds were content to retain their compactness and stay disciplined, watching the clock tick by.

Juve then changed to a 1-4-1-3-2 shape, with Emerson as a holding midfielder behind an attacking trio of Camoranesi on the right, Olivera central and Nedvěd on the left. Liverpool were able to easily adapt to this change, asking García to man-mark Emerson as Alonso and Biščan shut off the central space against Olivera. As Biščan came narrower to do this, Olivera and Camoranesi swapped over so that Camoranesi could receive slightly deeper and look to thread passes through to Olivera and Nedvěd out wide. Liverpool's offside trap stood strong, though.

Alonso then received a booking for failing to return the ball back to the home side when they wanted to take a quick free kick. He would now have to be careful when making a tackle, not that he looked like having to any time soon. Montero cynically tripped Núñez shortly afterwards, yet he was not yellow-carded. Juventus managed a couple of corner kicks, for which Liverpool had all 11 players back to defend and cleared the ball successfully.

Although Emerson began to dominate his individual battle with García, there was a lack of movement ahead of him and the Liverpudlian defence enjoyed a very comfortable end to the first half.

Half-time – Juventus 0 Liverpool 0

Like at Anfield, Capello made a half-time substitution. Trezeguet was out injured so Capello turned to Marcelo Zalayeta – a tall Uruguayan centre-forward known for his aerial ability. He was utilised as a right-winger here, tasked with being a wide target man against Traoré. Ibrahimović and Del Piero swapped sides, hoping that the big Swede would get some joy in the air against Carragher.

Liverpool had a huge chance to score early in the second half when Alonso threaded a pass between Thuram and Montero for Baroš to run on to. The Czech flicked the ball through the legs of Montero to move into the penalty area one v one against Buffon, but he misplaced his shot and it went wide of the far post. A Liverpool goal would have killed the tie – Juventus were never going to score more than once considering their pedestrian approach.

Zalayeta and Nedvěd swapped wings, before Del Piero moved to the right and Nedvěd came central behind

Ibrahimović. Like in Part 1, the Serie A outfit kept rotating in search of attacking solutions as the Premier League side stayed compact and disciplined in a simple defensive shape.

Benítez made his first change of the night in the 58th minute, swapping Šmicer for the exhausted Núñez and introducing fresh legs against Zambrotta, who had received a booking for a bad tackle on Baroš – he was evidently frustrated by how the Reds were shackling him. Juventus rotated again, putting Del Piero on the left, Zalayeta central and Nedvěd back on the right. They still found it hard to play through the compact Liverpudlian shape. Emerson went into the book for kicking Biščan – the Italian champions-elect could feel their European hopes slipping away from them.

In the 75th minute, Benítez gave Cissé his first minutes in almost six months in place of Baroš. The latter's role in this Liverpool side was clear – he was to selflessly chase channel balls and hassle defenders for between 60 and 75 minutes before being replaced by fresh legs. It was not a glorious role, but it was one that he did well. Cissé had one quality that Baroš did not possess – blistering pace. He added to Zambrotta's problems by speedily chasing direct through balls down the Liverpool right.

Cannavaro nearly made himself Juve's hero when he headed against the post from a free kick and Dudek was forced to parry the rebound off the goal line and out for a corner. Finnan had been yellow-carded for the foul that gave the kick away, providing added danger as Zambrotta threw caution to the wind and began to adventurously overlap again.

The home side made two substitutions in quick succession as Pessotto and Appiah came on for Montero and Camoranesi. They changed to a 1-4-2-1-3 shape, with Nedvěd as an attacking midfielder in front of Emerson and

Appiah. Del Piero, Zalayeta and Ibrahimović formed a line of three strikers looking to attack Liverpool's three centre-backs man-for-man. Cissé was running the right channel well, but García was too tired to offer any support and was replaced by Le Tallec. The visitors now had a tall player to play long balls to, giving them a different option for their forward passes. Juve had scored in all but two of their home games by that point in the season but they had run out of ideas on this occasion – a depleted Liverpool had come to Turin and successfully kept them at bay.

Full time – Juventus 0 Liverpool 0; Liverpool win 2-1 on aggregate

Liverpool disposing of Juventus sent shockwaves around Europe. How could a side so abject and inconsistent domestically better Italy's in-form team over 180 minutes of knockout football? Juventus had lacked dynamism and been far too one-paced, believing that they could control a dull second leg, score once and go through on away goals. With the benefit of hindsight, they would have been better served pushing for an equaliser at Anfield so that Liverpool had to try and score in Turin. Instead, the Reds were able to go through without having a single shot on target at the Stadio delle Alpi.

After his UEFA Cup success, Benítez was now showing his tactical nous on the biggest stage of all – his team caught Juventus offside ten times in the second leg and the way in which he limited the attacking threat of Zambrotta was magnificent. It remained to be seen how far he could take this group of players and his side would certainly not be favourites to win their semi-final.

Chapter 5

Semi-final – Liverpool 1 Chelsea 0 (aggregate)

First leg: Chelsea 0 Liverpool 0, 27 April 2005

As their disappointing league form continued, Liverpool were drawn to face runaway Premier League leaders Chelsea in the Champions League semi-final. The Londoners had fallen at this stage last season and were determined not to fall at the same hurdle again. Although they were not traditional rivals, matches between Liverpool and Chelsea were growing in importance as the Blues had spent a year trying to sign Steven Gerrard from his boyhood club. The intensity of the transfer speculation grew further after Gerrard scored an own goal to equalise for Chelsea in the 2005 League Cup Final, prompting José Mourinho to turn around and signal for the Liverpool fans to be quiet (Chelsea won 3-2 after extra time).

Speculation was rife that if Liverpool failed to qualify for the following season's Champions League then Gerrard would make the move down south. The media was also determined to portray a rivalry between Benítez and Mourinho, something that neither manager went out of their way to play down. Mourinho had never lost a semi-final and had won back-to-back European titles – the UEFA Cup in 2003 and the Champions League in 2004. Benítez was looking to match this achievement.

The team selections for the first leg at Stamford Bridge are shown by *Figure 28*:

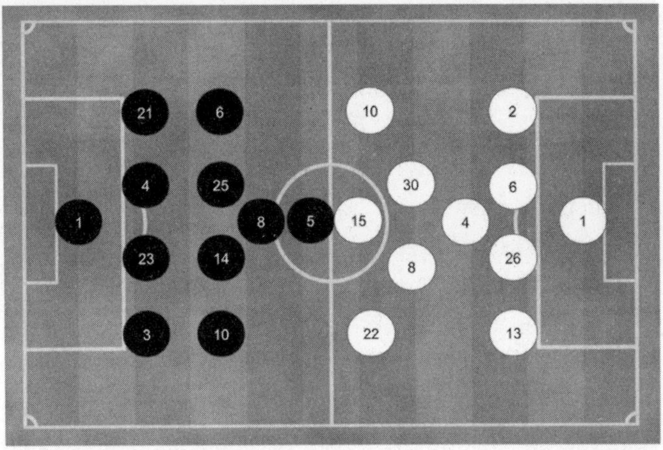

FIGURE 28

Liverpool (1-4-4-1-1): 1. Dudek; 3. Finnan, 23. Carragher, 4. Hyypiä, 21. Traoré; 10. García, 14. Alonso, 25. Biščan, 6. Riise; 8. Gerrard (captain); 5. Baroš.

Substitutes: 20. Carson, 7. Kewell, 9. Cissé, 11. Šmicer, 13. Le Tallec, 18. Núñez, 35. Warnock.

Head coach: Rafael Benítez.

Chelsea (1-4-3-3): 1. Čech; 2. Johnson, 6. Carvalho, 26. Terry (captain), 13. Gallas; 4. Makélélé, 30. Tiago, 8. Lampard; 10. Cole, 22. Guðjohnsen, 15. Drogba.

Substitutes: 23. Cudicini, 5. Smertin, 9. Kežman, 14. Geremi, 16. Robben, 24. Forssell, 29. Huth.

Head coach: José Mourinho.

Chelsea kicked off and patiently circulated possession between their defence and midfielders, giving themselves time to look at Liverpool's defensive shape and see if it was four or five at the back. This was a change of approach from the round of 16 and quarter-final, where they started rapidly and scored four first-half goals across their two home legs. They were perhaps wary of their Liverpudlian opponents, who had taken a first-minute lead against them in the League Cup Final.

Mourinho had taken the Premier League by storm with a powerful 1-4-3-3 formation that combined solid defending with offensive excellence. Petr Čech was a summer signing from Rennes and had taken over from Carlo Cudicini as Chelsea's first-choice goalkeeper. He was having an impressive first term, aided by the formidable centre-back pairing of Ricardo Carvalho and John Terry. Glen Johnson and William Gallas were trusted with filling in for the injured Paulo Ferreira and Wayne Bridge in the full-back positions. Claude Makélélé was arguably the best defensive central midfielder on the planet, sweeping up behind Tiago Mendes (known simply as Tiago) and Frank Lampard, the latter of whom was regularly compared to Steven Gerrard by fans and press alike. There was added tension because Lampard had been responsible for Alonso's broken ankle when the sides met three months ago. Damien Duff was out with a long-term problem and Arjen Robben was only fit enough for the bench, so Joe Cole started on the right with Eiður Guðjohnsen on the left. Ivorian striker Didier Drogba was the side's target man, a capable finisher who was good at holding the ball up with his back to goal. Despite the absentees, this was still a very strong Chelsea team.

Chelsea soon found their rhythm and began to try and progress the ball forward. Goal kicks went long and central to Drogba, with Cole and Guðjohnsen making runs beyond him in anticipation of flick-ons. When playing from defence into midfield, Tiago or Lampard would drop alongside Makélélé to help overload Gerrard and Baroš. Drogba could then move into the space vacated by the deeper midfielder and look to take a Liverpool centre-back with him, which in turn left space for Cole or Guðjohnsen to make a forward run into. Liverpool once again looked well drilled and it took until the 13th minute for Chelsea to create their first half-chance, after Drogba got a shot off from a Cole cross. Cole, who had scored the winning goal in both league matches between the sides that season, was two-footed and very difficult for Traoré to defend in one v one situations.

Like Liverpool, Chelsea did not press high up the pitch and prioritised limiting the space between their midfield and defence, allowing Makélélé to sweep laterally between the lines to intercept passes. This was preventing Gerrard from receiving the ball as often as Liverpool wanted, so they adapted their attacking shape, as shown by *Figure 29*. When the ball was on the Liverpool right, García would drift infield to occupy Makélélé, allowing Gerrard to drop deeper unfollowed. This would pull Guðjohnsen inside, allowing Finnan to make short, late overlaps out wide. Gerrard looked to receive and quickly switch play across to Riise,

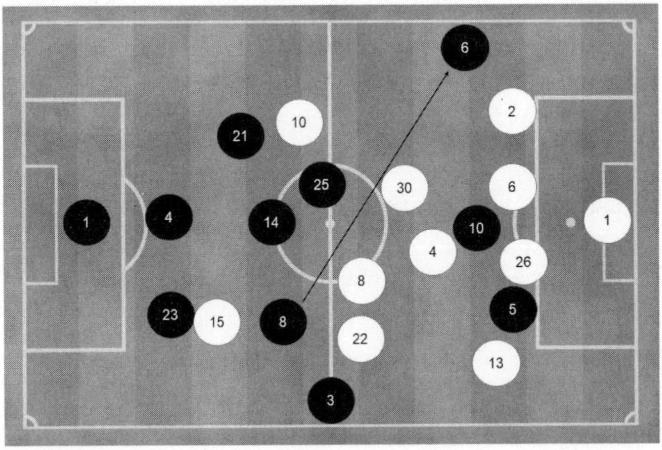

FIGURE 29

who attacked Johnson one v one and found success in doing so. He regularly beat the Chelsea right-back and got crosses into the box, however the Reds only had Baroš in there up against Carvalho and Terry. Two key one v one battles had been established and they were both on the same side – Cole v Traoré and Riise v Johnson.

Liverpool enjoyed 51 per cent of possession in the opening 20 minutes and looked very comfortable. The home fans were disgruntled until Lampard missed a gilt-edged opportunity, volleying over the crossbar from the edge of the six-yard box. This spurred Chelsea on to play with more purpose and the referee made a huge call when he decided not to book Bišćan when he cynically fouled Guðjohnsen to prevent a counter-attack. A yellow card would have left both Bišćan and Alonso one caution away from a suspension. Tiago showed some impetus in the 30th minute when he received the ball deep and drove forward against the Liverpool midfield, causing disarray and creating a shooting chance for Lampard. It was vital for Liverpool that they survived this wave of Chelsea momentum without conceding, so they slowed the game down by taking their time over set pieces and retaining the ball safely in wide areas. They nearly got the perfect reward when Gerrard found Baroš with a wonderful cross in the 37th minute, but Čech saved well to keep the match goalless.

Half-time – Chelsea 0 Liverpool 0

The key to Mourinho's managerial approach was always appearing to be in control. He had spent the first half calmly sat in the dugout, looking relaxed and trying to convince spectators that his side were in no rush and would outperform their opponents eventually. He had drawn the first leg of the Champions League semi-final 0-0 with Porto in the previous season and seemed prepared to accept the same result this time around. Liverpool were fine with this, content to make the tie a single 90-minute knockout match back at Anfield. The most important thing for both managers was that they did not concede the first goal because they knew how capable the other one was at setting his team up to defend.

Chelsea started the second half faster than the first, which was unsurprising because the home fans would have not reacted well to another laborious opening. Liverpool stood firm, though, with Biščan winning a lot of duels and Alonso and Gerrard showing their ability to escape pressure with the ball on transition. Biščan undid his good work by fouling Lampard and inexplicably throwing the ball away, for which he was booked. He had thrown the ball away to prevent Chelsea taking a quick free kick when they did not even want to. Now, that tightrope both he and Alonso were walking became of greater concern to Liverpool as there were still doubts over the fitness of Dietmar Hamann.

To try and suppress Gerrard and Alonso, Chelsea began to press higher to limit the space available in midfield. Makélélé tracked Gerrard closely to force Liverpool into needing different ideas in possession. Just before the hour mark, Tiago was replaced by Robben to try and provide some much-needed width to Chelsea's play. He was introduced on the left with Guðjohnsen becoming the left-sided central midfielder. Robben did not stick to the left for long though, rotating with Cole so that Finnan and Traoré could not settle and focus on just one opponent.

After another selfless shift up front, Baroš was swapped for Cissé as Benítez once again looked for an injection of pace to occupy the opposing back line. The referee then impacted the game once again when he failed to punish Terry for going over the top of the ball and crunching García's ankle.

In the 78th minute, striker Mateja Kežman, came on for Cole on the right wing in the absence of a more natural replacement. Traoré deserved credit for surviving the battle with Cole and encouraging Mourinho to make a change.

Liverpool began to tire and find it harder to retain possession, in no small part due to Makélélé's fantastic subduing of Gerrard. Benítez reacted to this with his second substitution of the night after 86 minutes as Kewell came on for Bišćan, with the Australian playing as the attacking midfielder and Gerrard dropping deeper. This also saved Bišćan from another booking and ensured his availability for the return game. Within seconds of this change, Alonso was booked after he was judged to have pulled back Guðjohnsen when the Icelandic international had simply taken a dive. Alonso was devastated at his suspension.

Kewell and Cissé combined well twice on Liverpool's right-hand side, forcing Gallas – who had begun to push forward in support of attacks – to retreat and be more defensive. Once again, Benítez showed his ability to effectively shackle opposition full-backs by giving them new situations to defend against. He elected to occupy Gallas further by sending on Šmicer for García. García was also the furthest player away from the dugout at the time of the substitution, so his leaving the pitch wasted valuable seconds as Liverpool looked to see the game out.

Full time – Chelsea 0 Liverpool 0

It was a forgettable match, but Liverpool had achieved exactly what they wanted – it was their first clean sheet against Chelsea that season after three previous attempts had proved unsuccessful. If they could repeat this feat in the second leg then they would give themselves a massive chance of reaching the final.

Second leg: Liverpool 1 Chelsea 0, 3 May 2005

A spectacular Steven Gerrard strike rescued a point for Liverpool at home to Middlesbrough in their next fixture, while Chelsea sealed their first league title for 50 years with a 2-0 win against Bolton Wanderers – Lampard scoring both goals. Only a fool would have completely ruled Liverpool out ahead of a knockout tie at Anfield, but Chelsea were still overwhelming favourites to qualify for the final in Istanbul.

The team selections are shown by *Figure 30*:

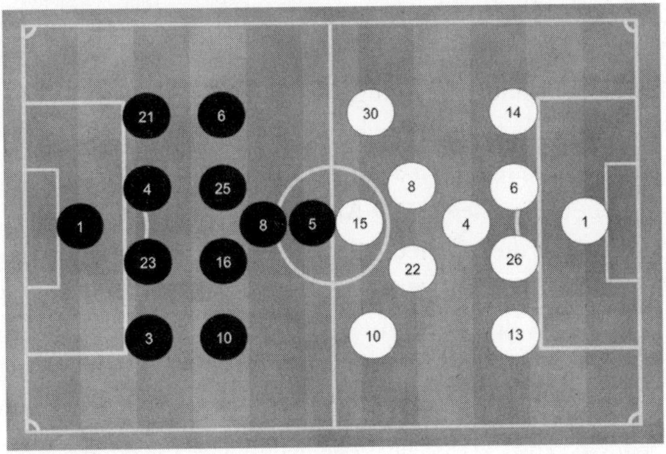

FIGURE 30

Liverpool (1-4-4-1-1): 1. Dudek; 3. Finnan, 23. Carragher, 4. Hyypiä, 21. Traoré; 10. García, 16. Hamann, 25. Biščan, 6. Riise; 8. Gerrard (captain); 5. Baroš.

Substitutes: 20. Carson, 7. Kewell, 9. Cissé, 11. Šmicer, 18. Núñez, 32. Welsh, 35. Warnock.

Head coach: Rafael Benítez.

Chelsea (1-4-3-3): 1. Čech; 14. Geremi, 6. Carvalho, 26. Terry (captain), 13. Gallas; 4. Makélélé, 8. Lampard, 22. Guðjohnsen; 30. Tiago, 10. Cole, 15. Drogba.

Substitutes: 23. Cudicini, 2. Johnson, 9. Kežman, 16. Robben, 24. Forssell, 29. Huth, 33. Morais.

Head coach: José Mourinho.

Liverpool made one enforced change from the first leg, with Dietmar Hamann making his first appearance in six weeks in place of Alonso. Hamann's return was huge for the Reds as his experience of playing in big occasions was invaluable. Chelsea had seemingly hoped that the German midfielder would not be available, with Guðjohnsen starting centrally, perhaps anticipating Gerrard beginning deeper, as he had done did against Juventus. The Iceland international was a good dribbler and would have wanted to occupy the Liverpool talisman to keep him from attacking himself, but now he was faced with two ball-winning midfielders in Hamann and Biščan. Geremi, a tough-tackling central midfielder by trade, was selected at right-back instead of Johnson, who had endured a tough night at Stamford Bridge.

The atmosphere inside Anfield was phenomenal – Terry would later describe it as the best that he had experienced. Mourinho had claimed pre-match that his side would not get caught up in the emotion of the game, still trying to appear in control of proceedings. Despite this, his team engaged with the crowd and continued the mind games at the coin toss by changing ends so that Liverpool would face the famous Kop stand in the first half, rather than in the second.

The game started frantically as Chelsea looked to match Liverpool's energy rather than play their way into things at a slower pace. By turning Liverpool towards the Kop first half and starting fast, Chelsea's message was clear – they wanted to show authority over the tie, that they were not afraid. They had won at Anfield as a visiting team already that season and had come to do it again. If the visitors were to score first, it would probably be tie over.

It was Liverpool who opened the scoring, though, once again raising the issue of how to approach the opening exchanges of European matches at Anfield. García, the man for the big European occasion, found the net once more. Riise received the ball wide on the left, beyond Tiago, so Lampard moved across to press and was nutmegged by the Norwegian. Makélélé then made a rare mistake and lost sight of Gerrard, allowing him to peel off and find space while Makélélé stood still and blocked a passing lane that no longer existed. Riise passed to Gerrard, who flicked the ball over Carvalho and Terry for Baroš to chase. Čech rushed out and clattered Baroš. García, who had run in from the right and reacted first to the loose ball, half-volleyed over Terry towards the goal. Instead of following García, Gallas had retreated to the goal line and cleared the ball away, but the Slovakian linesman, Roman Slysko, judged that it had already crossed the line, so the goal was given and Liverpool had the lead after just four minutes.

As much as the goal was controversial, it was probably the best-case scenario for Chelsea as Čech would have been sent off for his challenge on Baroš and Liverpool would have had a penalty. Regardless of the scrappy finish, credit must be given to Gerrard for his beautiful pass over the Chelsea centre-backs. The first moment of genuine quality across the whole tie had led to the opening goal.

When this moment is discussed, people focus on how the supporters at the Kop end began to celebrate before they had even received confirmation that the goal had been awarded. It is often forgotten, however, that it was thanks to Chelsea that Liverpool were attacking that end in the first place. Making Liverpool face the Kop in the first half is not a unique idea; many teams try it in an attempt to disturb their hosts. It had disastrous consequences for Chelsea here, though. Chelsea fans had been allocated half of the lower tier behind the other goal at the Anfield Road End – they would have simply stood still and applauded Gallas's attempted clearance if the incident had happened in front of them. There would have been no celebrations in the linesman's view to persuade him to give a goal. Sure, it may seem like a small detail, but fine margins count for a lot in elite sport.

Baroš went into the book for an adrenaline-fuelled tackle on Carvalho. Neither team had settled, and the game continued at a furious speed. In the absence of wingers Duff and Robben, Chelsea attacked very narrowly, with Tiago and Cole both tucking inside to try and create a central overload alongside Drogba and Guðjohnsen. Lampard played deeper than usual, looking to deliver forward passes into those in front of him. Liverpool retained their compactness, using their offside trap to snare Drogba and limit the space behind their midfield in which Chelsea wanted to operate. Tiago worked hard to try and prevent Liverpool passing wide to Riise on transition, having already failed to stop the pass that led to Liverpool's goal.

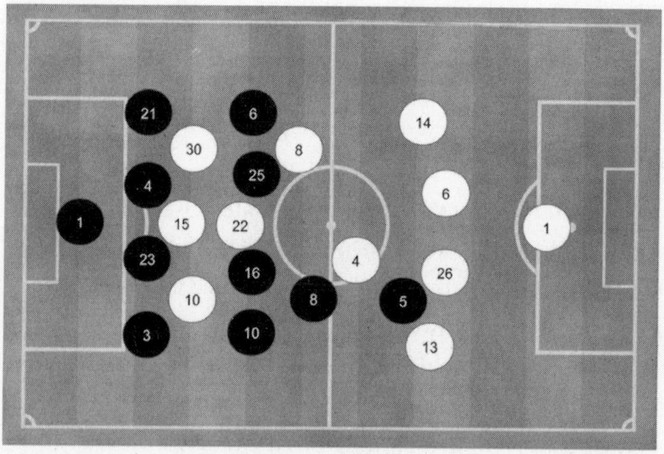

FIGURE 31

Figure 31 shows the two shapes matching up against each other when Chelsea had possession in Liverpool's half. Once Tiago settled into his role and defended better, Liverpool looked to the other side and found that they were able to exploit Cole's positioning instead. Because he was coming so narrow when the Blues had the ball, he could not cover the necessary ground to block Liverpool from looking to their right and finding Gerrard, who dropped deep to receive and combine with García. The diminutive Spaniard nearly went from hero to zero when he tried to nutmeg Lampard on the edge of the Liverpool area and lost the ball, only for Cole to receive and overhit his cross under pressure from Dudek.

Gallas pushed further forward in support of Chelsea possession as half-time approached, looking to create a wide option that could entice Liverpool out of their narrow defensive shape. As a right-footed centre-back playing on the left, he was not suited to this task and Liverpool found him easy to deal with. Chelsea were reluctant to take any risks in the first half, afraid that conceding a second goal would be a fatal blow. Mourinho continued to sit in the dugout like he had done in the first leg, determined to portray a feeling of control amid the chaos that surrounded him on the pitch and in the stands. In his pre-match press conference, the Portuguese manager had downplayed the potential impact of the crowd, who collectively responded by chanting 'we are the famous, the famous Kopites' as the Reds reached the interval unscathed.

Half-time – Liverpool 1 Chelsea 0

There were no substitutions at half-time. Robben was seemingly not fit enough for a full half of action, because Chelsea were in desperate need of some width and it would have made sense to bring him on. At this point in his career, he played in a different style to the one he later became famous for at Bayern Munich, where he would cut inside from the right and curl shots inside the far post. Instead, he was more of an old-fashioned winger who hugged the touchline and looked to cross from wide areas.

Liverpool pressed with less intensity at the beginning of the second half to avoid burning out early. They sat back in their 1-4-4-2 defensive shape, with Gerrard and Baroš working as a pair to try and stop the Chelsea back four passing to Makélélé. This led Lampard to move deeper when his defenders had the ball, to assist build-up play, but Gerrard and Baroš coped well with this two v two situation and Chelsea still found it hard to penetrate centrally. Tiago then moved deep and central too, hoping to attract a Liverpool midfielder into pressing forward and leaving space behind them for Drogba or Guðjohnsen to move into. Liverpool remained disciplined and undisturbed.

Chelsea had a decision to make – go all out early in the second half for an equaliser to try and blow Liverpool away, or patiently dominate possession and exhaust the Reds before delivering the killer blow late on. Of course, they only needed one goal. They opted for the latter option, keeping the ball in unthreatening positions instead of pushing forward and taking risks. They clearly believed in their ability to create several chances late on if necessary.

Benítez made the first substitution of the night after 59 minutes, and unsurprisingly Baroš made way for Cissé. Once again, Baroš had done his job by relentlessly pressing and chasing loose balls for an hour before being swapped for a pacier replacement. Chelsea finally had their first shot on target of the night in the 67th minute and even that was from a Lampard free kick rather than an opportunity created in open play. Liverpool were defending brilliantly and Chelsea needed new solutions. Plan A had been a resounding failure. They made a double substitution in the 68th minute, with Kežman and Robben replacing Tiago and Cole. It was bizarre

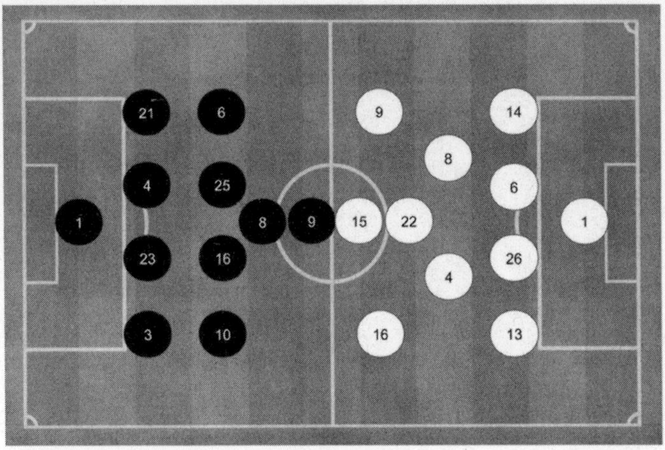

FIGURE 32

that Cole had not been deployed against Traoré after enjoying success against him at Stamford Bridge. Chelsea's new 1-4-2-3-1 shape is shown by *Figure 32*. Kežman played as a narrow right-winger, while Robben stayed touchline wide on the left. Both Geremi and Gallas now had licence to charge forward as their side looked for an away goal.

Hamann was immense on his return to action but was unable to last a full 90 minutes. Australian Harry Kewell came on for him – a player with unquestionable technical ability but, unfortunately, questionable levels of fitness and consistency. He missed the Juventus clashes through injury but was favoured by Benítez, who admired his quality on the ball. Kewell came on behind Cissé, and Gerrard dropped back into midfield next to Biščan.

Chelsea made their final change in the 76th minute and brought young centre-back Robert Huth on in place of Geremi. The 20-year-old German did not come on in the defence, though. He was sent up front alongside Drogba to act as a second target man as Chelsea scrapped their patient approach and began to play long balls forward instead. Their

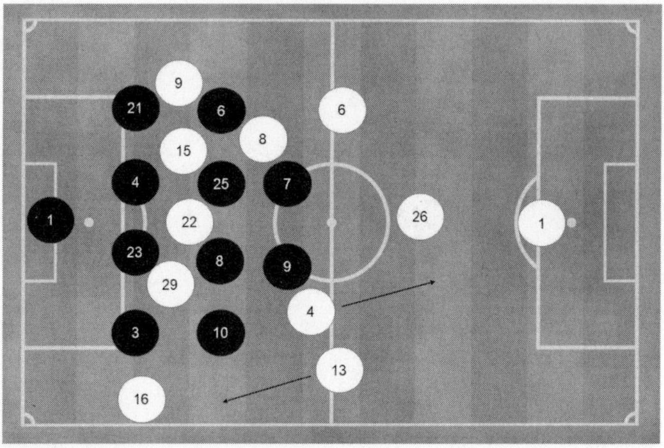

FIGURE 33

new shape is shown by *Figure 33*, with the black arrows illustrating the relevant movements of both Makélélé and Gallas. Makélélé dropped back on transition so that Terry was not left one v one against Cissé, while Gallas pushed forward from the left-sided centre-back position to support Robben on the left wing. Liverpool defended even deeper now, with the back four on the edge of their penalty area in anticipation of long balls to Drogba and Huth. The midfield stayed just in front of them so that they were ready to react to second balls and clear them away.

Cissé had a glorious chance to confirm Liverpool's place in the final in the 78th minute, but he headed Riise's cross straight at Čech. Although this miss frustrated him, he was doing a very good job defensively – hassling Chelsea's back three and not giving them time to calmly look for a direct passing option, forcing them to hastily boot it long instead. Chelsea then had a big chance themselves in the 83rd minute when Robben crossed in towards Drogba, whose header went wide of the back post. It was a perfect example of the threat that Chelsea had lacked without a natural winger on the pitch.

Liverpool made their third substitution as Núñez replaced García. They now had fresh legs on the side that Robben and Gallas were attacking, hoping to force Gallas back towards his own goal.

Unbelievably, the fourth official signalled that six minutes of additional time would be played, even though there had been no significant stoppages in the second half. Núñez, Kewell and Cissé were combining well to threaten Chelsea, with Cissé winning a corner in the 90th minute and Núñez doing the same in the 95th to relieve some pressure off their team-mates. Like against Juventus, Benítez showed his ability to masterfully use substitute attackers when his side were looking to see a game out in situations where many managers would be tempted to bring on extra defenders. Here, he combined the pace of Núñez and Cissé with the technical ability of Kewell – Núñez and Cissé ran with the ball into corners and wide areas and then Kewell kept it there to waste time.

Liverpool did so well to defend for 95 minutes but nearly threw their place in the final away with seconds remaining. They failed to deal with a deep cross into the box and the ball fell to Guðjohnsen, unmarked with time to shoot and Dudek off his line. Incredibly, he volleyed his effort across the goal and out for a goal kick. Anfield fell silent as Guðjohnsen took aim, and it took a second or two for the crowd to realise that the ball had actually gone wide. After a miss so incredible it felt impossible for Liverpool to lose and the party started in the stands. Liverpool sent the ball back upfield and the referee blew for full time before Čech could launch it forward again. Chelsea's decision to begin the second half patiently had left them with insufficient time to chase the tie late on. With hindsight, it may have been better for them to have attacked earlier against a Liverpool side that rarely looked like scoring a second goal.

Full time – Liverpool 1 Chelsea 0; Liverpool win 1-0 on aggregate

Beating such a strong Chelsea team and reaching the final in Istanbul was a wonderful achievement for Liverpool. For Benítez, taking the Reds to their first European Cup/Champions League final for 20 years made his domestic troubles suddenly feel irrelevant. Liverpool Football Club as an institution was built on European success – this win against Chelsea ranked alongside past victories against the likes of Inter Milan, Borussia Mönchengladbach, Club Brugge and Saint-Étienne as one of the greatest nights that Anfield had ever seen.

Benítez had proven his ability to set sides up to defend well in European competition, while Finnan, Carragher, Hyypiä and Traoré were all having the campaign of their careers. Across the last two seasons, Benítez had conceded just eight goals in 19 European knockout matches. His aforementioned use of substitute attackers was brilliant and, in midfield, the previously maligned Biščan was superb. Liverpool had undeniably benefited from the support of their fans during their home legs and it remained to be seen how they would cope in a one-off match in a neutral venue.

Chapter 6

Final – Liverpool 3 AC Milan 3; Liverpool win 3-2 on penalties, 25 May 2005

Five days after winning the semi-final, Liverpool travelled to Arsenal and started with the team that many expected Benítez to select in the final, as Hamann began next to Alonso in midfield, with Gerrard advanced behind Baroš, but a 3-1 defeat in London raised questions about this line-up. They then made eight changes for their final game of the league season, which was won at home to Aston Villa. They finished fifth in the table; one place lower than in 2003/04 under Houllier. The failure to finish in the top four was even harder to take for the Reds because Everton got there ahead of them. It was the first time that Everton had finished above Liverpool since 1987. Without a guaranteed place in next season's competition, Liverpool's presence in the Champions League Final felt even more extraordinary.

Liverpool were to face AC Milan, who had finished second in Serie A behind Juventus but had enjoyed a stellar European season so far. The *Rossoneri* topped Group F ahead of Barcelona before dispatching of Manchester

United in the round of 16 by a 2-0 aggregate score. In the quarter-final, they won the first leg against local rivals Inter 2-0 before being awarded a 3-0 walkover in the second leg because of crowd trouble instigated by Inter supporters. Their semi-final tie against PSV Eindhoven was far from straightforward and looked destined for extra time before a goal each in stoppage time gave Milan the victory on away goals.

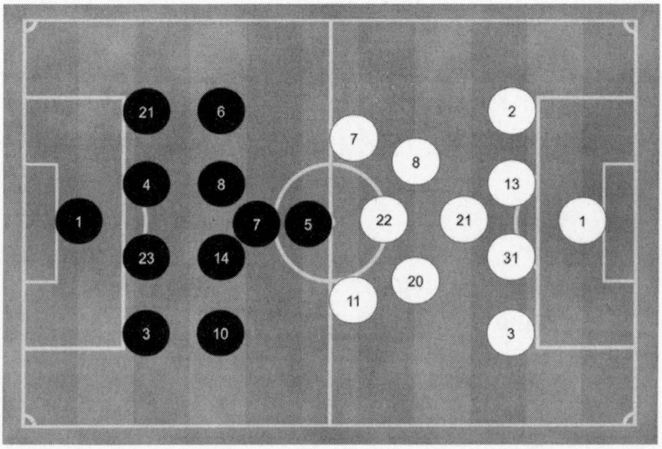

FIGURE 34

The team selections are shown by *Figure 34*. Benítez made a huge call by pairing Gerrard and Alonso in midfield with Kewell in front of them. Hamann and Bišćan were both on the bench. Despite reaching the final thanks to solid defending and avoiding defeat across two-legged ties, Benítez wanted to attack and put Milan on the back foot. Ancelotti lined his team up in their usual 4-3-1-2 shape – the starting 11 consisted of eight previous Champions League victors and three World Cup winners. Rather than sit back and show fear against this level of quality opposition, Liverpool would try and take the game to them instead. A brave move.

Liverpool (1-4-4-1-1): 1. Dudek; 3. Finnan, 23. Carragher, 4. Hyypiä, 21. Traoré; 10. García, 14. Alonso, 8. Gerrard (captain), 6. Riise; 7. Kewell; 5. Baroš.

Substitutes: 20. Carson, 9. Cissé, 11. Šmicer, 16. Hamann, 17. Josemi, 18. Núñez, 25. Biščan.

Head coach: Rafael Benítez.

AC Milan (1-4-3-1-2): 1. Dida; 2. Cafu, 13. Nesta, 31. Stam, 3. Maldini (captain); 8. Gattuso, 21. Pirlo, 20. Seedorf; 22. Kaká; 7. Shevchenko, 11. Crespo.

Substitutes: 46. Abbiati, 4. Kaladze, 5. Costacurta, 10. Costa, 15. Tomasson, 24. Dhorasoo, 27. Serginho.

Head coach: Carlo Ancelotti.

The pre-match atmosphere at the Atatürk Olympic Stadium was incredible, with Liverpool supporters occupying three-quarters of the ground. Liverpool got things underway, passing back and across to Traoré, who clipped a long ball down the line for Milan to collect with ease. They advanced forward and found Kaká, who dribbled wide and was hacked down by Traoré – the Malian left-back had made a very nervous start. Pirlo, who had developed into a world-class midfielder since his cameo in Part 1, took an out-swinging free kick towards the centre of the penalty area. Captain Paolo Maldini moved in unmarked from the edge of the area to volley past Dudek for 1-0. Liverpool had failed to effectively man-mark on a set piece in the first minute of the Champions League Final; it was a criminally bad goal to concede. Ancelotti had predicted pre-match that his side would score inside three minutes and his vision had come true.

Liverpool responded well and enjoyed two minutes of good, patient possession before winning a corner after Stam (who had left Manchester United for Lazio, then moved to Milan) came across to intercept a channel ball aimed for

Baroš. With the corner, Gerrard found Riise on the edge of the box, but his volley was blocked and cleared back out to the skipper, who crossed wonderfully for Hyypiä to head straight at Dida. Both sides had clearly worked on their attacking set pieces; unfortunately, Liverpool temporarily forgot about the need to defend them properly as well.

Milan's shape became clearer as the game settled down. *Figure 35* shows the shape of both sides with Riise in possession on the Liverpool left. The Milanese back four sat back, limiting the space behind them that Baroš wanted to

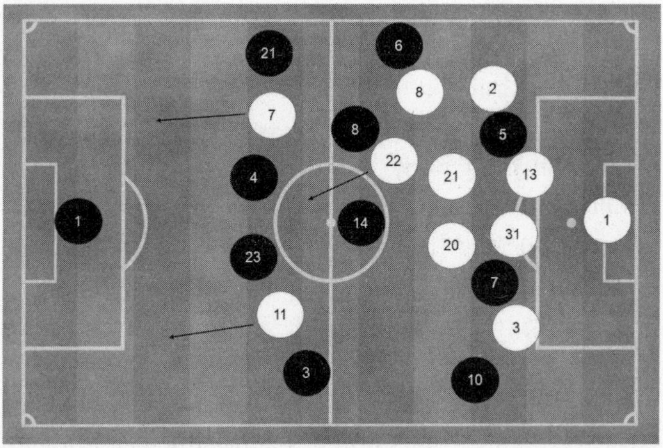

FIGURE 35

chase channel balls in. Here, the ball-side central midfielder, Gattuso, presses Riise to prevent him from playing inside to Gerrard, with Cafu ready if Riise runs down the line. If Liverpool had the ball on their right-hand side, then Seedorf would perform the same job as Gattuso. The pair showed their defensive intelligence, allowing Pirlo to sit centrally and focus on being the side's deep-lying playmaker. The black arrows show the movements of Kaká, Shevchenko and Crespo on transition once Milan won the ball and looked to play forwards. Kaká, Milan's *trequartista*, would move between or behind Gerrard and Alonso into space enlarged by the runs of Shevchenko and Hernán Crespo, who burst forward and forced the Liverpool back four deeper. While Gerrard and Alonso were both looking good on the ball, they were not naturally defensive-minded and struggled against Kaká's clever moment. Shevchenko and Crespo were both excellent forwards, timing runs between Liverpool's full-backs and centre-backs to perfection. The offside trap that had worked so well against Juventus and Chelsea was now looking vulnerable.

Milan almost scored from another set piece in the 14th minuten when García was forced into clearing a Crespo header off the line from a Seedorf corner.

The Italians were technically excellent, able to retain the ball in midfield if required, or utilise full-backs Cafu and Maldini. Liverpool were still holding their own in general play, though. As a *trequartista*, Kaká was not asked to work hard defensively and this afforded Gerrard and Alonso a lot of time on the ball. The Liverpool pair looked to receive off their back four, turn and switch play to the far-side full-back, moving Milan laterally across the pitch. García began to move inside as his side progressed the ball forward to form another central passing option next to Kewell. These periods of good possession were exactly what Benítez wanted from a Gerrard-Alonso midfield pairing.

When Milan had possession in deep areas, it was Kewell's job to man-mark Pirlo, to stop him receiving the ball and dictating play. The Australian was injured by a strong Gattuso challenge in the 19th minute and tried to play on but could no longer keep up with Pirlo, whose movement was hard to track at the best of times. García tried to help his team-mate, but this left an easy passing lane out to Maldini that Baroš had to rush back to defend against. Benítez reacted in the 23rd minute, with Kewell limping off to be replaced by Šmicer, who played on the right with García assuming Kewell's central position. Benítez clearly wanted to stand by his initial plan and stay on the front foot, otherwise he would have introduced Hamann or Biščan and pushed Gerrard forward.

Milan were moving through the half in first gear, happy to watch Liverpool play in front of them and then quickly use Kaká, Shevchenko and Crespo on the counter-attack. Unlike in the last two rounds, Liverpool had not raced into an early lead and would need to find different attacking solutions instead. Nesta and Stam were easily dealing with Baroš, while Gattuso and Seedorf were expertly blocking passing lanes into the central areas that Liverpool wanted to attack. Riise dropped deeper to receive switches of play from Gerrard and Alonso, but he was not troubling opponents, preferring to play easy passes rather than dribble forwards and take players on.

Liverpool had appeals for a penalty turned down in the 38th minute as Nesta slid to intercept a through pass and the ball touched his elbow. Milan launched a devastating counter-attack, with the strikers making forward runs so that Kaká could once again receive the ball in space in front of the Liverpool back four. The Brazilian playmaker threaded a pass between Hyypiä and Traoré for Shevchenko, who played a low cross to Crespo. The Argentine tucked the ball away for 2-0. Milan had looked ready to score this type of goal throughout the first half and it came as no surprise. Gerrard and Alonso had both pressed forward on the initial transition, leaving Kaká behind them. From there, three forward players of such quality were bound to create a goalscoring opportunity.

Crespo scored again six minutes later, prompting wild celebrations from everybody of a Milanese persuasion inside the ground. It was another counter-attacking goal and it surely put AC Milan's name on the trophy for a seventh time. Pirlo intercepted a Gerrard pass aimed for Baroš and retained possession with the help of Cafu. He then passed forward to Kaká, who turned away from Gerrard and played another sensational ball, this time curling his pass between Carragher and Hyypiä into the path of Crespo, who had made a run between Carragher and Finnan. The pass was so good that the on-loan Chelsea striker did not even need to control it; he simply chipped it over the onrushing Dudek and into the goal. Liverpool had played reasonably well for most of the half but found themselves 3-0 down because they failed to defend a set piece and then got cut open by two ruthless transitions. They were in the tie at 1-0, but the second and third goals felt like fatal blows.

Half-time – Liverpool 0 AC Milan 3

Liverpool had planned to take Traoré off at half-time but an injury to Finnan meant that the Malian had to hop out of the shower and get ready to play again. Hamann replaced Finnan

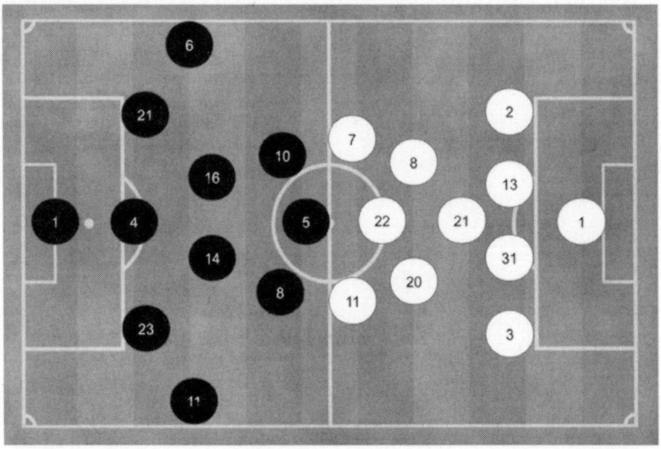

FIGURE 36

as Liverpool changed to 1-3-4-2-1 – a formation that they had not actually used under Benítez before. This new shape is shown by *Figure 36*. Carragher, Hyypiä and Traoré formed a back three, with Šmicer and Riise as wing-backs. Hamann joined Alonso in midfield and Gerrard moved forward next to García, forming an attacking duo behind Baroš. The players re-entered the field to the sound of 'You'll Never Walk Alone', sung by the Reds' supporters in an act of defiance.

Milan started the half positively; they were unchanged and playing well. In contrast, it took Liverpool a few minutes to settle into their new shape. Dudek made a good save from a Shevchenko free kick in the 52nd minute, which seemed to give the Polish custodian a boost after such a difficult first half. Then, in the 54th minute, Gerrard gave his team hope. The half-time tactical switch took all defensive responsibility off him and allowed him to roam about the pitch, exploring and exploiting space wherever he found it. Initially, he was deep to receive off Riise, who could not advance further up the left wing because he was pressed well by Gattuso. Gerrard played the ball inside to Alonso then drifted forward unmarked. Alonso and Hamann exchanged passes before switching back to Riise, who was now in a good crossing position. Baroš occupied Nesta and García pushed up on to Stam so that he could not mark Gerrard. Pirlo spotted that Gerrard was unmarked in the penalty area but did not bother to track him, appearing to assume that Maldini would tuck inside on to García so that Stam could mark Gerrard. In fairness, that is what should have happened. Riise's initial cross was blocked by Cafu, but his second found Gerrard, who headed brilliantly past Dida to give Liverpool a lifeline.

Maldini did eventually tuck inside to mark García and free Stam but it was too late – the cross had already come into the box. For defenders as experienced as Stam and Maldini, this was an extremely disappointing goal to concede. Gerrard, meanwhile, raced back to the halfway line, waving his arms up and down, asking for the Liverpool fans to keep singing in support of their side.

Milan had been here before. In the 2003/04 quarter-finals, they beat Deportivo La Coruña 4-1 in the first leg before going to Galicia and losing 4-0. Five days before this match they threw away a 3-1 lead at home to Palermo and drew 3-3. Lightning could not strike for a third time, surely? Well, conceding a goal visibly affected them and they gave the ball away from the restart, allowing Liverpool to attack again.

Suddenly, the Reds were passing the ball about with confidence and purpose. They advanced into the Milan area and Baroš was flagged offside, but the referee failed to notice his linesman and play continued with Milan clearing the ball straight back to Liverpool. As Alonso received off Riise, Kaká inexplicably stopped running and began removing the strapping from his socks. Shevchenko rushed back to try and cover for him, but the Ukrainian could not stop Alonso passing inside to Hamann. Gerrard and Šmicer had rotated,

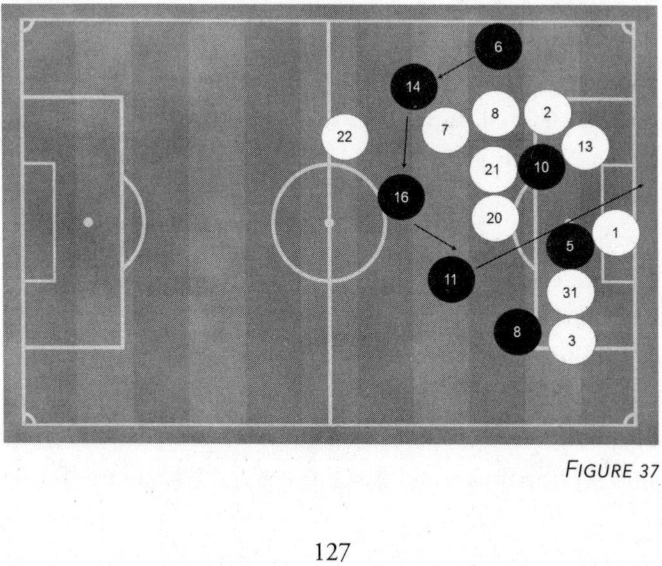

FIGURE 37

so that Gerrard was wide and the Czech central. Seedorf rushed across to close down Šmicer but he was too late – the Liverpool man laced the ball through the bodies and past Dida. Milan had conceded twice in two minutes for the second time in a week. Like with United's win against Juventus in Part 1, one side was gripped by the fear of failure and the other began to believe that anything was possible. This goal is shown by *Figure 37*.

Milan were in bits. They gave the ball away from the restart again and Liverpool stormed forward to win a corner. Šmicer continued to drift inside when Liverpool had the ball, allowing Carragher to advance forward on the overlap. Not normally known for his ball-playing abilities, Carragher was pushing higher here and giving the Milan forwards a problem. The three Liverpool centre-backs combined with Alonso, Hamann and Šmicer to create a six v three overload over Shevchenko, Crespo and Kaká when circulating possession between defence and midfield. Carragher carried the ball into Milan's half and became the first player in a well-performed 'third man' sequence that resulted in a Liverpool penalty.

Carragher played forward to Baroš with a pass that Pirlo should have blocked. García took Stam away from the ball with a clever dummy run, leaving Baroš isolated against Nesta. With his back to goal, Baroš flicked the ball into the path of Gerrard, who was surging forward as Gattuso tried to catch him. As Gerrard looked to receive the ball in the Milan box, he was tripped by Gattuso and went down – penalty given. Alonso, who had never taken a penalty before in his professional career, stepped up. Benítez had removed Gerrard from penalty duties because he had recently missed one against Tottenham Hotspur. Dida managed to save Alonso's initial effort but could not prevent the Basque midfielder smashing in the rebound for 3-3. Liverpool had scored three goals in six of the craziest minutes the Champions League had ever seen.

Milan finally regained some composure but were uncomfortable playing through midfield and began to play more directly. Hamann was shutting off passing lanes to Kaká in a way that Gerrard and Alonso had been unable to do in the first half. In the stands, the Liverpool fans sang 'You'll Never Walk Alone' once more, this time as a 'thank you' to the players for the best six minutes that they had ever witnessed. Traoré then put his name in Liverpool folklore with a clearance off the line from Shevchenko after Dudek had spilled a Kaká cross. A fourth Milan goal so soon after Liverpool's equaliser would have killed the Liverpudlian momentum.

Šmicer began to stay wider in possession, looking to entice Maldini forward and create space for channel balls for Baroš to chase against Stam. Gerrard continued to cover every blade of grass, impossible for the Milanese to keep up with. Milan made no changes, hoping that the 11 on the pitch could put things right themselves. Carragher went into the book in the 76th minute after a poor challenge on Shevchenko, as did Baroš five minutes later. He was exhausted and had stayed on the pitch for longer than usual because his side had been forced into two early substitutions. His last selfless shift of the season finally came to an end in the 85th minute when, as usual, he was replaced by Cissé. Milan then made a double substitution, taking off Crespo and Seedorf and introducing Jon Dahl Tomasson and Serginho. Tomasson was an intelligent attacker who made up for his lack of pace with excellent movement and discipline. Serginho was a Brazilian wing-back well renowned for his speed, energy and crossing ability. They matched Liverpool's 1-3-4-2-1 shape, as shown in *Figure 38*.

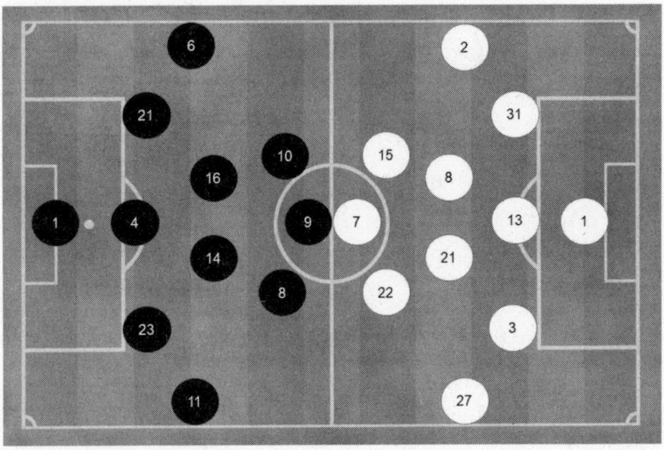

FIGURE 38

This formation change lifted Ancelotti's men; the wing-backs gave them more width and Cafu was seeing more of the ball. They passed wide to Serginho as much as possible so that he could attack Šmicer, who was not a natural defender. Benítez reacted to this by swapping him with Gerrard. Milan dominated the closing stages of regulation time, but Liverpool held out until the final whistle.

Full time – Liverpool 3 AC Milan 3

What a half of football. Although Liverpool did remarkably well to score three goals in quick succession, they were shattered and Milan looked ready to go again – a fourth Liverpool goal seemed unlikely. The Italians also had another substitution left, whereas as the Reds did not. A careful, disciplined 30 minutes was now in order.

Milan changed to 1-3-4-1-2 early in extra time, with Kaká behind Tomasson and Shevchenko. Tomasson and Shevchenko looked to occupy Liverpool's side centre-backs – Carragher and Traoré – so that Cafu and Serginho could attack one v one against Riise and Gerrard. Liverpool looked to play forward to Cissé on transition; however, the Frenchman struggled to keep hold of the ball and was caught offside several times. García made forward runs to support him, while Šmicer stayed back to press Pirlo and Gattuso if Milan looked to counter through midfield. The Italians were very much on top but found creating clear-cut chances difficult as Gerrard and Riise defended well in wide areas. Liverpool's back three also began to use their offside trap more effectively, forcing Shevchenko and Tomasson to drop deeper to receive the ball. Šmicer went down with cramp and received treatment, helping the clock reach 105 minutes. Shevchenko hit a feeble volley straight to Dudek at the end of the half and was comforted by Gerrard as the players left the pitch.

Half-time of extra time – Liverpool 3 AC Milan 3

Liverpool started the second half of extra time well, finding Cissé with a channel ball down the right for him to win a corner after engaging with both Gattuso and Nesta. After that, it was all Milan for ten minutes, with Liverpool in survival mode. Carragher went down with cramp twice but continued to make heroic blocks and interceptions. Hamann was still subduing Kaká, and Gerrard was keeping up with the fresher Serginho. Ancelotti made his final substitution in the 112th minute, bringing on Portuguese star Rui Costa for Gattuso. Costa was a good passer of the ball and would act as a second midfield playmaker alongside Pirlo. Gattuso's ball-winning role had become redundant because of Milan's utter domination of possession.

The Reds were defending deeper in the face of relentless Milanese pressure. They adopted a 1-5-4-1 defensive shape, with Šmicer on the right of the midfield and García on the left. If Liverpool did win the ball back then the pair would

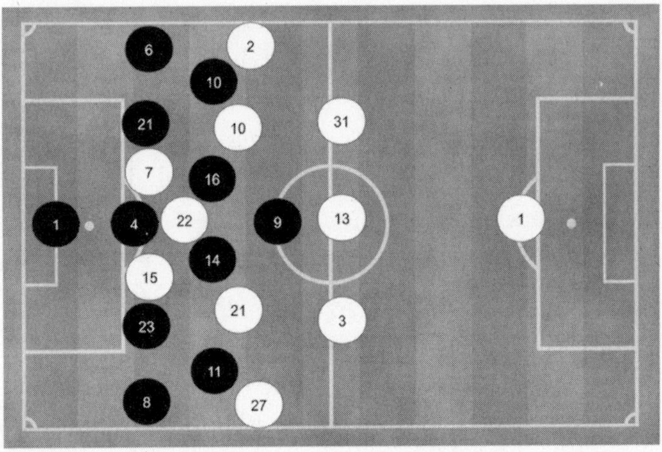

FIGURE 39

look to make inwards runs in support of Cissé, who himself was coming deep to help his team-mates defend. *Figure 39* shows the shape of both sides, with Milan pushing forward in pursuit of a winning goal.

Dudek pulled off the double save of his life in the 118th minute, adding further to Shevchenko's woes. Serginho received the ball further back than usual to create some space in front of Gerrard and crossed into the Liverpool area. The Ukrainian striker got between Hyypiä and Traoré and headed the ball into the ground. Dudek dived and palmed the ball back into the path of the striker, who blasted it goalward from two yards out. Somehow, Dudek got a hand to it and Liverpool survived.

Willed on by the Liverpool fans, Hamann won the ball in the last minute of extra time and drove forward into the Milan half to drag his team up the field. The ball came to Šmicer and Costa chopped him down on the edge of the area – free kick Liverpool. After defending desperately for the best part of 50 minutes, keeping Milan from scoring a fourth was a fantastic achievement. Now, Liverpool would have the final goalscoring opportunity of the match. Unfortunately, they wasted the free kick and the referee blew the full-time whistle …

Full time of extra time – Liverpool 3 AC Milan 3

As the sides prepared for penalties, Carragher took Dudek to one side and appeared to instruct him to try and put the Milan players off when they were taking their kicks, which were to be at the end housing the Italian fans.

Serginho, who scored his penalty in the 2003 final, took the first one here. Dudek waved his arms and jumped from side to side along the goal line, responding to Carragher's instructions. The Brazilian overhit his shot and it flew over the crossbar. Hamann then stepped up and scored – he would later discover that he had done so with a broken foot. As Pirlo walked forward to take the next kick, Dudek grabbed the ball and started bouncing it up and down before handing it to the Italian. He waved his arms and side-stepped along the line, then dived and palmed away the penalty – admittedly from very far off his line. In contrast to the Pole, Dida stood still on the goal line and could do nothing to prevent Cissé doubling Liverpool's advantage at 2-0. Tomasson then scored, and Riise tried to place his effort to Dida's right and saw it saved, before Kaká found the roof of the net to make it 2-2.

Šmicer, aware that he was making his last competitive kick in a Liverpool shirt, placed the ball to Dida's left to make it match point to Liverpool. Strangely, Dida dived to his right for all four Liverpool penalties. Having endured a torrid night, Shevchenko now had to score to keep his side's hopes alive. Dudek gave him the ball and then began frantically waving his arms up and down as the Ukrainian ran up to the spot. The Milan striker attempted a Panenka penalty, chipping it down the middle, but Dudek got a hand to it and won the Champions League for Liverpool.

Liverpool win 3-2 on penalties

With this victory, Benítez became the third manager to achieve successive UEFA Cup and European Cup/Champions League triumphs after Mourinho and Liverpool's own Bob Paisley. He was the first ever to win the successive titles with two different clubs. Not only had he earned a place in the history of European club football, but he had earned a status of immortality in the eyes of the adoring Liverpool fans. From half-time of the final group match, through the round of 16 and the ties against Juventus and Chelsea, his tactical performance was immense. Even though his initial selection for the final was defensively weak, he adapted well at half-time and gave his players the platform to get themselves back into the match. Of course, he received a massive helping hand in Istanbul from the same man who scored the goal that took them into the knockout stages – Steven Gerrard had come of age and earned his spot as one of the greatest players on the planet.

This final is rightly remembered as a wonderful comeback story, but the Reds began upsetting the odds long before Gerrard headed past Dida. Defeating the champions of both Italy and England was a remarkable achievement, and conceding only one goal across those four legs was simply phenomenal. Of course, there was then an element of fortune in how the Istanbul comeback has made people forget the flawed starting line-up, but Liverpool were still tactically resolute for 75 minutes of the 120. Credit must go to Benítez for his half-time team talk which, by all accounts, was calm and concise. Already-devastated players do not need a dressing-down when they are trailing 3-0 in the biggest game of their lives; they need to be provided with solutions, which the change to 1-3-4-2-1 offered. It gave Gerrard the freedom to attack freely while others limited the respective impacts of Pirlo and Kaká. Switching Gerrard and Šmicer was another good move, using the captain to defend Serginho and restrict the Brazilian to just a few crossing opportunities.

This Liverpool victory was extremely significant because it was their fifth European Cup/Champions League triumph. They became the first English team to reach that total and earn the right to keep the trophy for themselves. At this point in time, only they, Real Madrid and AC Milan owned a European Cup/Champions League trophy. Liverpool were now European royalty.

Benítez won the 2005 European Football Coach of the Year Award and shared the 2004/05 European Football Coach of the Season title with Valery Gazzaev, who won the UEFA Cup with CSKA Moscow.

Steven Gerrard finished third in the Ballon d'Or vote, with Carragher 20th and García joint 23rd with Nedvěd. Gerrard also finished seventh in the FIFA World Player of the Year standings.

Part 3

Manchester United 2007/08

A year after Liverpool's incredible victory, Arsenal reached their first Champions League Final but lost 2-1 to Barcelona. In 2006/07, Liverpool reached the final once again and lost to AC Milan as Ancelotti's men avenged the Miracle of Istanbul. Still managed by Ferguson, Manchester United had failed to progress to a Champions League Final since 1999, falling twice at the semi-final stage. By 2007/08, the Scot was rebuilding a squad that had fallen short of the Premier League title between 2003/04 and 2005/06 before reclaiming their crown in 2006/07.

The pressure was on to make the 2007/08 term a memorable one for the football club because it marked two important anniversaries – 50 years since the Munich air disaster and 40 years since the club's first European Cup/ Champions League triumph. Ferguson had a squad capable of achieving great things and if there was a time for them to reach their collective potential then this was it. In the summer of 2007, Owen Hargreaves, Anderson, Nani,

Tomasz Kuszczak and Carlos Tevez were signed as Alan Smith, Gabriel Heinze, Kieran Richardson, Giuseppe Rossi and Ole Gunnar Solskjær left.

By April 2008, United had lost four leagues games, including home and away against Manchester City, but were top of the table in a three-horse race with Chelsea and Arsenal. Despite losing to Portsmouth in the sixth round of an FA Cup that had looked like theirs to lose, they looked strong in Europe, topping their Champions League group above Roma, Sporting Clube de Portugal and Dynamo Kyiv. In the round of 16, a 1-1 draw away against Olympique Lyonnais was followed up with a 1-0 win at Old Trafford to secure a 2-1 aggregate victory. Having never scored more than 25 club goals in a season before, Cristiano Ronaldo looked on course to break a whole host of records and was, at this time, undoubtedly the world's best player. United were in a rich vein of form and determined to write more history.

Chapter 7

Quarter-final – Manchester United 3 Roma 0 (aggregate)

First leg: Roma 0 Manchester United 2, 1 April 2008

Just like in Part 1, United were drawn against Italian opposition in the quarter-final. Roma were familiar opponents – the sides faced each other in the 2006/07 quarter-final and the 2007/08 group stage. In 2006/07, Roma won the first leg in Italy before United triumphed 7-1 at Old Trafford in one of the most extraordinary European matches of the era. Earlier on in 2007/08, United won 1-0 in Manchester before the teams drew 1-1 in a dead rubber tie on matchday six. Roma were having a good season, challenging Inter for the Serie A title and confident in Europe, having beaten Real Madrid in the round of 16. They were seeking revenge for the previous year's embarrassment at the hands of Ferguson's men.

The team selections are shown by *Figure 40*:

Manchester United (1-4-1-4-1): 1. van der Sar; 6. Brown, 5. Ferdinand (captain), 15. Vidić, 3. Evra; 16. Carrick; 13. Park Ji-Sung, 18. Scholes, 8. Anderson, 10. Rooney; 7. Ronaldo.

Substitutes: 29. Kuszczak, 4. Hargreaves, 11. Giggs, 19. Piqué, 22. O'Shea, 27. Silvestre, 32. Tevez.

Head coach: Sir Alex Ferguson.

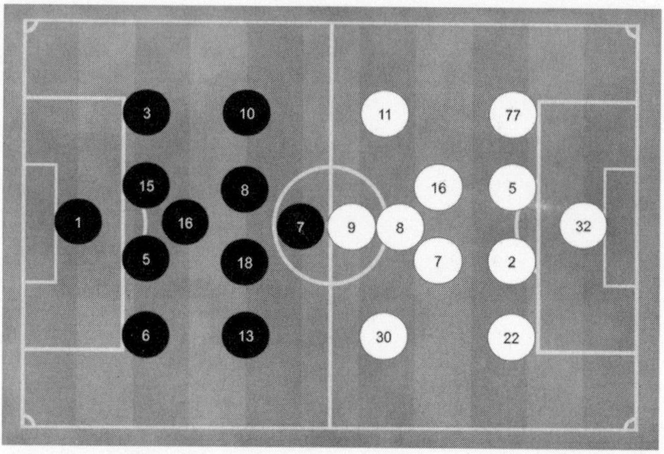

FIGURE 40

Roma (1-4-2-3-1): 32. Doni; 77. Cassetti, 5. Mexès, 2. Panucci (captain), 22. Tonetto; 16. de Rossi, 7. Pizarro; 11. Taddei, 8. Aquilani, 30. Mancini; 9. Vučinić.

Substitutes: 1. Curci, 3. Cicinho, 14. Giuly, 15. Antunes, 18. Esposito, 21. Ferrari, 33. Brighi.

Head coach: Luciano Spalletti.

Capable of lining up his team in several formations, Ferguson opted for a 1-4-1-4-1 shape that matched Roma's midfield three v three. As he liked to do in big matches, particularly away from home, he started Ronaldo up front so that the Portuguese star did not have a lot of defensive responsibility and could focus on being an attacking threat. Ronaldo had developed from a talented but unpredictable dribbler into a goalscoring machine focused on ruthless efficiency. Of course, he was aided by the excellence of his team-mates. There was 37-year-old Edwin van der Sar, who had won the 1994/95 Champions League with Ajax and was in his third season at United. Wes Brown had been a young squad member in 1998/99 but had established himself as first-choice right-back in the long-term absence of club captain, Gary Neville. Rio Ferdinand was one of the best all-round centre-backs of his generation and was partnered by the physically imposing Nemanja Vidić. Patrice Evra was an attacking left-back who used his high energy levels to sprint up and down the flank. Michael Carrick was an intelligent passer, as was Scholes, which we know from Part 1. Park Ji-Sung and Anderson were extremely energetic players who relentlessly covered ground both in and out of possession. Wayne Rooney was a wonderfully gifted attacker capable of playing central or in wide areas.

The game started calmly, with Roma looking to be positive but failing to trouble their visitors. They did not press high, allowing United to settle into the match and enjoy some comfortable possession. When they had the ball in their own half, the visitors utilised a 1-4-3-3 shape, with Park Ji-Sung and Rooney pushing high and wide in support of Ronaldo. Things then became much more fluid once the ball was progressed into Roma's half. Ronaldo looked to receive between Roma's lines of midfield and defence, with the rest of the side geared around facilitating this. If Ronaldo moved left of centre, Rooney would go touchline wide to occupy Cassetti, while Park Ji-Sung would move high and central to deter the Roma centre-backs from tracking Ronaldo into deeper areas. This allowed Brown to push forward wide on the United right.

Carrick and Scholes were man-marked in deep possession by Mirko Vučinić and Alberto Aquilani respectively, but used their superior ability to retain and recycle possession effectively. Anderson pushed in front of the English pair, in line with Roma central midfielders Daniele De Rossi and David Pizarro. His presence would deter the ball-side Roma central midfielder from dropping to mark Ronaldo because doing so would leave him space to receive the ball himself. These movements are shown by *Figure 41.*

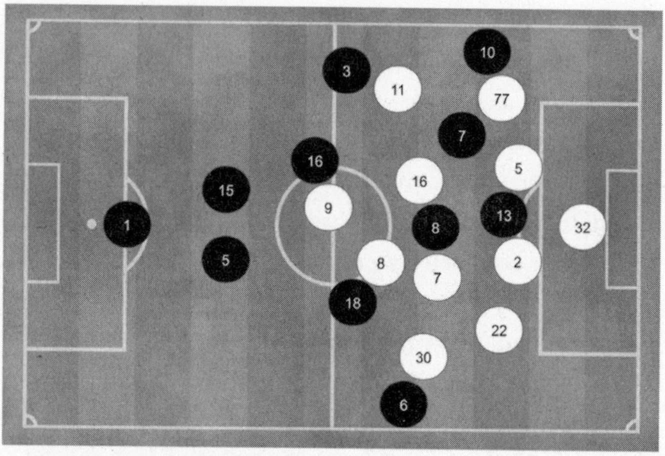

FIGURE 41

United's rotations did not end there. Both Ronaldo and Rooney would look to offer for the ball between the lines if Scholes made a run forward, which he had licence to do. He would occupy Roma's back line alongside Park Ji-Sung, preventing them from pushing forward and engaging with Ronaldo and Rooney. Anderson would move deeper in Scholes's place, which helped progress the ball forward but

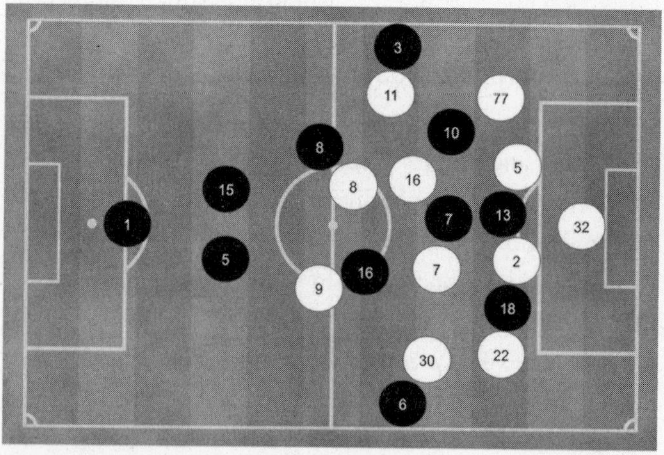

FIGURE 42

also meant that he could use his energy to cover the 33-year-old on transition if United lost possession. The full-backs pushed wide in support, giving the Roman wingers reason to track back and defend. They did not venture as high as some of the full-backs who will be discussed later in this book, but they were more advanced than Neville and Irwin had been at the start of matches in Part 1. *Figure 42* shows this. United played with patience, while still making it clear that they could force Roma into a 1-4-4-2 defensive shape and then play through it. Ferguson's tactical evolution was clear, influenced both by the players at his disposal and his team of coaches – Carlos Queiroz, Michael Phelan and René Meulensteen.

If United lost the ball, their defensive transition was impressive thanks in no small part to the energy and selflessness of Rooney and Park Ji-Sung, who would spring back from attacking positions to defend against the Roma full-backs, both of whom liked to push forward and be involved in offensive moves. Along with Anderson protecting the centre, Ferguson's side were set up well to limit Roma's counter-attacking potential.

Roma played in a generic 1-4-2-3-1 shape, relying on Taddei, Aquilani and Mancini to try and dribble with the ball to create chances. They were without their injured talisman, Francesco Totti, and consequently lacked a cutting edge. Technically, the Romans were a decent side capable of keeping possession, but killer passes were hard for them to come by. They were faced with a solid United defensive shape, shown by *Figure 43*.

Here, Mexès has possession for the home side. United allowed Roma's centre-backs to have possession and focused on limiting their forward passing options. This encouraged Roma's full-backs to push forward and leave space that

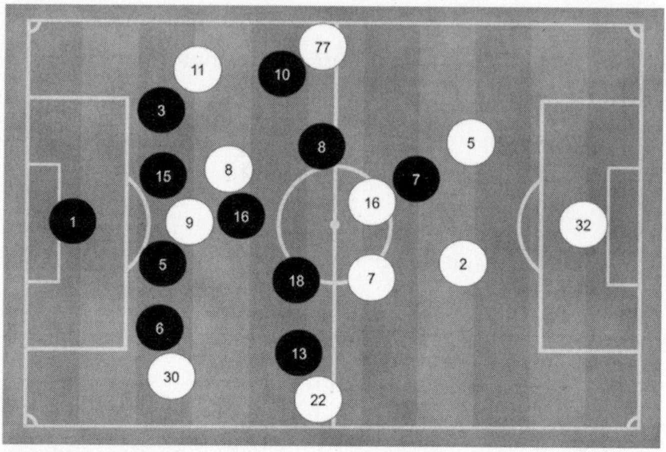

FIGURE 43

the visitors could look to exploit on the counter-attack. Ronaldo's task was simple – close the passing lane from the ball-carrying centre-back to the ball-side central midfielder (De Rossi in this case). If De Rossi escaped from Ronaldo and received from Mexès, Anderson was on hand to press forward. United's far-side central midfielder – Scholes here – would loosely mark his Roman counterpart from behind, ready to push higher and prevent him from receiving the ball without pressing too early and leaving space in midfield.

Unlike the Premier League at the time, the UEFA competitions employed a multi-ball system, having multiple official match balls available for use rather than just one. This allowed for the quick redistribution of balls when one went out of play. Roma used this system to try and increase the speed of the match when it was their throw-in or corner kick and their play quickened. United maintained careful possession themselves, dictated mostly by Carrick. On their goal kicks, they employed a 1-4-2-3-1 shape, with Anderson behind Ronaldo. Van der Sar would then kick long and leftward towards Rooney, hoping to get United into Roma's half and either achieve a transition or establish possession high up the pitch.

In the 29th minute, Vidić landed awkwardly from an aerial challenge with Vučinić and required treatment, forcing United to temporarily play with ten men. Park Ji-Sung moved to right-back and Brown moved inside to cover for Vidić's absence. Four minutes later, Vidić was replaced by John O'Shea, a versatile defender capable of playing across the defence as well as in midfield. O'Shea operated as the left-sided centre-back, with Ferdinand to his right. Roma enjoyed some good passages of play as United resettled, but they never looked particularly threatening.

Ferguson's side opened the scoring in the 39th minute with a magnificent goal. After dealing with Roma's periods of possession, they provided the first moment of true quality in the half and took the wind out of the Roman sails. The home side had sat back deeper, seemingly with the intention of reaching half-time goalless. This allowed United to patiently progress the ball from van der Sar and into midfield via Ferdinand and O'Shea, allowing Carrick to be at the heart of the initial move. Park Ji-Sung and Scholes made forward runs so that Ronaldo and Rooney could look to drop and receive.

Carrick played one-twos with Scholes and Brown, giving Scholes time to safely move up the field. He then played a one-two with Park Ji-Sung and Anderson, looking to provoke gaps in Roma's lines, all the while giving the attacking players time to rotate and explore different spaces. As Carrick passed back across to O'Shea, Ronaldo dropped short to offer for the ball, attracting De Rossi forward and creating space for O'Shea to break Roma's midfield line and pass to Rooney. Mexès rushed forward to challenge him but Rooney span on the ball and left him stranded, before playing a pass into space for Scholes on the right-hand side of the Roma penalty area. Scholes controlled the ball and chipped it back across the box into space, behind the runs of Rooney and Park Ji-Sung. Ronaldo sprinted into the penalty area, unmarked as he charged forward from a deep position, hung in the air and powered a header passed Doni.

It was a fantastic goal that highlighted so many of this side's strengths. Carrick dictated play wonderfully as the players ahead of him moved around with intelligence and purpose. Rooney turned brilliantly to beat Mexès and create the chance to enter the Roma box. Only Scholes knows if his cross was purposeful, but there are no question marks at all over the header from Ronaldo, whose athletic ability was truly outstanding.

Having sat back in anticipation of the half-time break, Roma conducted a tepid ending of the opening period, though Anderson and Pizarro both went into the referee's book for cynical fouls. From United's perspective, it had been a textbook European away performance so far.

Half-time – Roma 0 Manchester United 1

Roma began the second half fast, looking to force the issue and get themselves back in the tie. Considering a 2-1 first-leg home win had not been enough for them against United last season, their situation was now precarious. They should have equalised in the 52nd minute when Panucci peeled off the unaware Scholes to meet a flick-on from a long throw-in, only to blast his effort over the bar from short range. With this chance encouraging the home crowd to be more vocal in support of their team, United had to remain disciplined and focused. They made their second substitution of the night three minutes later, replacing the yellow-carded Anderson with Hargreaves – a talented and versatile England international midfielder who had previously won the competition with Bayern Munich. This substitution slowed the game down and allowed the away side to catch their breath. Roma then brought on a former European champion themselves, introducing Ludovic Giuly in place of Taddei.

Van der Sar made a great save from a corner in the 62nd minute as pressure continued to grow on United. Forced to defend deep, they had left Ronaldo isolated up front on his own and he was finding it difficult to retain possession and counter-attack by himself. This prompted Ferguson to change formation to 1-4-4-2, with Rooney and Ronaldo up front together. Hargreaves moved to the right of midfield and Park Ji-Sung switched to the left. This was clever from the Scot – Park Ji-Sung was tireless and Hargreaves was fresh, so both could track Roma's full-backs while Rooney and Ronaldo simply focused on counter-attacking. This new shape is shown by *Figure 44*.

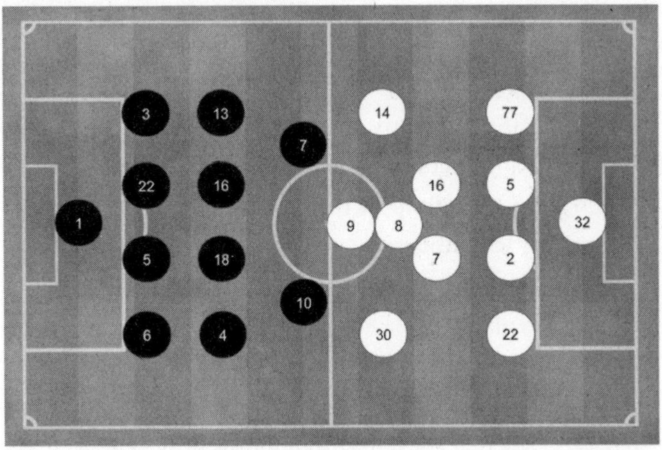

FIGURE 44

Almost immediately after changing their system, United doubled their advantage and all but confirmed their place in the semi-final. Like with Ronaldo's opener, they responded to a period of pressure by capitalising on a key moment and scoring a goal. Brown played a deep cross for Park Ji-Sung to attack at the far post, with Ronaldo and Rooney central. Park Ji-Sung headed across the box and Doni spilt the ball into the path of Rooney, who tapped the loose ball home to send the away end into raptures. It had taken a matter of seconds for the formation change to pay dividends.

Roma responded by swapping Tonetto for Cicinho – an extremely attacking full-back who could play on either side. Ronaldo and Rooney hardly worked at all when Roma had the ball, so it was important that the United midfield maintained their horizontal compactness to shut off potential passing lanes to Aquilani, Vučinić and Giuly (who was moving inside from the wing). Hargreaves and Park Ji-Sung had to work very diligently – they were the team's legs for the remainder of the night. Roma made their third change in the 77th minute, with Mauro Esposito coming on for Aquilani. Esposito played on the right and Giuly moved inside to assume Aquilani's position behind Vučinić.

Roma lacked the dynamism to really trouble United, who posed an enormous counter-attacking threat thanks to Ronaldo and Rooney. The pair had a chance to score a third in the 83rd minute as they attacked two v two against Mexès and Panucci. Rooney shot wide instead of passing to Ronaldo, to the clear annoyance of the Portuguese star. It was Rooney's last action of the match, as he was replaced by Tevez seconds later. Roma began to send the ball forward early, but United were able to sit back and easily deal with this strategy – they were used to this in the Premier League. They happily spent the two minutes of additional time defending on the edge of their own penalty area, soaking up pressure and denying access to their goal.

Full time – Roma 0 Manchester United 2

United were deserving victors in this match, putting in a brilliant away performance. They were solid defensively, clever and disciplined in midfield and clinical in two key attacking moments. Not only were they now huge favourites to go through to the semi-final, the maturity that they had shown in Rome made many people believe that Ferguson had finally assembled a squad capable of winning the Champions League again.

Second leg: Manchester United 1 Roma 0, 9 April 2008

In between the two quarter-final legs, United drew with Middlesbrough, dropping points in the title race. After the second leg, their next league match was at home to Arsenal – a must-win game in pursuit of top spot. Arsenal were also in the Champions League quarter-final but had drawn the first leg at home to Liverpool and had far more pressure on their second leg than United did. Ferguson was expected to rest players for the Roma match in readiness for Arsenal, something Wenger could not afford to do. In Serie A, Roma kept pressure on Inter by beating Genoa 3-2.

The two chosen teams are shown by *Figure 45*:

Manchester United (1-4-3-3): 1. van der Sar; 6. Brown, 5. Ferdinand (captain), 19. Piqué, 27. Silvestre; 16. Carrick, 4. Hargreaves, 8. Anderson; 13. Park Ji-Sung, 11. Giggs, 32. Tevez.

Substitutes: 29. Kuszczak, 2. Neville, 7. Ronaldo, 10. Rooney, 18. Scholes, 22. O'Shea, 47. Welbeck.

Head coach: Sir Alex Ferguson.

Roma (1-4-2-3-1): 32. Doni; 2. Panucci (captain), 5. Mexès, 4. Juan, 77. Cassetti; 16. de Rossi, 7. Pizarro; 11. Taddei, 20. Perrotta, 30. Mancini; 9. Vučinić.

Substitutes: 1. Curci, 3. Cicinho, 8. Aquilani, 14. Giuly, 18. Esposito, 22. Tonetto, 33. Brighi.

Head coach: Luciano Spalletti.

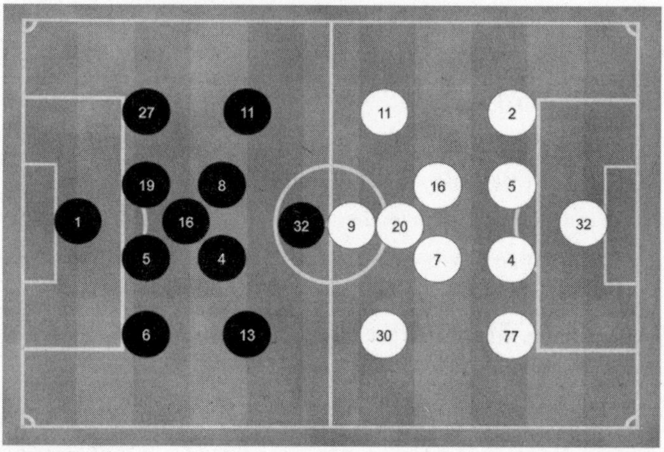

FIGURE 45

Ferguson made changes as expected, but he did keep Ronaldo and Rooney in reserve just in case they were needed. Gerard Piqué replaced the injured Vidić, while Silvestre, who had signed from Inter in 1999, came in for the rested Evra. Hargreaves was chosen from the start and Ryan Giggs, now 34 years old, started on the left. Whereas United had fallen back into a 1-4-1-4-1 defensive shape in Rome, they pressed higher here and formed a 1-4-3-3 instead. Brazilian centre-back Juan came in for Roma, so Panucci started at right-back and Cassetti replaced Tonetto on the left. Simone Perrotta started instead of Aquilani as Spalletti looked for more muscle and tenacity in the centre of the pitch.

The players were greeted by a good atmosphere at Old Trafford, although the stadium was far more relaxed than it had been when hosting Italian opposition in Part 1. United had one foot in the semi-final already and this match required professionalism to simply finish off the work started in Rome. Both sides started quickly, with Roma needing goals to get back into the tie and United looking to get on the front foot to increase their lead further. Like in the first leg, United went long to their left with goal kicks from van der Sar, but Giggs was not as effective in the air as Rooney had been. By this stage of his career, the Welshman was a very different footballer to the one seen in Part 1. Physically less able, he focused more on clever passing and good positioning rather than flying up and down the left flank.

United's rotations were more straightforward in the absence of Ronaldo and Rooney, but movements were still performed to good effect. Hargreaves and Park Ji-Sung rotated on the right, with Giggs and Anderson doing the same on the left. Hargreaves's movements into wide areas placed him in positions where he could showcase his excellent crossing ability, with Park Ji-Sung poised centrally should he be needed to press on transition. Giggs moved inside to receive the ball and help Carrick dictate possession, so Anderson moved to the left to ensure that United had someone occupying that area of the pitch. There was a third rotation – Park Ji-Sung would make runs towards the Roma centre-backs, like he did in the first leg, so that Tevez could drop deeper to receive behind Roma's midfield. To maintain balance, Hargreaves would then move to the right.

With so many energetic players on the pitch, United still possessed a counter-attacking threat without Ronaldo and Rooney. Anderson, Hargreaves and Park Ji-Sung worked tirelessly to burst forward and provide the lively Tevez with opportunities, the first of which came after six minutes when Tevez headed wide. As had been the case the week before, Roma often looked technically sound but incapable of matching Ferguson's side in moments when possession transferred from one team to another. They were physically incapable of keeping up with the runs of their opponents – United were simply faster and more dynamic. Doni made some good early saves to keep the match goalless.

Spalletti still wanted his three attacking midfielders to dribble with the ball in threatening areas, and this strategy paid dividends in the 29th minute when his side won a penalty. Mancini dribbled against Brown, who went to ground and appeared to miss both the ball and the player. Regardless, referee Tom Henning Øvrebø pointed to the spot and gave Roma the chance to get back into the tie. Unfortunately for the Italians, De Rossi blasted the penalty over the crossbar and United kept their two-goal advantage. Justice had arguably been served, but it was a warning to the home side that they would eventually be punished if they continued to miss chances to extend their lead. Roma played better after the penalty and increased the speed of their possession. Taddei was getting joy one v one against Silvestre, who was returning from injury and looking rusty. Ferdinand had picked up a knock against Middlesbrough and began limping as he struggled to shake off the pain. Van der Sar's distribution was wasteful, allowing Roma to reclaim possession and build another move. After a blistering start to the match, United were now holding on and edged their way to half-time.

Half-time – Manchester United 0 Roma 0

There were no substitutions at the interval, with Ferdinand able to continue after receiving treatment during the break. Roma started the second half with clear intent – they had 45 minutes to rescue their continental campaign. Vučinić began to play slightly deeper for the Italians, moving away from the United back four so that he could receive the ball in front of them and turn to face goalward. He did this in the 49th minute and released a good shot from long range. Van der Sar failed to hold the ball at the first attempt and only just beat the marauding Cassetti to the loose ball. The full-back then fell awkwardly in the 54th minute and injured his shoulder, causing him to be replaced by Tonetto.

After watching him dictate much of the first leg, Roma pressed Carrick much harder at Old Trafford and he had a poor game. Hargreaves and Anderson burst forward less in the second half, helping Carrick in the middle instead. The lack of clear-cut chances resulted in a lull in the crowd before Roma began to establish another positive period of possession with about 25 minutes left. Giuly came on for Pizarro, with Perrotta dropping back next to De Rossi and Giuly operating behind Vučinić.

Then, just as they had done in Rome, United took away their opponents' hopes with a well-taken goal seconds after a change had been made. Perrotta received a throw-in from Tonetto, but his return pass went straight to Brown, who passed forward first-time to Tevez. Perrotta had not settled into his new deeper position, giving the ball away and then failing to stop the line-breaking pass to Tevez. The Argentine striker turned and ran at the Roma back line before releasing Hargreaves on the United right (covered by Park Ji-Sung who stayed back with Anderson). Hargreaves drove forward with the ball, giving Tevez time to make a run into the box. He then crossed towards the front post, where Tevez was able to head the ball past Doni for a 3-0 aggregate lead. The goal was aided by poor defending from Spalletti's men. Juan had rushed out to press Hargreaves and Mancini tucked inside to cover him, but Mexès did not move across to mark Tevez, leaving him free to head home.

Tevez's goal ended the tie – Roma lost all purpose and United were able to relax. The crowd was back in a buoyant mood, singing about their rivals, Liverpool, in the hope of facing them in the final of the competition. They had hoped to in the previous season, but only Liverpool reached the showpiece in Athens while United were beaten in the last four by AC Milan. They did not want to lose out again.

Ferguson had instructed Rooney and O'Shea to warm up as soon as he saw Tevez's header hit the back of the net, and the pair were brought on for Giggs and Carrick in the 74th minute. One of the biggest cheers of the night greeted United's third change as Gary Neville made his first appearance in 13 months after recovering from a broken ankle. He came on for Anderson in the 81st minute and was given the freedom to play central midfield. There was no danger of losing the tie; Neville was simply allowed to stroll about and exchange some safe passes. Every single one of his touches was cheered boisterously by the home fans. Roma made their final change, bringing on Esposito for Taddei, but it was too little too late. United played keep-ball for the last few minutes and saw the tie out successfully.

Full time – Manchester United 1 Roma 0; Manchester United win 3-0 on aggregate

Although Roma had decent spells in both legs, they never looked superior to a United team that always carried a greater attacking threat. Van der Sar proved his worth out in Italy, making some good saves that helped his side survive some difficult moments. The tone of the second leg would have changed completely if De Rossi had scored his penalty, but United would have still had enough in their squad to see things through – Ronaldo and Scholes were not needed and Rooney only came on towards the end. Now, Ferguson was to return to the scene of his greatest ever triumph – Barcelona.

Chapter 8

Semi-final – Manchester United 1 Barcelona 0 (aggregate)

First leg: Barcelona 0 Manchester United 0, 23 April 2008

United went on to beat Arsenal 2-1, setting the north Londoners back in the title race in the same week that Liverpool had knocked them out of the Champions League. The Red Devils then rescued a point with a late Carlos Tevez strike away at Blackburn Rovers to stay top of the table. Their next European opponents were Catalan giants Barcelona who, as previously mentioned, beat Arsenal in the 2005/06 final. By April 2008, things were looking much bleaker for Barça – they were out of the La Liga title race, instead duelling with Atlético de Madrid and Sevilla in a battle for third. Having also lost to Valencia in the semi-final of the Copa del Rey, they were desperate to win the Champions League to rescue what had otherwise been a thoroughly disappointing campaign.

Managed by Dutchman Frank Rijkaard, Barça's squad was well stocked with world-class talent. Twenty-year-old Lionel Messi was improving all the time, rapidly developing into one of the best players in the world. The club also held high hopes for the 17-year-old Bojan Krkić, who had burst on to the scene and made a real impact. With Thierry Henry, Samuel Eto'o and ex-Chelsea man Guðjohnsen also at his disposal, Rijkaard was not short of attacking options, even with former Ballon d'Or and FIFA World Player of the Year winner Ronaldinho out injured.

The teams for the first leg at the Camp Nou are shown by *Figure 46*:

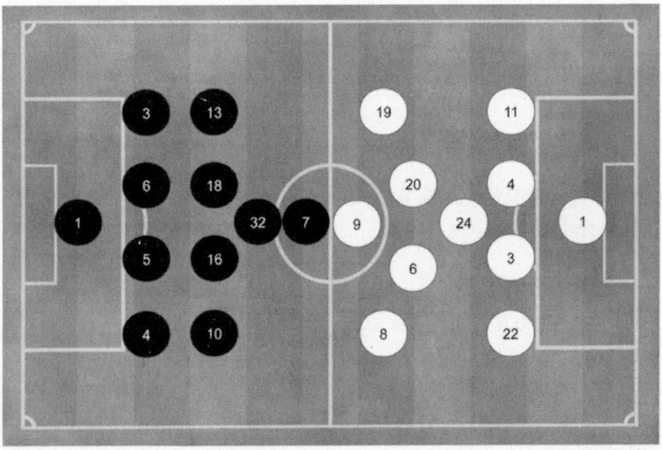

FIGURE 46

Manchester United (1-4-4-1-1): 1. van der Sar; 4. Hargreaves, 5. Ferdinand (captain), 6. Brown, 3. Evra; 10. Rooney, 16. Carrick, 18. Scholes, 13. Park Ji-Sung; 32. Tevez; 7. Ronaldo.

Substitutes: 29. Kuszczak, 8. Anderson, 11. Giggs, 17. Nani, 19. Piqué, 22. O'Shea, 27. Silvestre.

Head coach: Sir Alex Ferguson.

Barcelona (1-4-3-3): 1. Valdés; 11. Zambrotta, 4. Márquez, 3. Milito, 22. Abidal; 24. Touré, 20. Deco, 6. Xavi (captain); 19. Messi, 8. Iniesta, 9. Eto'o.

Substitutes: 13. Pinto, 7. Guðjohnsen, 14. Henry, 16. Sylvinho, 17. dos Santos, 21. Thuram, 27. Bojan.

Head coach: Frank Rijkaard.

Vidić had suffered another injury against Blackburn and was consequently unavailable here. It was initially rumoured that Barcelona academy graduate Gerard Piqué would start against his boyhood club. O'Shea and Silvestre were also both capable of playing at centre-back, but Ferguson elected to move Brown inside and start the versatile Hargreaves at right-back instead. All three of United's attacking trident (Ronaldo, Rooney and Tevez) started the match in the hope of providing a strong counter-attacking threat. Once again, it was a line-up able to change between 1-4-4-2 and 1-4-1-4-1 if necessary.

Despite doubts over his fitness, Messi was chosen to start for the hosts – he and Ronaldo would play against each other for the first time. Ex-Juventus man Gianluca Zambrotta was at right-back and had licence to support the diminutive Argentinian when Barça attacked. The physically strong Yaya Touré started in midfield behind the technically excellent Xavi and Deco. Captain Carles Puyol was suspended, so Gabriel Milito partnered Rafael Márquez at centre-back. Eric Abidal was a powerful left-back, good at defending one v one situations and then sprinting forward to support attacks.

United settled into their defensive shape immediately. Like against Roma, Ferguson matched the opposition midfield three v three, this time using Tevez to mark Touré so that Ronaldo could just try and block the passing lanes between Touré and the Barça centre-backs. Ferguson gave Ronaldo as little defensive responsibility as possible in these difficult European away matches, and understandably so – he was their key attacking outlet and his team-mates were capable of defending well behind him. Tevez marking Touré allowed Carrick and Scholes to focus on Deco and Xavi. Rooney and Park Ji-Sung were again tasked with selflessly tracking adventurous full-backs.

The Mancunian outfit almost had a dream start when they were awarded an early penalty, only for Ronaldo to see his effort hit the woodwork and bounce clear. He had been fouled in the opening minute of the match and shown his desire to impose himself on the game by shooting with a free kick despite being a considerable distance from the Barça goal. His shot was deflected out for a corner. Rooney swung it out from United's right for Ronaldo to attack – his header was blocked by the hand of Milito and the referee instantly pointed to the spot. The Portuguese attacker tried to be precise with his penalty and place it in the top-right corner, but he was off target. A golden opportunity to seize control of the tie had been squandered and the home fans were ecstatic.

Barcelona were very comfortable in possession, forcing United into a 1-4-4-2 defensive shape by making Tevez leave his central slot and press elsewhere. They did this by using Deco and Xavi in roles we will describe in this book as 'false full-backs' – they positioned themselves outside of their centre-backs to receive the ball in spaces historically

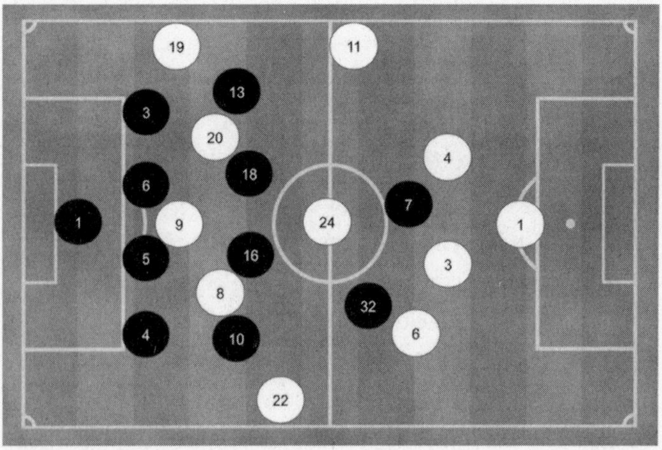

FIGURE 47

occupied by full-backs – like Edgar Davids for Juventus in Part 1. Please note that the term 'false full-backs' can also be used to describe other roles within a team's set-up, however this is the definition that this book will employ. *Figure 47* shows Xavi positioned as a false full-back outside Milito, who has the ball. Xavi's movement has allowed Abidal to advance forward and Iniesta to move deep and central. Tevez has pressed towards Xavi so that he is not free to receive, which consequently leaves Touré unmarked. Deco and Iniesta have positioned themselves on the outside shoulders of Scholes and Carrick respectively, preventing one of the English pair from pushing forward on to Touré because it would leave the man outside them free. Rooney and Park Ji-Sung needed to move inside to retain the midfield line's horizontal compactness and help deal with Deco and Iniesta, both of whom were dangerous if given time and space. Therefore, they conceded space in wide areas to the Barça full-backs instead. If the Catalans then moved the ball wide, United's ball-side winger would have to rush out and press the receiving full-back.

Messi began the match with a wide starting position to occupy Evra and stop him from pressing Zambrotta. If the Argentinian wanted to receive the ball in a more central area, he either waited until Deco became a false full-back, or rotated positions with the Portugal midfielder so that Evra was not free to follow him inside. It became very clear that Barcelona would dominate possession across this tie and that United would have to put in two monumental defensive efforts to go through.

Not only were they good at retaining possession, but Rijkaard's side pressed well when they lost it and United struggled to cope. The home side swarmed the ball carrier in transition and forced mistakes well. If United conceded a throw-in, ball boys were on hand for the home team to use the multi-ball system effectively and restart play as quickly as possible. If it was a throw-in or a corner to United, the balls were redistributed much slower.

Van der Sar nearly cost his side in the 13th minute when he cleared the ball straight to Messi, who passed through to Eto'o. Luckily for van der Sar, Scholes got back in time to cut out Eto'o's attempted return pass to Messi. Seconds later, though, Tevez clattered Touré on the edge of the United penalty area and conceded a free kick. United survived, but they were under serious pressure. They desperately needed to see out the opening 25 minutes unscathed.

After failing to score an early goal, Barça settled down into a more patient passing rhythm. United were nearly rewarded for making it through the first 30 minutes with a second penalty when Márquez barged Ronaldo over in the box following a misplaced Iniesta back pass, but the referee decided against giving a foul. Touré had an excellent first half, winning challenge after challenge to break up United play and launch new periods of Barcelona possession. The more patient this possession became, though, the easier it was for United to defend.

The visitors retained their vertical and horizontal compactness, watching Barcelona harmlessly pass the ball in front of them. The *Blaugrana* lacked pace and did not sufficiently threaten the space behind United's defence. Hargreaves was a midfielder playing right-back, but the absence of Henry was giving him an easy ride. Rooney worked his socks off in front of him, closing space desired by both Iniesta and Abidal. If Rooney needed to focus solely on Abidal, Hargeaves would follow Iniesta into midfield, safe in the knowledge that the Spaniard would not beat him for pace. Ferguson's side ended the half on a positive note as Ronaldo dribbled forward and drew a foul from Márquez, for which the Mexican defender was booked. With a quarter of the tie played, things were very much in the balance.

Half-time – Barcelona 0 Manchester United 0

United complained to UEFA officials at half-time regarding the inconsistent use of the multi-ball system, but Barça continued to receive the ball back quicker and they started the second half well. In midfield, Xavi and Deco had swapped sides. Xavi settled into his new position with a nutmeg on Scholes, though he continued to operate as a false full-back so that Messi could tuck inside with Zambrotta advancing on the overlap. Messi was involved in the creation of two good chances – firstly with a slide tackle that found its way to Eto'o and secondly by dribbling inside and passing to Xavi, who flicked the ball over Ferdinand and Evra for Eto'o to receive. The Cameroonian shot wide, letting United off the hook. Barça wanted an early goal in this half to relieve pressure and take control of the tie. If the score was still goalless with ten minutes left, they would have to choose between taking risks in search of a goal or settling for 0-0 at the halfway point of the tie. United were not offering much of a counter-attacking threat – Ronaldo was isolated up front on his own and repeatedly gave the ball away when he tried to dribble forward.

Messi was struggling by the hour mark, evidently not fit enough for a full 90 minutes, so he was replaced by Bojan in the 62nd minute. Iniesta moved to the right, with Bojan on the left. As the game slowed down again following Barcelona's quick start, United showed their defensive solidity once more. The home side became desperate and began to shoot more from long range, especially Xavi, who was uncharacteristically impatient. United were still not offering a lot themselves, though, and Carrick had a very wasteful spell midway through the half, prompting Phelan to shout at him to calm down. Rooney and Park Ji-Sung swapped wings as Zambrotta pushed even further forward. Ronaldo was asked to drift more to the left so that he and Rooney could look to combine on transition in the space being vacated by Barça's Italian full-back. The pair did manage to combine on the odd occasion, only for Ronaldo to give the ball away. He was trying too hard to perform the spectacular and steal the headlines for himself.

Bojan played touchline wide on the Barcelona left, forcing Hargreaves further away from where he was comfortable. The United man was booked for a late tackle on the Barça youngster – a cheap yellow card in the circumstances and one that served to make the final 20 minutes of the match harder for him.

By the 75th minute, Barcelona had enjoyed 65 per cent of possession and the home crowd was singing the club's anthem to try and will them forward. Ferguson gave his players a breather by bringing off Rooney, who was the furthest player away from the dugout. He was replaced by Nani – a flamboyant winger in his first season at the club – who provided fresh legs on the side of Zambrotta. Like Benítez in Part 2, Ferguson was hoping to either force the Italian to stay deeper or exploit the space that he left behind if he continued to attack. Barcelona made their second change, introducing ex-Arsenal star Henry in place of Deco. The mercurial Frenchman was returning from injury, but if fit possessed the pace to trouble United's weary defenders. He initially came on up front with Eto'o on the left before the pair swapped over. Bojan moved to the right. It did not take long for Henry to receive on the left, dribble inwards and draw a good save from van der Sar.

Meanwhile, his team-mates played more patiently, refrained from getting the ball forward early and took fewer long-range shots. As much as they wanted a lead to take to Old Trafford, it was not worth risking too much in case they were punished on the break. Having said that, it seemed like common sense to get the ball to Henry early so that he could attack against the tired, yellow-carded Hargreaves. United slowed things down again by bringing Giggs on for Tevez in the 85th minute. Park Ji-Sung and Nani swapped wings, as Ferguson prioritised defending against Zambrotta over hoping to counter-attack. Barcelona stayed patient, accepting that they had not done enough to score but that they still had the opportunity to go again in the second leg.

Full time – Barcelona 0 Manchester United 0

The first leg was a disappointing one for the neutral – the first meeting of Messi and Ronaldo had seen them both struggle to perform. United proved that, despite their attacking stars, their success was built first and foremost on defensive discipline and work rate. They survived early pressure at the beginning of both halves before settling into a compact, organised shape that was difficult to break down. Hargreaves filled in well at right-back, Ferdinand and Brown were brilliant and Evra hardly put a foot wrong all night. Scholes and Carrick marshalled the midfield well, shuffling side to side to shut off passing lanes as Barça moved the ball laterally. Park Ji-Sung and Rooney hardly attacked at all, but selflessly shackled Zambrotta and Abidal.

Frankly, it had been more '2005 Liverpool' than '1999 Manchester United', but this was understandable given the circumstances. Like Benítez, Ferguson had shown an ability to react to the actions of the opposition's full-backs

– something that could have resulted in an away goal if Ronaldo had been more careful with the ball in the second half. Their commendable defensive display had effectively made this semi-final a 90-minute tie at Old Trafford.

Second leg: Manchester United 1 Barcelona 0, 29 April 2008

The Premier League title race was blown wide open when United made six changes from the side that started in Barcelona and lost 2-1 away to Chelsea, bringing the teams level on points with two games remaining. The Red Devils had dropped points in three of their last four league games and they were suddenly looking much less imperious than before. There was further cause for concern regarding the wellbeing of Nemanja Vidić, who made his comeback against Chelsea but only lasted for 14 minutes before getting concussed. Rooney had also been forced off with a hip injury. A win against Barcelona, who spent the weekend losing 2-0 to Deportivo La Coruña, would change everything, though. A Premier League and

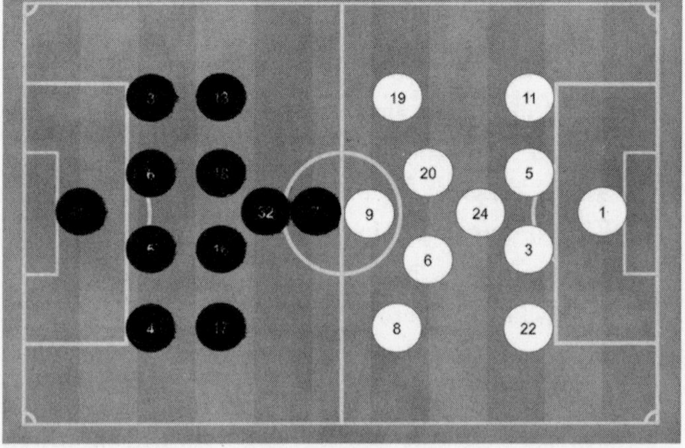

FIGURE 48

Champions League double was still in sight for Ferguson and he was not prepared to let this opportunity pass him and his side by.

The teams selected for the start of the second leg at Old Trafford are shown by *Figure 48*:

Manchester United (1-4-4-1-1): 1. van der Sar; 4. Hargreaves, 5. Ferdinand (captain), 6. Brown, 3. Evra; 17. Nani, 16. Carrick, 18. Scholes, 13. Park Ji-Sung; 32. Tevez; 7. Ronaldo.

Substitutes: 29. Kuszczak, 8. Anderson, 11. Giggs, 22. O'Shea, 24. Fletcher, 27. Silvestre, 47. Welbeck.

Head coach: Sir Alex Ferguson.

Barcelona (1-4-3-3): 1. Valdés; 11. Zambrotta, 5. Puyol (captain), 3. Milito, 22. Abidal; 24. Touré, 20. Deco, 6. Xavi; 19. Messi, 8. Iniesta, 9. Eto'o.

Substitutes: 13. Pinto, 7. Guðjohnsen, 14. Henry, 15. Edmílson, 16. Sylvinho, 21. Thuram, 27. Bojan.

Head coach: Frank Rijkaard.

The six players rested from the start against Chelsea – Hargreaves, Evra, Scholes, Park Ji-Sung, Tevez and Ronaldo – all returned for United. Rooney had not recovered in time to feature, so Nani started on the right in his place. Brown deputised for Vidić again, with Hargreaves at right-back instead of O'Shea (Gary Neville was still a long way from full fitness and had not made a single appearance since his cameo against Roma). The Catalans made one change, with Puyol returning from suspension.

The atmosphere at the start of the first leg had been impressive due to the sheer size of the crowd, but the noise that greeted the players at Old Trafford was far more intense. The United faithful truly believed that they had another group of players capable of going all the way in Europe and they were determined to play their part. It was Barcelona who started the better, though, as Messi dribbled forward and was fouled by Scholes on the edge of the United penalty area. United cleared and continued to tackle strongly, earning a cheer from the crowd each time they performed a successful challenge.

After their rigid performance at the Camp Nou, United wanted to impose themselves on the second leg and their attackers therefore rotated more frequently. Tevez and Park Ji-Sung looked to swap positions with each other so that Tevez could receive in space – he had struggled to impact the first leg and needed to be more effective here. Sometimes the rotations went a step further, with Park Ji-Sung central behind Tevez so that Ronaldo could move to the left. Scholes and Carrick were free to rotate as appropriate, which created passing lanes from United's back four to their attackers because the English midfield pair were marked tightly by Deco and Xavi.

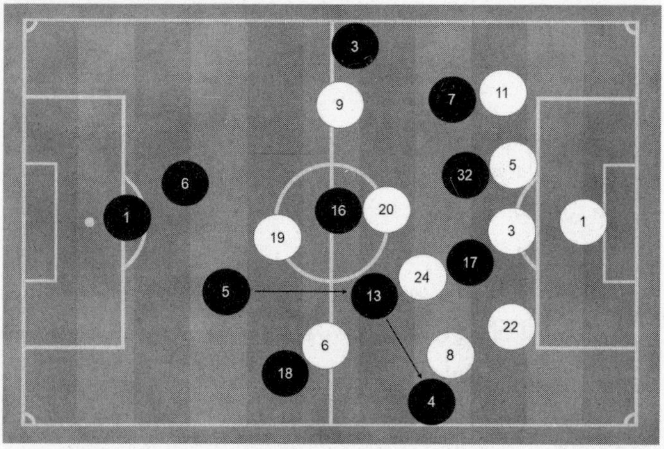

FIGURE 49

Figure 49 shows Scholes performing similar movements to those of Xavi and Deco, moving to the right and becoming a false full-back outside of Ferdinand, pulling Xavi away from the centre. This created space for Ferdinand – afforded time by the temporarily central Messi – to play through to Park Ji-Sung, who in turn passed wide to Hargreaves.

From here, Hargreaves dribbled against Iniesta and won a throw-in for his side. As much as they did not expect to dominate possession for long periods of the night, United still showed a preparedness to rotate and be brave when the opportunity arose.

Out of possession, Tevez was again tasked with marking Touré, with Ronaldo able to shuffle a few yards from side to side when Barça's centre-backs had the ball. Ronaldo would be activated from a defensive perspective if Barcelona had been forced into passing backwards to a centre-back; if this happened then he would sprint to close the receiving defender down and force them into an early decision. Iniesta had some early joy against Nani in space created by Xavi becoming a false full-back outside of Milito. This prompted Hargreaves to follow Iniesta into midfield like in the first leg. Deco also acted as a false full-back again, creating space for Messi to move to Carrick's outside shoulder and receive the ball. The Argentine looked much sharper than he had done six days previously. His side settled into the game first, establishing some good periods of possession that forced United back into their compact defensive shape. The away team were able to toy with their hosts – passing back to Valdes and encouraging Tevez and Ronaldo to push forward on to a centre-back each in the hope of intercepting a short pass. This allowed Touré to drop, create a four v two overload and receive the ball with time to turn and progress the ball forwards. Concern began to grow in the stands as United looked technically second best.

The feeling in the ground was then completely changed in the 14th minute thanks to a moment of brilliance from Scholes. Eto'o tried to run on to a long ball from Milito but could only head it on to van der Sar, who quickly rolled the ball back out to Ferdinand. Comfortable in possession,

Ferdinand played a rapid one-two with Carrick before finding Ronaldo to his left, able to receive the ball and turn thanks to Zambrotta slipping over. This forced Touré to move across and cover. Zambrotta recovered to win the ball off Ronaldo but he could not pass back to Puyol because Park Ji-Sung – central due to United's rotation – was on hand to press the Catalan defender. So, Zambrotta panicked and played a blind pass into midfield, hoping that Deco would be there to receive. Scholes reacted first, though, running on to the ball and controlling it before unleashing a brilliant strike from 25 yards out. His effort flew past Valdes and into the top corner for 1-0. United's rotations paid dividends, getting Ronaldo into a position where he could dribble forward and cause problems. This had dragged Touré across, forcing him to leave the space that Scholes would then occupy unopposed at the time of his shot. Ferdinand's distribution at the beginning of the move also deserved credit.

The home side were much better after scoring. Hargreaves and Evra supported attacks more confidently, forcing Iniesta and Messi to track back rather than focus on attacking. Messi then reminded everybody of the threat that he posed by picking the ball up in a deep position, dribbling past Scholes and Brown before forcing van der Sar into a good save with his shot from the edge of the United box. After surviving this warning, Ferguson's side settled back into their disciplined shape and made it difficult for Barcelona to play through them.

Barça had an issue as Puyol and Milito were less capable in possession than their team-mates and regularly played unsuccessful long passes that gifted the ball back to the home side. The goal certainly boosted Scholes and Carrick, who were doing better at keeping the ball at a fast pace than Deco and Xavi were. The pair were also benefiting from the effective rotations taking place in front of them, making passes between Deco and Touré for whichever one of Park Ji-Sung, Ronaldo or Tevez was occupying the space in that moment.

Eto'o and Iniesta began to rotate to see if they could isolate Eto'o against Hargreaves. United did not fall for the trap – Hargreaves tracked Iniesta inside and Ferdinand moved wide with Eto'o, sticking tight to the Cameroonian so that he could not run with the ball into space. Ferdinand defended excellently and Iniesta did not receive the ball in central areas enough to make an impact against Hargreaves. Brown accidentally kneed van der Sar in the head as United tried to defend a cross, but luckily for United the Dutch goalkeeper was able to carry on.

United defended deeper for the last few minutes of the first half, determined to reach the break with their one-goal lead intact. This afforded Barcelona more possession but they could do nothing with it, faced with a wall of red bodies in front of them. After effectively turning this semi-final into a one-legged affair, United were now halfway to Moscow.

Half-time – Manchester United 1 Barcelona 0

Ferguson's team now had a choice – push for a second goal or continue to defend deep. They went with the latter, prioritising the protection of their lead over the temptation of increasing it. This made sense because they were well suited to this approach – they were defensively excellent and possessed incredible ability on the counter-attack. Barcelona were unchanged and started the half on the front foot, but their crosses into the penalty area were easily dealt with by their hosts. By the 50th minute, Barcelona had enjoyed 60 per cent of possession but they were struggling to create anything with it.

Zambrotta was yellow-carded in the 52nd minute for a poor tackle on Evra, who had advanced forward in support of a United counter-attack. Deco received a booking two minutes later for pushing Park Ji-Sung as the South Korean prevented the taking of a quick free kick – Barcelona were getting frustrated. Messi still looked dangerous, receiving a short corner and dribbling past Scholes, before crossing for Puyol. Brown blocked the cross well and United survived.

Barcelona made their first substitution in the 61st minute, swapping Iniesta for Henry. Like in the first leg, Barcelona had been desperate for a faster forward who could run into space behind United. Had the Frenchman been fully fit, he almost certainly would have played a bigger role in the tie. Iniesta's ineffectiveness vindicated Ferguson's decision to deploy Hargreaves at right-back. Whereas a more natural defender would have preferred to stay in the back line and concede space in front of them, Hargreaves was comfortable following Iniesta into midfield and engaging with him there.

Conserving his energy for attacking situations, Messi stopped tracking back, inviting Evra to attack and leave space behind him. United reacted by moving Ronaldo to the left, with Park Ji-Sung central behind Tevez, so that Barcelona had to decide if they wanted to leave the yellow-carded Zambrotta exposed two v one against Evra and Ronaldo. Evra continued to support counter-attacks, hoping to occupy Zambrotta defensively and believing that he had the energy levels to rush back and defend against Messi.

Carrick and Ronaldo then received bookings, as did Touré. Rijkaard made his second change in the 72nd minute, replacing Eto'o with Bojan. After a difficult few minutes in which they played some sloppy passes, Carrick's yellow card seemed to refocus him and Scholes. They began to hold on to the ball more effectively, eating up valuable time that

Barcelona wanted to spend attacking rather than defending. When the La Liga outfit did have the ball, their main threat was still Messi, who wanted to receive wide and dribble inwards into Zone 14. It was up to Carrick and Scholes to prevent easy access into Zone 14, protecting the space in front of Ferdinand and Brown. They did this well, intercepting attempted through balls from Messi, Deco and Xavi, before making good decisions with the ball themselves on transition.

Ferguson decided that he wanted Zone 14 to have even more protection, so he made two substitutions and changed formation – Fletcher and Giggs replaced Scholes and Nani as

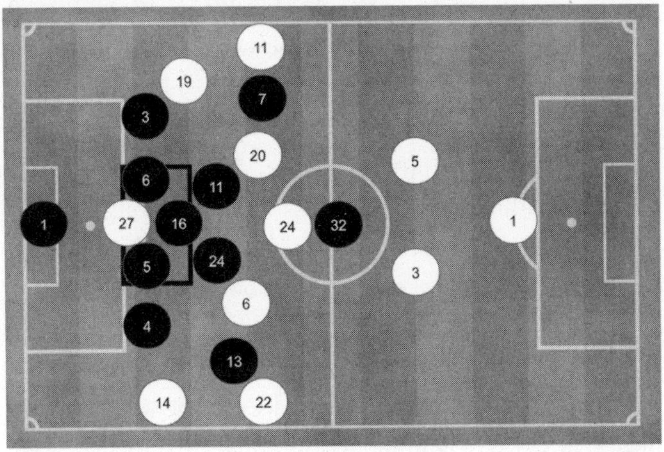

FIGURE 50

United changed to 1-4-1-4-1. As shown by *Figure 50*, Fletcher and Giggs played in front of Carrick, allowing him to solely focus on blocking access to the space in front of Ferdinand and Brown. As had been the case in Part 1, Ferguson replaced Scholes with a more natural ball-winning midfielder when looking to defend deep and maintain a compact shape.

Van der Sar made another big save in the 78th minute, this time thwarting Henry after the Frenchman had been left free on a Barça corner and managed to head the ball towards goal. This chance aside, the visitors were struggling to create genuine chances. Henry was rusty and Bojan lacked presence up front against the physically strong Ferdinand and Brown.

Whereas van der Sar had been comfortable distributing to his centre-backs in the first half, he was now booting goal kicks long to Ronaldo to occupy Zambrotta and get his side into the Barcelona half.

The Old Trafford crowd remained loud and encouraging. United once again proved that for all their attacking strength their defending was equally as important. They defended their penalty area well and continued to block crosses and through balls. Defending deep is fine as long as the goalkeeper and defence perform effectively, and they did so here. Barcelona made their final substitution in the 88th minute, taking off Touré and introducing Guðjohnsen, who had joined from Chelsea in 2006. Xavi moved back into Touré's position and Guðjohnsen played as the left-sided central midfielder. Touré had performed well over the two legs but was now redundant as his side totally dominated possession and no longer needed somebody breaking play up in midfield.

United's exhausted players had a chance to catch their breath in the first minute of additional time as Evra went down injured. Unfortunately, he had to be stretchered off and was replaced by Silvestre. Barcelona began to panic, abandoning their philosophy and lumping the ball forward instead. This was ideal for United, who were used to dealing with long central passes at domestic level. Between their two centre-backs and three central midfielders, they dominated aerial challenges and battles for second balls. Ronaldo gifted Barça one last chance by fouling Bojan and giving a free kick away. Valdes came up for the set piece but could not impact the situation like Schmeichel did in the final for United in

Part 1 – the hosts cleared the ball and the referee blew for full time.

Full time – Manchester United 1 Barcelona 0; Manchester United win 1-0 on aggregate

United were back in the final of the Champions League after nine years of continental underachievement. Although they were expected to beat Roma, the Red Devils were clinical in the away leg and earned the ability to cruise through the return fixture. In defeating Barcelona, they displayed their ability to defend with discipline, limiting their talented opponents to very few clear-cut chances. Scholes's goal was the most high-quality moment of the tie and it was fitting that a man who missed the 1999 showpiece had earned himself a shot at redemption. As much as Barça were on a poor run of form, they still had an array of talent at their disposal – United's spot in the final was well earned.

One day later, Chelsea beat Liverpool 3-2 after extra time to secure a 4-3 aggregate win and their first final appearance. The final that the United fans had sung for against Roma had not materialised, but a meeting between the Premier League's best two teams that season was equally as mouthwatering.

Chapter 9

Manchester United 1 Chelsea 1; Manchester United win 6-5 on penalties, 21 May 2008

After beating Barcelona to reach the final, United were suddenly three wins away from a Premier League and Champions League double. A Cristiano Ronaldo hat-trick inspired a 4-1 victory over West Ham United before a Ryan Giggs goal rounded off a 2-0 win away at Wigan Athletic, confirming United's 17th top-flight title. Switching their focus back to Europe, the build-up to the Champions League Final was emotional, with the team determined to mark the anniversaries of Munich and the 1968 triumph in style.

These anniversaries encouraged the Mancunian outfit to believe that it was their destiny to become champions of Europe again. However, Chelsea had their own reasons to believe that this was their time. After making their Champions League debut in 1999/00, they were losing semi-finalists in 2003/04, 2004/05 and 2006/07 and had now finally reached the final for the first time in their history.

After controversially replacing Mourinho with Avram Grant in September 2007, the Blues topped their group ahead of Schalke 04, Rosenborg BK and Valencia. Faced with Olympiakos in the round of 16, Chelsea drew 0-0 in Greece before winning 3-0 at Stamford Bridge. Turkish outfit Fenerbahçe were beaten 3-2 on aggregate in the quarter-final as Chelsea recovered from a 2-1 defeat in the first leg in Istanbul to win 2-0 at home. Semi-final losses to Liverpool in 2005 and 2007 were then avenged. A Riise own goal in stoppage time of the first leg gifted Chelsea a 1-1 draw at Anfield and, after tying by the same scoreline after 90 minutes eight days later, goals from Drogba and Lampard secured a dramatic 4-3 aggregate victory in extra time. After losing that season's League Cup Final to local rivals Tottenham Hotspur and falling short of the Premier League title by two points, Grant was desperate to deliver a trophy.

The rivalry between United and Chelsea had grown in intensity thanks to the Londoners' rise to the top of English football. The pair had been first and second in the Premier League in every season from 2005/06 to 2007/08 and had also met in the 2007 FA Cup Final, which Chelsea won 1-0 after extra time. Now, they were to meet in European competition for the first time in the first all-English final of the Champions League.

Adding to Chelsea's belief that they were destined for victory was the fact that the final was to take place in Russia, the homeland of their owner, Roman Abramovich. The Luzhniki Stadium in Moscow was the easternmost host of a final in the competition's history and was an extremely long way for fans from London and Manchester to travel. There were question marks over the state of the pitch – the venue's original artificial surface had been replaced by grass just days before the match.

The two starting line-ups are shown by *Figure 51*:

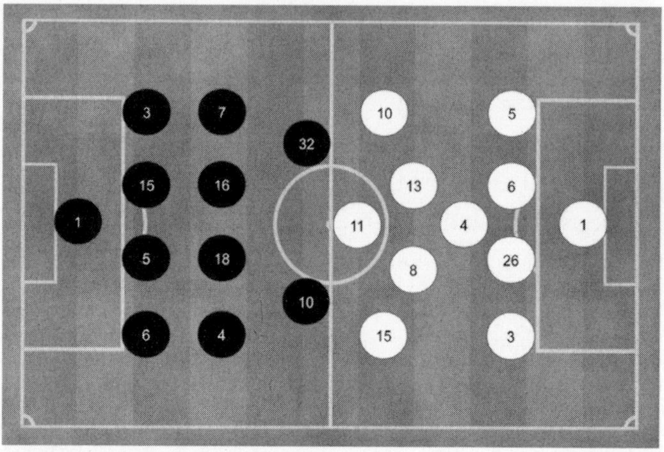

FIGURE 51

Manchester United (1-4-4-2): 1. van der Sar; 6. Brown, 5. Ferdinand (captain), 15. Vidić, 3. Evra; 4. Hargreaves, 18. Scholes, 16. Carrick, 7. Ronaldo; 10. Rooney, 32. Tevez.

Substitutes: 29. Kuszczak, 8. Anderson, 11. Giggs, 17. Nani, 22. O'Shea, 24. Fletcher, 27. Silvestre.

Head coach: Sir Alex Ferguson.

Chelsea (1-4-3-3): 1. Čech; 5. Essien, 6. Carvalho, 26. Terry (captain), 3. A. Cole; 4. Makélélé, 13. Ballack, 8. Lampard; 10. J. Cole, 15. Malouda, 11. Drogba.

Substitutes: 23. Cudicini, 7. Shevchenko, 12. Mikel, 21. Kalou, 33. Alex, 35. Belletti, 39. Anelka.

Head coach: Avram Grant.

One of the major talking points in the days prior to the match was whether Ferguson would start with a 1-4-1-4-1 or 1-4-4-2 formation. He chose the latter, deciding that attack was better than defence. This was fair enough – United were known for starting fast and Chelsea had developed a reputation for growing into games and killing them off in the second half. If United were to win then they would most likely need to score first, and early. Excluding a penalty shoot-out victory in the 2007 Community Shield, United had only won two of their last ten meetings with Chelsea and they had taken a first-half lead on both of those occasions.

The decision to use 1-4-4-2 was also dictated by Ferguson's desire to put Ronaldo in the position that gave him the best chance of influencing the match. The Portuguese star had played as a right-winger against Chelsea left-back Ashley Cole for both club and country, finding it difficult to outplay the Englishman. Ronaldo could have started centrally but would have faced the domineering centre-back pairing of Carvalho and Terry. So Ferguson instead started him on the left because he correctly predicted that Chelsea would pick Michael Essien at right-back instead of Paulo Ferreira or Juliano Belletti. Essien was naturally a central midfielder and Ronaldo would fancy his chances of giving the Ghana international a hard time.

The hardest decision for Ferguson was selecting his substitutes and there was no place in the matchday squad for Park Ji-Sung, despite his heroic efforts against Roma and Barcelona. Ferguson decided that he had other players who could act as better impact subs in a one-off final.

Chelsea played in their usual shape, selecting Florent Malouda instead of Salomon Kalou on the left side of the attack. German central midfielder Michael Ballack had replaced Tiago, adding more power and strength to a star-studded midfield.

Remarkably, neither of these two starting 11s had ever been used before. The two teams knew each other so well and were desperate to try and find a new tactical edge. The teams had also had longer to prepare for this meeting than usual – the Premier League season had ended ten days prior to the final. Whereas these two sides were used to facing each other in the middle of hectic schedules, this time they had enjoyed the opportunity to thoroughly work on their game plans.

The Luzhniki Stadium was a marvellous sight when full and the players were greeted by a fantastic pre-match atmosphere. For most of them, this was the biggest night of their careers so far. The weather was far from ideal – it was raining heavily and it remained to be seen how well the pitch would cope in such conditions.

Essien made an early statement by clattering Ronaldo in the second minute. Overall, the opening five minutes saw football typical of two English sides, with plenty of direct passes and strong challenges for second balls. After these initial duels, Chelsea showed their intent to spend the first half trying to suffocate United's inevitable attempt at a fast start. They fell back into a 1-4-1-4-1 defensive shape, allowing United to retain possession in their own half. United responded to this by playing short from van der Sar to see if they could entice their opponents into pushing forward and leaving space behind them.

Chelsea resisted, so Ronaldo dropped deep to receive the ball off his defence and dribble forward. Essien had used up his 'free hit' on Ronaldo in the opening stages and could no longer intentionally foul him. Ronaldo beat Essien on several occasions to advance forward into dangerous positions, often supported by Evra on the overlap. United were therefore the first team to settle and establish an attacking threat. They managed to perform some dangerous crosses that troubled the London side. In terms of rotation, Tevez and Hargreaves initially looked to swap positions while Ronaldo and Rooney retained theirs. If both wingers stayed wide, Rooney and Tevez were free to rotate with each other before making dangerous runs into the box to attack crosses.

United adopted a 1-4-4-1-1 shape when Chelsea had possession, hoping to encourage Essien and Ashley Cole to advance high and wide so that they left space behind them. Tevez dropped on to Makélélé, with Ferguson hoping to create a central three v three like he had done in the two previous rounds. Tracking Makélélé was difficult, though, as the Frenchman used excellent off-the-ball movement to create space for himself, similar to Juventus's midfield in Part 1. Makélélé aside, Chelsea struggled to retain the ball in the first 20 minutes of the match.

In the 21st minute, Scholes and Makélélé were both booked after clashing in pursuit of a loose ball. Scholes, who had suffered with vision problems in the past, had blood coming from his head and required treatment. This temporarily gave Chelsea a one-man advantage, which allowed them to finally settle down and enjoy some periods of possession. Tevez had moved to the right, with Hargreaves covering centrally for Scholes, so Makélélé was free – giving Chelsea a three v two central overload. Anderson was sent to warm up, but Scholes was determined to stay on and returned to the field of play.

United were rewarded for their superior start with a goal in the 26th minute. Makélélé fouled Tevez just inside Chelsea's half. Scholes took the set piece and passed square to Carrick, which attracted Lampard to push forward and press. With Makélélé blocking the passing lane through to Tevez, Rooney dropped into space behind Chelsea's midfield to receive a pass that Carrick could play through the area abandoned by Lampard. Rooney turned and passed wide to Hargreaves, who won a throw-in off Ashley Cole. Scholes drifted over to receive Brown's throw, which forced Lampard across to press him. He played a clever one-two with Brown that took both Lampard and Malouda out of the game, leaving Brown in space to cross left-footed towards Ronaldo on the far side of the Chelsea six-yard box. Tevez made a run inside Ronaldo to occupy Carvalho. One v one with Essien, Ronaldo leapt into the air and powered a header past Čech for his 42nd goal of an incredible season. Brown's cross and Ronaldo's header are shown by *Figure 52*.

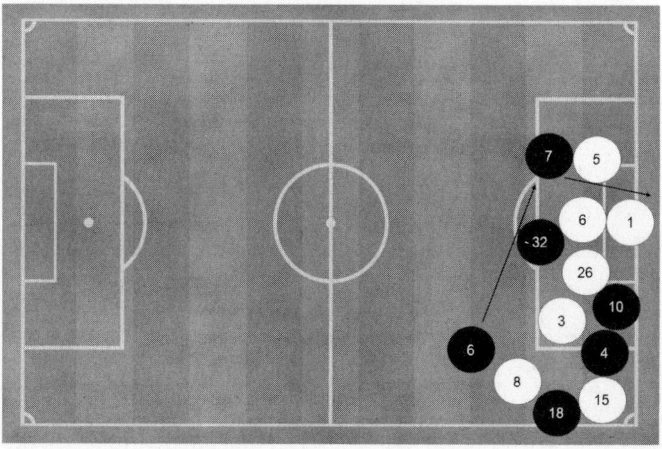

FIGURE 52

This is the last United goal in this book and, fittingly, it has some similarities to the first. Both moves were able to accelerate forwards from midfield because a short pass from Scholes tempted an opposition central midfielder into pressing forwards and sacrificing space that United could then pass the ball through. Brown crossed from the United right as Beckham had done in 1999, with Ronaldo heading in like Yorke. Ferguson clearly loved his teams scoring from crosses, although pre-match he probably envisioned Hargreaves getting an assist rather than Brown. That said, it was a very good cross from the United right-back.

By the 30-minute mark, United had enjoyed 65 per cent of possession. In the next 15 minutes, Chelsea finally began to enjoy some good time on the ball for the first time at

11v11, but United remained a threat on the counter-attack, transitioning forward at frightening speed in the 34th minute and then again in the 42nd. Ferdinand was then yellow-carded in the 43rd minute for a foul on Lampard, who had a made a run forward to try and reach a through ball.

As much as positioning Ronaldo on the left had helped United from an attacking perspective, it contributed to their concession of Chelsea's equaliser just before half-time. Van der Sar had pushed his team forward and sent a goal kick long into Chelsea's half in the hope of keeping the ball away from danger for the rest of the half. Hargreaves flicked the ball on, but it ran straight out of play for a Chelsea throw-in. Ashley Cole threw down the line to Drogba for the Ivorian to hold off Brown and lay the ball to Malouda to receive and dribble forward. After making it past Brown and moving centrally, Malouda was tackled by Ferdinand and the clearance fell to Lampard. He headed the ball onwards towards Ballack. As the ball travelled to the German midfielder, Essien burst over the halfway line, with Ronaldo unaware of his whereabouts. The ball ran away from Ballack, but Essien was central and able to assume possession. He shot powerfully from long range as Malouda made a diagonal run infield and into the box, tracked by Ferdinand. Essien's shot hit Ferdinand's back and fell into the path of Lampard, in space because neither Carrick nor Scholes had tracked his run. Van der Sar slipped as he rushed out to meet the ball, allowing Lampard to half-volley the ball over the Dutchman and into the goal.

Had Essien been tracked, he would not have received the ball in such space. Ronaldo had been absolved of defensive responsibility against Roma and Barcelona, but starting him in midfield in the final inevitably ran the risk of him not tracking his full-back properly.

United had been superior for 44 minutes, but it only took one chance for Chelsea to get back on level terms. Carvalho was yellow-carded for an aggressive tackle on Ronaldo before the referee brought a breathless first half to a close.

Half-time – Manchester United 1 Chelsea 1

The second half started scrappily, just like the first had done, with both teams playing early passes and challenging strongly for second balls. In the 52nd minute, United began to go short from goal kicks again and Chelsea continued to let them. However, Chelsea were now pressing with much more intensity in the midfield area, boosted by their equaliser and keen to dominate second halves like they so often did. The first threatening attacking situation of the half was a Chelsea one in the 57th minute, with Vidić clearing a dangerous cross from Ashley Cole. Tevez was losing his battle with Makélélé to the point that Chelsea practically had a three v two overload in midfield. Like he had done in the lead-up to Lampard's goal, Essien tucked inside next to Makélélé when Chelsea progressed the ball through midfield, giving them a four v two overload at times. United were forced to play long to Ronaldo to try and pin Essien back and get themselves into Chelsea's half of the pitch. Chelsea remained the better side, though, winning several corners that their powerful players could attack with menace.

Ferdinand went down with cramp in the 68th minute after slipping on his landing from a header. Silvestre was told to get ready but the England international recovered. Shortly afterwards, Lampard slipped over while making a recovery run. Remember also that van der Sar slipped when attempting to stop Lampard from equalising – the pitch was deteriorating under pressure from the torrential rain and it was difficult for players to maintain their grip on the surface.

Tevez was penalised for dragging Makélélé to the ground, but escaped caution. Having seen enough of Chelsea's second-half dominance, Ferguson changed shape to 1-4-1-4-1 in the 75th minute. Rooney moved to the right and Hargeaves went into central midfield alongside Scholes and in front of Carrick. This shape is shown by *Figure 53*.

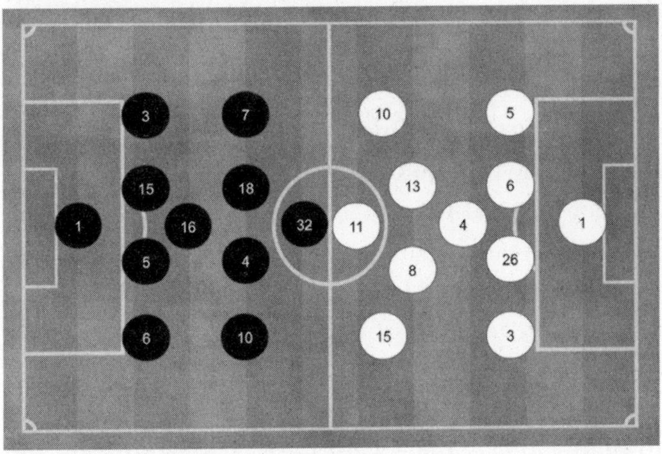

FIGURE 53

Terry was the next player to slip over as he played a long ball forward. Drogba threatened when he hit the post with a shot from long range in the 78th minute before Ferdinand slipped over again in the 80th. Neither side had made a substitution in the first 80 minutes, clearly wary that the game could go all the way to extra time and penalties. The last ten minutes of regulation time were messy, with the pitch proving problematic and nobody wanting to make an error that could cost their team glory. United made the first substitution of the night in the 87th minute, with Giggs coming on in place of Scholes, who was having breathing difficulties after his earlier collision with Makélélé. By coming on to the field, Giggs broke Sir Bobby Charlton's all-time Manchester United appearance record.

Full time – Manchester United 1 Chelsea 1

A scoreline of 1-1 was fair – United were the better team in the first half and Chelsea were in the second. The game had gone as many had expected it to, with United starting fast and Chelsea then growing into the game as time passed. The frustration for the Red Devils was that they had created several good crossing situations in the first half and only scored from one, before allowing to Chelsea to capitalise on their first significant attacking moment.

United began extra time promisingly and settled back into their rhythm quicker than the Blues. Chelsea, who had not required tactical changes so far because of their positive second-half display, made their first substitution two minutes into extra time by swapping Florent Malouda for Salomon Kalou. Grant had tried to make this change just before the end of regulation time, but Kalou had not got ready quick enough. Kalou was involved immediately, dribbling down the Chelsea left against Brown and winning a throw-in deep in United's half. From the throw-in, Ashley Cole played a one-two with Kalou and dribbled into the United penalty area. He passed to Ballack, who set-up Lampard with a deft reverse ball as both Ferdinand and Vidić rushed towards him in anticipation of a shot. Lampard crashed a shot against the crossbar, with van der Sar rooted to his line. Chelsea had missed an enormous chance to take the lead.

Joe Cole then went down with a calf problem and United kicked the ball out of play so that he could receive treatment. Instead of then giving possession back to United when play resumed, Chelsea threw the ball on to the pitch before kicking it back out themselves, forcing United to take a throw-in from deep in their own half. Ferguson, Quieroz and Phelan all voiced their disgust at this behaviour.

As Kalou continued to look dangerous, Grant decided to introduce fresh legs on the other wing as well. Anelka came on for Joe Cole in the 99th minute, with Cole failing to fully recover from his calf complaint. Both United full-backs were now faced with fresh wingers blessed with pace. It was United who had the next big chance, though, with Terry clearing a Giggs shot from his own goal line. Ferguson substituted Rooney in the 101st minute, bringing on Nani so that United had some fresh legs in wide areas themselves.

Half-time of extra time – Manchester United 1 Chelsea 1

The pace of the match reduced significantly as the players' tiredness caused several poor decisions to be made, both on and off the ball. Vidić was booked for a mistimed tackle on Anelka before Terry, Ashley Cole, Carvalho, Ballack and Ferdinand all had issues with cramp at the same time, prompting Čech to kick the ball out of play so that treatment could be given. They expected United to give possession back to them, but Tevez simply kicked the ball back out of play like Chelsea had done earlier. Several Chelsea players rushed over to confront him, despite the fact they had of course done the exact same thing themselves. More players came over to get involved and Drogba inexplicably slapped Vidić across the face right in front of the referee. He was sent off, leaving Chelsea with ten men to see out the match. Tevez was booked for his role in the trouble.

Grant reorganised in the aftermath of the red card, changing to 1-4-3-2, as shown by *Figure 54*. They soaked up pressure as United, unsurprisingly, began to look like the stronger of the two sides. In the 118th minute and with full time approaching, Essien decided that he had finally had enough of defending against Ronaldo and fouled him, consequently receiving a booking.

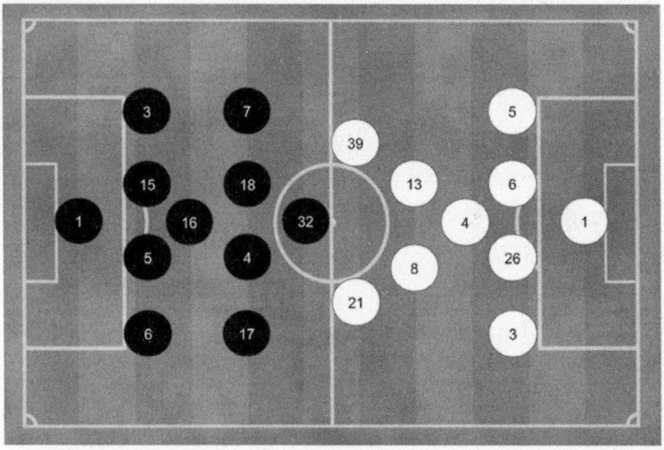

FIGURE 54

Nani and Ashley Cole both received treatment after clashing with each other while competing for a cross. This stoppage calmed things down and led to further additional time being played. Both sides had avoided rushing into their third substitution in case they needed to bring on a reliable penalty-taker, and they used this time to do just that. Belletti replaced Makélélé for Chelsea and Brown then made way for Anderson.

Full time of extra time – Manchester United 1 Chelsea 1

A season that had started with a penalty shoot-out between United and Chelsea would now end with the same contest. United won that first shoot-out 3-0, with van der Sar saving all three of Chelsea's penalties (taken by Claudio Pizarro, Lampard and Shaun Wright-Phillips). Two of the three saves were made with dives to his preferred right-hand side. All three Chelsea kicks had been struck at mid-height, rather than high or low. Ferdinand, Carrick and Rooney had scored for United.

United won the toss and elected to go first. Tevez stepped up and placed the ball to his right, then Ballack took Chelsea's first kick and scored a penalty against United for the second time that season (he had scored both Chelsea goals in the league match in April). Van der Sar had dived the correct way – to his left – but could not get a hand on the strike. Carrick tucked his penalty home before Belletti, subbed on for this single kick, scored to make it 2-2.

Chelsea had done their homework on Ronaldo – the Red Devils' primary penalty-taker. They knew that he sometimes paused in the middle of his run-up and that it was vital for the goalkeeper to remain still if he did so, because Ronaldo would see the keeper's slight movement and place his shot the other way. He paused as expected, but Čech stood still and unnerved the Portuguese before diving the right way to make the save. Lampard then blasted home to put his side in front. Next up was Hargreaves, whose excellent penalty found the top corner. Van der Sar dived the correct way (left) for Ashley Cole's effort, but he could only help the ball into the bottom corner. It was match point Chelsea and Nani had to score, but he stayed calm under pressure and did so to make it 4-4.

The responsibility of Chelsea's fifth penalty was given to the captain, John Terry. The Blues had been forced into changing their order of takers by Drogba's red card and Grant had initially pencilled in Kalou to take their fifth effort, but Terry had volunteered to take it himself. Terry slipped over as he struck the ball and could only watch as his shot rebounded away off the post. A night of slips had just produced its costliest one yet.

Anderson and Kalou scored the opening two penalties of sudden death to make it 5-5. It was interesting that Anderson had been brought on for United's sixth penalty in case of sudden death, rather than being used as one of the initial five takers. Giggs then tucked his penalty away to make it 6-5. Anelka stepped up for Chelsea's seventh effort. He took a short run-up before striking mid-height to van der Sar's left. The Dutch keeper saved the penalty to secure his club's third European Cup/Champions League title.

Manchester United win 6-5 on penalties

Credit must go to Ferguson for his incredible longevity, as winning two Champions Leagues with the same club nine years apart is a commendable achievement. As much as he would have liked one or two more European titles, the two best sides that he created at United had now both won the top crown once each. Claiming victory 50 years after the Munich disaster and 40 years after the club's first European Cup made the triumph even more special.

It is interesting to note the tactical differences between the 1999 win and this one. Ferguson stayed loyal to the idea of a back four that could defend deep if necessary, and he loved for his teams to counter-attack with pace, power and flair. But whereas he was enamoured with a flat 1-4-4-2 in Part 1 that just occasionally saw Dwight Yorke drop behind Andy Cole, he was now open to changing the shape of his midfield based on the opposition. Against Roma, he played one deep-lying central midfielder behind a pair, matching Roma's combination of two behind one more advanced central midfielder. Barcelona and Chelsea played with a single defensive midfielder behind a pair, so Ferguson played with a pair behind one attacking midfielder – at least in some phases of play. His class of 2007/08 were also more fluid and capable of rotating with each other, which is a testament to both the versatility of the players and the evolution of Ferguson's ideas, aided by his coaching staff.

As a reward for winning the double, Ferguson was named LMA Manager of the Year, Premier League Manager of the Season, Coach of UEFA Team of the Year, Onze d'Or Coach of the Year, European Coach of the Year and IFFHS World's Best Club Coach.

Ronaldo received acclaim for his remarkable season, winning both the Ballon d'Or and the FIFA World Player of the Year titles. Vidić finished tied for 21st in the Ballon d'Or shortlist, with van der Sar tied for 24th. Aside from Ronaldo, no other United player made the final FIFA World Player of the Year shortlist.

Part 4

Chelsea 2011/12

The Premier League came extremely close to further European success in the 2008/09 season, with three English clubs reaching the semi-final stage for the second successive term. United beat Arsenal and Chelsea lost to Barcelona in controversial circumstances before Barcelona defeated Ferguson's side 2-0 in the final thanks to goals from Samuel Eto'o and Lionel Messi. After the league failed to supply a semi-finalist in 2009/10, United reached the final again in 2011. Like in 2009, they were beaten by a Messi-inspired Barcelona, managed by Josep Guardiola, who had replaced Rijkaard as manager in the summer of 2008.

After suffering semi-final heartbreak in 2003/04, 2004/05, 2006/07 and 2008/09, in addition to losing the 2008 final, some Chelsea fans began to wonder if their side would ever win the Champions League. In the summer of 2011, owner Abramovich hired 34-year-old André Villas-Boas, who had previously worked for the club in a scouting capacity under Mourinho and was fresh off the back of a treble with Porto. In preparation for the 2011/12 season, the club signed Thibaut Courtois (loaned out to Atlético

Madrid), Oriol Romeu, Romelu Lukaku, Juan Mata, Ulises Dávila (loaned to Vitesse Arnhem) and Raul Meireles. Popular squad members Nicolas Anelka and Alex were transfer-listed and eventually sold in January 2012.

Villas-Boas endured a difficult start to life as Chelsea boss, tasked with phasing out ageing players and implementing a more attacking playing style. Initial attempts at playing a high defensive line earned derision from sections of the media as captain John Terry struggled to adapt. Midfield hero Lampard, by now aged 33, was also playing less because Villas-Boas wanted a more dynamic midfield. In the Champions League, the Blues topped their group ahead of Bayer Leverkusen, Valencia and Genk. By the time of the round of 16 in February 2012, they were winless in four games and out of the Premier League title race. Pressure was mounting on Villas-Boas, both internally and externally, with rumours of squad discontent being pounced upon by the press.

Alex Ferguson celebrates the 1999 triumph with his players.

Rafael Benítez in conversation with his assistant Pako Ayestarán ahead of a Champions League match.

Steven Gerrard celebrates Liverpool's 2005 victory over AC Milan. His role in the Reds' comeback remains iconic.

Sir Alex Ferguson celebrates with Carlos Queiroz and Michael Phelan, May 2008.

Ferguson enjoys a laugh with René Meulensteen, who played a key role in the development of Cristiano Ronaldo.

André Villas-Boas in deep discussion with his assistant, Roberto di Matteo.

Di Matteo celebrates Chelsea's semi-final victory over Barcelona with assistant Steve Holland, April 2012.

Petr Čech saves Arjen Robben's extra-time penalty, May 2012.

Chelsea are 2011/12 UEFA Champions League Final winners, having defeated Bayern Munich.

Jürgen Klopp celebrates with members of his backroom staff, May 2019.

Chapter 10

Round of 16 – Chelsea 5 Napoli 4 (aggregate)

First leg: Napoli 3 Chelsea 1, 21 February 2012

Just like in the previous sections, analysing Chelsea's journey to European glory begins with a tie against Italian opposition. Chelsea had been drawn against Napoli, who were in the Champions League for the first time in their history and had finished second in a strong group behind Bayern Munich and ahead of Manchester City and Villarreal. The Neapolitans drew away to City before beating the Premier League billionaires 2-1 in Italy. While surprising, this was not too spectacular because City were still finding their feet in Europe – Chelsea were definitely superior to Napoli on paper and had enough to win the tie, but they were on a bad run of form and travelled to Naples low on confidence ahead of the first leg.

The team selections are shown by *Figure 55*:

Chelsea (1-4-2-3-1): 1. Čech; 2. Ivanović, 24. Cahill, 4. Luiz, 17. Bosingwa; 7. Ramires, 16. Meireles; 23. Sturridge, 10. Mata, 15. Malouda; 11. Drogba (captain).

Substitutes: 22. Turnbull, 3. Cole, 5. Essien, 8. Lampard, 9. Torres, 12. Mikel, 21. Kalou.

Head coach: André Villas-Boas.

Napoli (1-3-4-2-1): 1. De Sanctis; 14. Campagnaro, 28. Cannavaro (captain), 6. Aronica; 11. Maggio, 88. Inler, 23. Gargano, 18. Zúñiga; 17. Hamšík, 22. Lavezzi; 7. Cavani.

Substitutes: 83. Rosati, 2. Crava, 8. Dossena, 20. Džemaili, 21. Fernández, 29. Pandev, 85. Britos.

Head coach: Walter Mazzarri – suspended.

Assistant Manager: Nicolò Frustalupi.

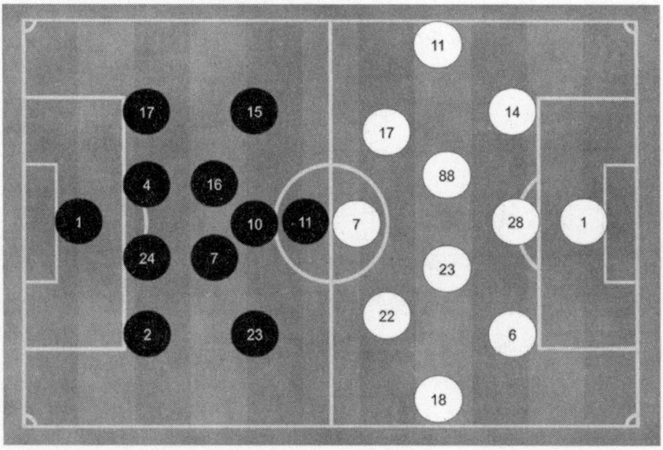

FIGURE 55

Terry was ruled out due to injury just a few hours before kick-off, so Gary Cahill – signed the previous January from Bolton Wanderers – partnered David Luiz at centre-back. Branislav Ivanović was a strong defender capable of playing at right-back or in the middle of the defence. At left-back, the right-footed José Bosingwa was preferred over Ashley Cole, who was returning from a spell on the physio's bench. The midfield that started the 2008 final was nowhere to be seen here – Claude Makélélé and Michael Ballack had departed while Frank Lampard was only a substitute. In their place, Raul Meireles and Ramires started together with Malouda lining up alongside Daniel Sturridge and

Juan Mata in an attacking line of three behind stand-in captain Drogba.

There was a fiery atmosphere inside Napoli's Stadio San Paolo, though the pitch was wet and bobbly after two days of rain. Napoli kicked off and played long down their right. Bosingwa headed the ball out of play and the home side achieved a throw-in in Chelsea's half – clearly looking for a positive start. The visitors began well, though, and looked assured. They played direct to Drogba and had runners bursting beyond him in anticipation of second balls, particularly Mata and Sturridge. Both teams challenged for the ball aggressively, not wanting to concede any ground in the opening stages and give their opponents an upper hand mentally. This prompted the referee to award several early fouls in the hope of calming things down. The players had a breather in the fifth minute when Drogba and Hugo Campagnaro clashed heads in an aerial duel, causing both to require treatment.

Napoli were without manager Walter Mazzarri, who had been suspended by UEFA after pushing an opposition striker in a group match in December. In his place, his assistant Nicolò Frustalupi led the side from the touchline and paced up and down his technical area, shouting regular instructions at his players. *Gli Azzurri* sat deep when defending to, firstly, protect their slow back three and, secondly, to try and lure Chelsea into pushing forward and leaving space available for counter-attacks.

Morgan De Sanctis was an erratic goalkeeper, talented but capable of committing sloppy mistakes. Campagnaro, Paolo Cannavaro and Salvatore Aronica were all physically strong, but they were error-prone and lacked pace. They did not act like Italian back threes of the past – whereas Inter in Part 1 used two man-markers, Napoli used three aggressive defenders that shared the responsibility of dealing with opposition strikers. Wing-backs Maggio and Zúñiga were defensively competent and able to push forward in support of attacks. Gökhan Inler and Walter Gargano played functional roles, looking to win the ball and release it wide to the wing-backs or forward to Marek Hamšík, Ezequiel Lavezzi and Edinson Cavani. Initially, Hamšík and Lavezzi looked to receive the ball in front of the Chelsea back four and play through passes for Cavani to run on to. The Uruguayan striker started livelily and forced Čech into an early save.

Chelsea had to make a substitution in the 12th minute when Bosingwa injured his hamstring as he stretched for a pass, so he was replaced by Cole. The Blues did not press as high as they had done in other periods of the season, allowing the Napoli back three to have possession, with Mata and Drogba trying to prevent passes being played into Inler and Gargano. Sturridge and Malouda tracked their wing-backs so that Ivanović and Cole were able to stay back instead of pressing high and sacrificing space behind them. The Chelsea wingers were struggling to effectively defend against Zúñiga and Maggio, though, with Maggio particularly able to perform some early crosses from dangerous positions.

Villas-Boas's side were calm in possession, aided by Napoli's deep defensive starting position. Cahill and Luiz formed a safe box with Ramires and Meireles, with only Cavani pressing in Chelsea's half. As the ball eventually progressed down one side of the pitch, the Blues' ball-side full-back would overlap while the far-side one stayed deep with the centre-backs. Gargano marked Mata when Chelsea looked to play from defence into midfield, which limited Chelsea's ability to play through the lines. Sturridge, Drogba and Malouda pushed high on to the Napoli back three in readiness for balls over the top.

Napoli's defence looked shaky and they gifted Chelsea the opening goal of the tie in the 27th minute. Čech sent a goal kick long and central towards Drogba, who beat Cannavaro in the air as Mata and Sturridge ran beyond him. Aronica won the second ball and passed to Gargano. Ramires pressed Gargano from behind and tackled him, and the loose ball ran to Malouda. He passed forward first-time to Drogba and the Ivorian relayed the ball on to Sturridge on the Chelsea right. Seeking to maintain the fast pace of the attack, Sturridge tried to pass first-time back inside to Ramires, who had made a run forward after tackling Gargano. However, the pass was behind Ramires and ran through to Cannavaro. The Napoli captain tried to clear with his left foot, but completely miskicked his clearance, which lobbed over his head and into the path of Mata, who volleyed past De Sanctis from ten yards. It was terrible play by Cannavaro, but Mata took the chance very well. The Londoners had secured their dream start.

Chelsea continued to look good and almost doubled their lead in the 36th minute when David Luiz headed over an open goal after De Sanctis had come rushing out on a corner and missed the ball. Napoli wanted to equalise as soon as possible and played out from the back quickly, while using the multi-ball system to take fast throw-ins. The leveller came in the 38th minute, facilitated by terrible Chelsea defending. Cannavaro had the ball deep for Napoli, and instead of stopping the pass into midfield, Mata ran leftward to stop the pass across to Campagnaro. This allowed Cannavaro to play forward to Inler, who turned and played a diagonal pass over Cole to Maggio, who was free of Malouda. Maggio flicked the ball back to Hamšík. Meireles moved across to defend against Hamšík and attempted to clear the ball away, but he inadvertently booted the ball straight up into the air. Cahill jumped highest and headed the ball forward to Inler, who was free to control the ball and pass left to Cavani, who had dropped in front of the Chelsea back line. Ramires and Meireles failed to close the passing lane between Cavani and Lavezzi, allowing the former to pass inside to the latter. Lavezzi faked to go on his left foot and tricked Meireles, creating space to shoot with his right from just outside the area. The ball flew past Čech for 1-1.

Both teams had contributed to their own respective downfalls, committing individual errors that allowed goalscoring opportunities. This goal exposed Chelsea's lack of a natural ball-winning midfielder. Villas-Boas had selected Ramires and Meireles – both technically gifted – in the hope of dominating possession and getting the ball forward early. However, the pair were defensively vulnerable and failed to defend Zone 14 in the build-up to this goal.

Chelsea resettled after conceding and began passing the ball around again, showing the benefits of a Ramires-Meireles midfield partnership. The positivity did not last long, though, as Napoli took the lead in stoppage time at the end of the first half. Campagnaro dribbled forward down the Napoli right, easily bypassing Malouda. He then passed to Hamšík, who recycled possession back to Inler – free in space to cross because Meireles was slow to move out and press him. He crossed round the back of Chelsea's back four towards the far post, where Cavani got in front of Ivanović to score from close range. Meireles, who also picked up a booking just before half-time, was poor defensively for both goals. Ivanović was disappointing here too, allowing Cavani to beat him to the ball and score. After a solid opening, Chelsea were suddenly a goal behind at the break and they looked shell-shocked.

Half-time – Napoli 2 Chelsea 1

Chelsea found their feet again at the beginning of the second half, winning an early corner and having a couple of shots from outside the area. However, they began to look wide open on transition and Lavezzi should have made it 3-1 when he was allowed to shoot from the edge of the box under minimal pressure. Cahill was then booked in the 56th minute for a poor challenge on Lavezzi, before missing a chance to equalise from a corner, just like Luiz in the first half. Despite fielding three centre-backs, Napoli were clearly vulnerable to set pieces.

Lavezzi scored Napoli's third goal in the 65th minute and again the hosts were helped by some questionable Chelsea defending. De Sanctis distributed the ball short to Campagnaro and Mata moved across to press, but he did not arrive in time to prevent Campagnaro playing long between Luiz and Cole for Cavani to chase. Cavani's energy was a nightmare for Chelsea all game – he was capable of rotating with Lavezzi and receiving in deeper positions as well as making quick bursts into space behind the Chelsea back line. In this instance, he latched on to the ball on the edge of the Chelsea penalty box and Čech decided to rush out towards him. Cavani squared to Lavezzi – whose run had not been tracked by a Chelsea player – and the Argentine scored into the empty goal. The match was 65 minutes old and Chelsea had still not got to grips with dealing with Hamšík, Lavezzi and Cavani. The central midfielders were not effectively tracking runners or closing down space. The back four were struggling, both when the ball was in front of them and when it was in space behind them. Defensively, the core of Chelsea's side looked far too weak.

Villas-Boas reacted by making a double substitution in the 70th minute, with Lampard and Essien replacing Malouda and Meireles. Chelsea changed to 1-4-3-1-2, as shown by

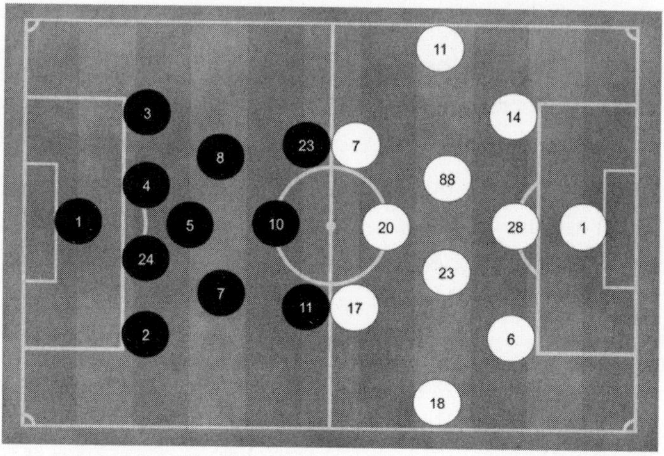

FIGURE 56

Figure 56. Essien came on to protect the central space in front of the back four, finally giving Chelsea someone capable of doing so. Ramires and Lampard looked to get on the ball in midfield, with the full-backs overlapping outside them. Meanwhile, Sturridge and Drogba looked to make early runs into space between Napoli's side centre-backs and the wing-backs, with Mata central trying to receive behind Inler and Gargano. Frustalupi was happy to shut up shop and settle for a 3-1 advantage going into the return leg, so in the 74th minute he replaced Lavezzi with the more industrious Blerim Džemaili. *Gli Azzurri* changed to a 1-3-4-1-2 formation, with Džemaili behind a front pair of Cavani and Hamšík.

The hosts sat very deep for the final 15 minutes, retaining a vertically compact shape with the whole side defending in their own half. This allowed Luiz to dribble forward with the ball and carry it into midfield, however it was difficult for the Blues to break through the wall of Napoli players stood in front of them. The home side were still a threat on the counter-attack and Cole cleared a Maggio shot off the line in the 81st minute, effectively keeping Chelsea in the tie. A minute later, striker Goran Pandev replaced Hamšík for Napoli.

Chelsea dominated possession in the latter stages but continued to find clear-cut chances hard to come by. Lampard had a shot from long range in stoppage time, which De Sanctis saved and celebrated his doing so. The final whistle that the home fans craved finally came soon after, and Chelsea's European hopes were hanging by a thread.

Full time – Napoli 3 Chelsea 1

Chelsea were easily capable of bettering Napoli in open play, but they simply made too many defensive errors and were punished for them. While the decision to go with an attack-minded central midfield pairing had its benefits, the consequences had proven severe. Napoli were vulnerable to direct attacks and set pieces, so Chelsea would undoubtedly get chances in the second leg. They needed to avoid the concession of silly goals in the process, though, otherwise an embarrassing round-of-16 exit was in store.

Second leg: Chelsea 4 Napoli 1, 14 March 2012

Chelsea responded to their defeat in Naples with a 3-0 victory against Bolton Wanderers, but a defeat away at West Bromwich Albion on 1 March spelled the end of Villas-Boas's brief time at the helm – he was sacked and replaced by Roberto Di Matteo, who had been his assistant manager and was given a short-term deal until the end of the season. Di Matteo was a club legend, having won the FA Cup, League Cup, the UEFA Cup Winners' Cup and the UEFA Cup with the Blues as a player. He began his managerial reign with victories against Birmingham City and Stoke City. Napoli only had three matches between the two legs; beating Inter Milan, Palma and Cagliari to continue their rich vein of form.

The starting line-ups for the second leg are shown in *Figure 57*:

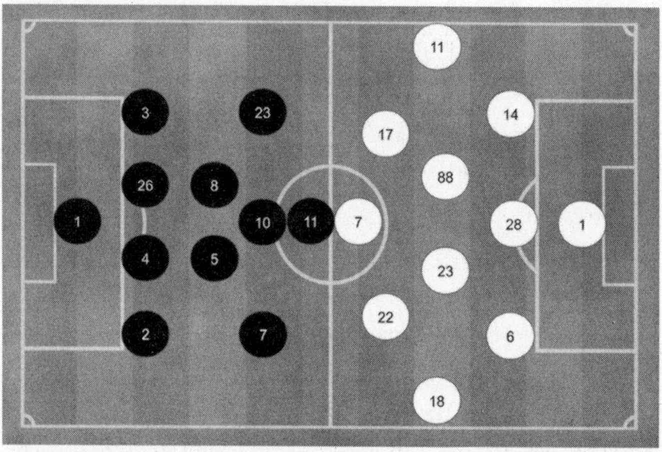

FIGURE 57

Chelsea (1-4-2-3-1): 1. Čech; 2. Ivanović, 4. Luiz, 26. Terry (captain), 3. Cole; 8. Lampard, 5. Essien; 7. Ramires, 10. Mata, 23. Sturridge; 11. Drogba.

Substitutes: 22. Turnbull, 9. Torres, 12. Mikel, 15. Malouda, 17. Bosingwa, 21. Kalou, 24. Cahill.

Head coach: Roberto Di Matteo.

Napoli (1-3-4-2-1): 1. De Sanctis; 14. Campagnaro, 28. Cannavaro (captain), 6. Aronica; 11. Maggio, 88. Inler, 23. Gargano, 18. Zúñiga; 17. Hamšík, 22. Lavezzi; 7. Cavani.

Substitutes: 83. Rosati, 8. Dossena, 16. Vargas, 20. Džemaili, 21. Fernández, 29. Pandev, 85. Britos.

Head coach: Walter Mazzarri.

Di Matteo made several changes to the team that started in Naples but retained the 1-4-2-3-1 formation. Terry was fit to start and assumed his role as captain alongside Luiz in the centre of defence. Cole started instead of Bosingwa, while in midfield, Lampard and Essien were reinstated instead of Ramires (who moved to the right wing) and Meireles (who was suspended). Sturridge moved to the left-hand side of Chelsea's attacking trio. Napoli were unchanged, although manager Mazzarri had his ban reduced so that he could be present for this match.

As expected, the game began with a quick tempo and it took less than five minutes for Sturridge to force a save from De Sanctis and win a corner. Ramires, Mata, Sturridge and Drogba had permission to rotate, giving them positional fluidity and making them harder for Napoli to pin down. Sturridge and Ramires regularly swapped wings, but the rotations sometimes went even further, with Drogba and Mata moving wide and Ramires and Sturridge central. Ivanović and Cole were positioned deeper in possession than they had been in the first leg, looking to receive short passes off the Chelsea centre-backs in front of Napoli's midfield. They wanted to attract Hamšík and Lavezzi forward to press them, leaving space in the middle for Chelsea's midfield to exploit.

Napoli started well themselves and Cavani struck into the side-netting at the end of a frighteningly quick counter-attack in the 13th minute. The Neapolitans were a serious threat on transition, as they had showcased in the first match. After the opening 15 minutes here, they had already had six attempts, three of which were on target.

The visitors adopted a 1-5-3-2 shape when defending in their own half, with Hamšík on the right of a midfield three behind Cavani and Lavezzi. Right wing-back Maggio tucked inside close to Campagnaro to deter Chelsea from playing through passes into the space between the pair, leaving space wide on Chelsea's left. After initially trying to press high up the field and build pressure, Chelsea responded to Napoli's good start by dropping back into a 1-4-4-2 defensive shape, leaving Mata central with Drogba.

Chelsea curtailed their attacking rotations, utilising Ramires as a permanent left-winger because Napoli were looking to use Maggio to overload Cole two v one when they attacked. This decision made sense because Ramires was more energetic and industrious than Sturridge, but it provided an added benefit by contributing to Chelsea's opening goal of the night in the 29th minute. Cole received the ball in a narrow position, deep enough that he had space to move forward with the ball unopposed. Hamšík had been caught on the Napoli left when Chelsea won possession, giving Cole even more space than usual. As Inler rushed across to try and cover, Cole passed the ball to Ramires, who was wide on the Chelsea left. As a naturally right-footed player, Ramires received the ball and immediately cut inside on to his stronger foot so that he could cross into the Napoli penalty area, and Maggio could not move out and close him down quickly enough. In the box, Drogba got in front of Aronica and brilliantly headed past De Sanctis. The crowd was alive, and Chelsea were back in the tie.

Chelsea nearly scored again four minutes later, with Campagnaro narrowly preventing Drogba from converting a low cross from the right. Napoli went straight up the other end on another rapid counter-attack, but Cavani shot wide. By 34 minutes Chelsea had enjoyed 63 per cent of possession, but the visitors were fine with this for as long as they sustained their threat on transition. Mazzarri was then forced into an early change because of an injury to Maggio. Ex-Liverpool player Andrea Dossena replaced him, with Zúñiga moving to the right and Dossena playing as the left-sided wing-back. Lampard, who had received a warning from the referee after a bad tackle on Cavani in the opening stages, was booked in the 43rd minute after making another poor challenge – this time on Zúñiga.

Chelsea had time for one final chance in the first half – this time Cannavaro blocked a Luiz shot and De Sanctis gratefully pounced on the loose ball.

Half-time – Chelsea 1 Napoli 0

Neither side made a substitution at half-time and Chelsea began the second period in control of possession. In the 47th minute, the vulnerability that Napoli showed in the first leg when defending set pieces was exploited by Chelsea to great effect. Lampard took an outswinging corner from the right-hand side and Terry – excellent in the air in both boxes – burst free of his marker, Inler, and powered a header past De Sanctis. Lampard's cross and Terry's header were both very good, but they do not excuse Inler's bad marking. Why did Napoli task a central midfielder with marking Terry when they had three centre-backs on the pitch? Chelsea now led the tie on away goals and had transferred the pressure that they began the night with on to their opponents.

Napoli responded well to this setback and it only took them eight minutes to produce a precious away goal. Terry headed away a Dossena cross from the Napoli left, but his clearance only went as far as Inler on the edge of the Chelsea box. Inler was unmarked because both Lampard and Essien had retreated into the Chelsea area, so the Napoli man controlled the ball in space and volleyed it past Čech. Chelsea's away goals lead lasted eight minutes; now they had to push forward and score again …

Striker Fernando Torres was immediately told to warm up by Di Matteo as the visitors dropped back into a deep 1-5-4-1 defensive shape. This made it difficult for Chelsea to play through them, as they displayed extreme compactness between their lines of midfield and defence. Torres replaced Sturridge in the 63rd minute and assumed the role of right-winger. Torres was goalless since early February; however, he still possessed the ability to trouble defences on his day.

The away side began to play slower and longer, content to frustrate Chelsea and wait for counter-attacking opportunities to arise. Čech had to make another important save when Cole slipped over and allowed Zúñiga to enter the Chelsea box and unleash a shot goalward. Within five minutes of the Chelsea custodian keeping his team in the tie, they were back on level terms. Lampard took another corner, this time an in-swinger from the left. Ivanović headed towards goal, only for his effort to be blocked by Dossena's hand – penalty. Again, Napoli had failed to effectively defend a set piece. A player known for scoring big goals in big moments, Lampard was never going to miss and duly blasted home to make the score 3-1 on the night and 4-4 on aggregate.

Chelsea spent the remaining minutes of regulation time in pursuit of a winning goal, whereas Napoli were happy to defend deep and take the tie to extra time, as it would give them 30 extra minutes to score one away goal. Chelsea were favourites to go through now, though – they had their tails up and it was unlikely that Napoli would go half an hour without conceding at least once more. Essien was playing well, breaking up play in central areas to blunt Neapolitan counter-attacks. This was something that the Blues had dearly missed in the first leg. Neither side made another substitution in the 90 minutes, keen to stay patient and save their replacements for when players became tired in the additional 30 minutes.

Full time – Chelsea 3 Napoli 1

Di Matteo waited to see if Napoli made any changes for extra time, which they chose not to do, before making his second substitution of the night in the 95th minute.

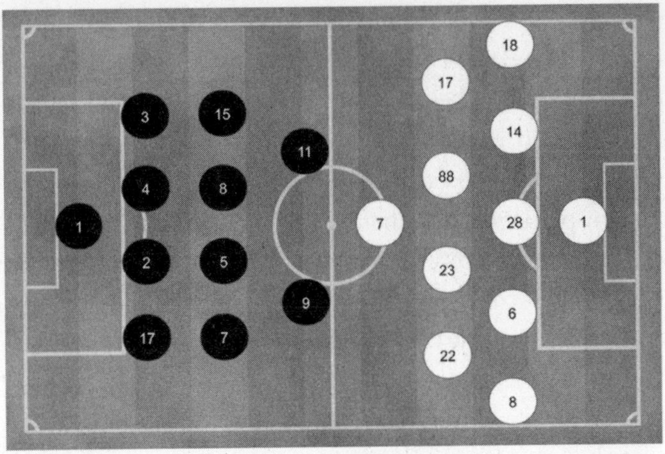

FIGURE 58

Malouda replaced Mata, who had not had the desired impact on proceedings. Chelsea changed to 1-4-4-2 with Torres up front alongside Drogba. Terry limped off injured three minutes later and Bosingwa came on in his place, with Ivanović moving to centre-back. The formations at this stage of the game are shown by *Figure 58*.

Chelsea abandoned the idea of playing through Napoli and began playing long, aerial balls over the top of the Neapolitans instead, looking to get Torres and Drogba threatening the space behind the three centre-backs. This resulted in a chance for Torres in the 100th minute when De Sanctis rushed out so vigorously that the ball bounced over him. Unfortunately for the Blues, the angle was too acute for Torres to score from. Playing early balls forward from deep also meant that Chelsea's full-backs could stay back rather than pushing forward in support of more patient possession. This limited the space that Napoli wanted to counter-attack into.

Drogba then used his wit to win a soft free kick in the 104th minute after Aronica briefly placed his arms around the Ivorian's chest. Taken from Chelsea's right, the initial delivery was cleared by Napoli, as was Ramires's attempted cross on the second phase. The ball came back out to Ramires and he dribbled down the right before passing to Drogba, who turned and speculatively played a low cross towards the Napoli penalty spot. There, Ivanović was unmarked and the Serbian superbly stroked the ball into the roof of the net. Like with Terry's goal, it was Inler who had failed to man-mark properly. He was completely unaware of Ivanović's whereabouts and failed to pick him up at any point. Napoli's defending was simply not good enough for the knockout stages of the Champions League. Chelsea were now 15 minutes away from the quarter-final and looked certain to progress.

Half-time of extra time – Chelsea 4 Napoli 1

Mazzarri made a half-time change, removing Hamšík and introducing Pandev. Hamšík had been disappointing across the two legs, failing to impose himself on either. Chelsea took control of proceedings at the beginning of the second

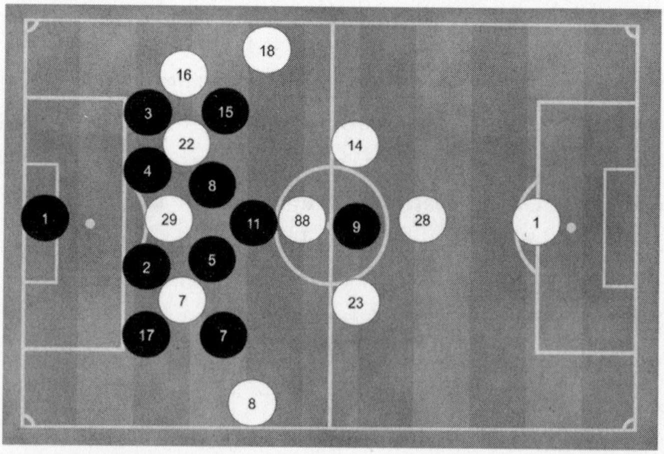

FIGURE 59

half, sitting back in a 1-4-4-1-1 shape and placing the onus on Napoli to find new attacking solutions. *Gli Azzurri* made their third and final substitution in the 110th minute, replacing Aronica with Chilean forward Eduardo Vargas, who was yet to score in a difficult first season at the club. This change saw Napoli gamble and change to an expansive 1-3-3-4 shape, shown by *Figure 59*. Chelsea held firm and now had an increased counter-attacking threat thanks to Napoli's lack of midfielders. This led to Inler being yellow-carded for cynically fouling Torres to prevent a quick counter. Drogba won a couple of soft free kicks, fooling the referee into believing that he had been fouled and buying valuable time and territory for his side.

Chelsea comfortably navigated their way towards full time and the only complication came when Luiz picked up an injury. With no more substitutions available, Essien and Luiz swapped over so that Luiz could simply focus on standing in front of Zone 14 and cutting out any attempted through balls into the space between or in front of Ivanović and Essien. Napoli managed to win a late free kick and piled men forward, but Chelsea cleared it with ease. Drogba moved to the right-hand side next to Ramires, giving Chelsea an overload to play the ball to on transition. There, Drogba and Ramires could safely retain possession between themselves and waste time. Napoli's 1-3-3-4 attacking shape did not have the impact that Mazzarri had hoped for – his side looked out of ideas and lacked creativity when they needed it most. The final whistle was greeted by wild celebrations from both the home fans and Di Matteo, who ran on to the pitch to hug his players.

Full time of extra time – Chelsea 4 Napoli 1; Chelsea win 5-4 on aggregate

Di Matteo had enjoyed the dream start to life as Chelsea's caretaker manager and with this victory he made himself a contender for the job on a more permanent basis. He had proven his ability to win big European matches and, although bigger tests would inevitably follow, coming from behind to beat Napoli was an enormous confidence boost for this Chelsea side. His tactics had contributed to the victory – moving Ramires to the left brought about the opening goal of the night, and the decision to start Essien provided much more balance in midfield. The Blues also managed extra time well, giving themselves a platform from which to find a winning goal by wisely limiting Napoli's counter-attacking threat. As hard a season as Chelsea were having, they had players used to reaching the latter stages of the Champions League and any team that reaches the quarter-final stage is capable of winning the competition – Liverpool had proven this in 2004/05 when they went all the way despite a tough domestic campaign.

Chapter 11

Semi-final – Chelsea 3 Barcelona 2 (aggregate)

First leg: Chelsea 1 Barcelona 0, 18 April 2012

The Blues were the only Premier League side to make it to the quarter-final of a European competition in the 2011/12 season and were drawn against Benfica of Portugal in the last eight. They won 1-0 away in the first leg by virtue of a Kalou goal in the 75th minute before winning 2-1 at Stamford Bridge thanks to another Lampard penalty and a long-range strike from Meireles. Their good form under Di Matteo continued domestically with just one defeat, away at Manchester City, by the time of the semi-final first leg against Barcelona.

Chelsea and Barcelona had history, having met in the knockout stages of the Champions League in 1999/00, 2004/05, 2005/06 and 2008/09. The Londoners were victorious in 2004/05, with the Catalans going through on the other three occasions. The 2008/09 semi-final had been extremely controversial – Barcelona scored a stoppage-time equaliser in the second leg at Stamford Bridge that took them through on away goals on a night when Chelsea believed that they should have been awarded at least two penalties. As has been previously mentioned, the Catalans went on to beat

United in the final before then beating Sir Alex Ferguson's side again in the final two years later.

Regarded by many as one of the greatest sides in the history of club football, if not the greatest, in 2011/12 Barcelona topped a group consisting of AC Milan, Viktoria Plzeň and BATE Borisov before dispatching of Bayer Leverkusen in the round of 16. They then met AC Milan again in the quarter-final and beat them 3-1 on aggregate. After failing to light up the semi-final against United in 2008, Messi had developed into a true superstar and won the Ballon d'Or three years running. Locked in an incredible La Liga title race with the José Mourinho-managed Real Madrid, Barça were the team to beat and defeating them would be an enormous achievement for anybody, let alone a Chelsea team stuck outside the Premier League's top four.

Figure 60 shows the starting line-ups for the first leg at Stamford Bridge.

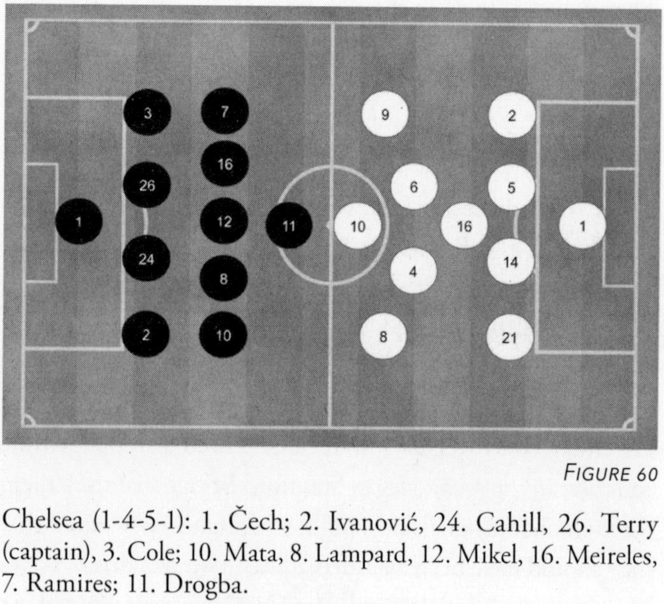

FIGURE 60

Chelsea (1-4-5-1): 1. Čech; 2. Ivanović, 24. Cahill, 26. Terry (captain), 3. Cole; 10. Mata, 8. Lampard, 12. Mikel, 16. Meireles, 7. Ramires; 11. Drogba.

Substitutes: 22. Turnbull, 5. Essien, 9. Torres, 15. Malouda, 17. Bosingwa, 21. Kalou, 23. Sturridge.

Head coach: Roberto Di Matteo.

Barcelona (1-4-3-3): 1. Valdés; 2. Alves, 5. Puyol (captain), 14. Mascherano, 21. Adriano; 16. Busquets, 6. Xavi, 4. Fàbregas; 9. Sánchez, 8. Iniesta, 10. Messi.

Substitutes: 13. Pinto, 3. Piqué, 11. Thiago, 15. Keita, 17. Pedro, 32. Barta, 39. Cuenca.

Head coach: Josep Guardiola.

Barcelona were inevitably going to dominate possession, so Di Matteo chose an extremely compact side containing three holding midfielders. Luiz was injured, meaning Cahill started at the back alongside Terry. Mata began on the right of midfield with Ramires on the left. The visitors lined up in a fluid 1-4-3-3 shape, with former Arsenal captain Cesc Fàbregas in midfield alongside the exceptional Xavi. Iniesta was on the left, with Alexis Sánchez on the right and Messi through the middle. In defence, ex-Liverpool star Javier Mascherano, naturally a defensive midfielder, started next to Puyol instead of Piqué, who had signed from Manchester United in 2008. Guardiola had often deployed Mascherano in defence due to his ability to assist playing out from the back – something that Puyol and Milito struggled with at times at Old Trafford in Part 3. Striker David Villa was unavailable after breaking his tibia earlier in the season.

As expected, Barça enjoyed the lion's share of possession right from the off. While their system was laced with fluidity, *Figure* 61 illustrates their standard positioning when in possession. Right-back Dani Alves, known for being offensively excellent, pushed higher and wider than left-back Adriano, who looked to receive deeper and entice Mata forward from his right-midfield slot. Iniesta and Sánchez provided the width, allowing Fàbregas and Messi – who dropped off the Chelsea back line rather than acting like a traditional striker – to explore the central and half-spaces. The half-spaces are the areas inside the long black lines – Lanes 2 and 4. From the perspective of Barcelona, Lane 1 is the wide right space, Lane 3 is the central space and Lane 5 is the wide left space. As we know from previous matches, the black box on the edge of the Chelsea area represents Zone 14.

The idea of 'half-spaces' became popularised in the late 2000s and early 2010s because elite teams were defending Zone 14 more effectively. Using the width of the pitch in possession is an age-old theory, but instead of teams using width to create space in the centre, the 'half-space' theory uses width to create space *between* the wide and central areas, via horizontal passes that shift the opposition from side to side until a gap is created in their defensive shape. As *Figure 61* shows, Barcelona had players occupying all five horizontal

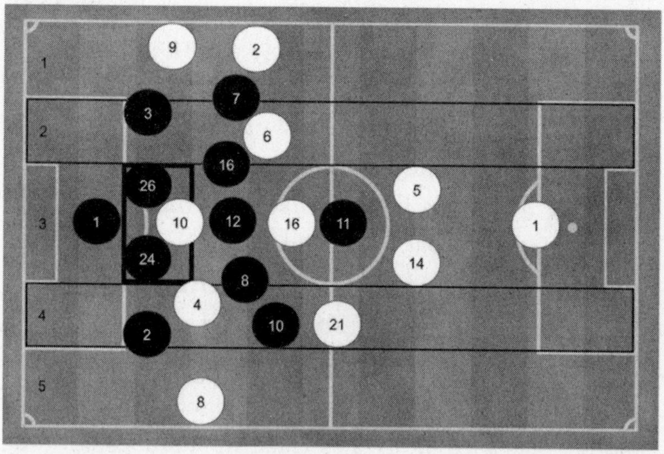

FIGURE 61

lanes, giving them the ability to move the ball quickly from side to side. Chelsea's defensive shape would move across to follow the ball, and if they accidentally left a gap between two team-mates then Barça would use that moment to play a pass through the space. As teams often defend the centre of the pitch so well, these gaps between defensive team-mates tend to appear in the half-spaces.

At the start of this match, Barça wanted to find Fàbregas in the left half-space, creating space for him by keeping Adriano deep and Iniesta wide. For example, if Adriano received the ball and Mata pressed him, he could pass wide to Iniesta, who could play the ball to Fàbregas in space left by Mata – utilising the 'third man' theory. If Fàbregas received the ball in such a situation, a central Chelsea player might move across to press him – potentially creating space for Messi in or around Zone 14.

Chelsea sat deep, retaining vertical compactness between their defence and midfield as well as horizontal compactness to avoid leaving too many gaps that would allow the Catalans to play into the half-spaces. Their key outlet was Drogba, who they looked for with quick, direct passes through the centre. In the third minute, Čech booted a long ball over the top of Barcelona for Drogba to latch on to on the edge of Barça's area, but unfortunately for the Blues his touch was too heavy and the ball ran away from the Ivorian. Barça implemented an extremely high line; their back four rushed towards the halfway line whenever a deep Chelsea player readied themselves to perform a long ball. This high line had a reasonable level of success in the first half, catching Drogba offside on several occasions. Chelsea's alternative outlet was passing into the space that Alves would leave by advancing forward in possession.

Di Matteo backed Ramires to perform a very demanding role, but he was the Chelsea player most suited to this task because of his exceptional energy levels. Ramires would initially tuck inside next to his central midfielders, shutting off central passes. He would then move to the wing to press

Alves if necessary and, if Chelsea won the ball back, he would sprint into the space left by Alves so that Chelsea could play direct passes for him to chase. The hope was that Ramires's energy would help him to reach the passes before Alves did. Of course, by playing early, direct passes from deep, Chelsea ensured that their defenders and midfielders did not have to venture forward to progress possession higher – they could stay deep and prevent space from being open on counter-attacks, like they did in extra time against Napoli.

Despite initially settling well into their defensive shape, Chelsea nearly fell behind in the ninth minute when they afforded Barcelona too much space in key areas. Fàbregas had temporarily dropped deep in front of Chelsea's midfield, which allowed Iniesta to move inside into the left half-space. Iniesta received the ball from Fàbregas and played a one-two with Messi, who was in front of the Blues' back four. Messi's receiving of the ball in space brought Terry forward to press, leaving space in Chelsea's back line. Sánchez made a run in from the right, into the space vacated by Terry, and Iniesta found him with a delightful, lofted pass, only for Sánchez to hit the crossbar. Once Barça spotted the initial space for the progressive pass to Iniesta, it took them three passes to beat the midfield, disorganise the defence and create a one v one situation against Čech.

There was a collision in the 12th minute when Sánchez ran into Terry, who made absolutely no effort to get out of the Chilean's way. Sánchez went to ground and tried to exaggerate the situation, but the pair were evidently unamused with each other.

Chelsea's central midfield trio settled into their shape well, maintaining horizontal compactness. This forced Messi to drop deeper and receive the ball in front of them. Messi having possession is never ideal for a defending team, but if you have both your midfield and defence lines between him and your goal then that is probably as ideal as it gets. To facilitate Messi dropping deeper, Xavi or Busquets became a false full-back on the Barcelona right, vacating space centrally and allowing Alves to remain high and wide.

The visitors had a penalty appeal rejected in the 25th minute when Iniesta received the ball and dribbled infield against Cahill. The Barça man went down in the penalty area after some slight contact from Cahill, but it would have been a very soft penalty. Pressure was building on the hosts, as Barcelona's high press limited the time that Chelsea had to perform direct passes, forcing mistakes that relinquished possession back to the Catalans. The Blues finally had a breather just before the half-hour mark as Barça temporarily sat back and allowed Chelsea's defenders to pass the ball between themselves in harmless, deep areas. Every Chelsea pass drew an olé from the home fans, who had endured a tense start to the tie. Eventually, the Londoners went long to Drogba and he was caught offside once again.

Fàbregas almost gave his side the lead in the 43rd minute. Messi tackled Mikel in the middle of the pitch and dribbled fiercely at Chelsea's back four, with Fàbregas supporting him to his left. The Argentinian threaded a lovely pass between Ivanović and Cahill for Fàbregas to receive in his stride. The ex-Arsenal man tried to dink the ball over Čech but he did not make enough contact with the ball, so Cole was able to recover and clear off the line. This was a huge let-off for the hosts, as well as being a reminder that they could not afford to dwell on the ball – they needed to play it forward early. It had been a tiring half for the Blues and the players looked like they wanted the half-time whistle.

One minute into stoppage time at the end of the first half, Messi slipped over when he tried to change direction. He stayed down, appearing to suffer from some groin pain, before recovering to his feet and playing on. Evidently uncomfortable, he received the ball a minute later and was dispossessed by Lampard in the centre of the pitch. Lampard played a chipped pass into the space behind Alves, and Ramires successfully latched on to the ball ahead of Xavi, who had been in the false full-back position. Drogba ran to his right and pulled Puyol across with him, further enlarging the space for Ramires to advance into. After entering the Barça penalty area, Ramires squared the ball to Drogba, who shot past Valdés for 1-0.

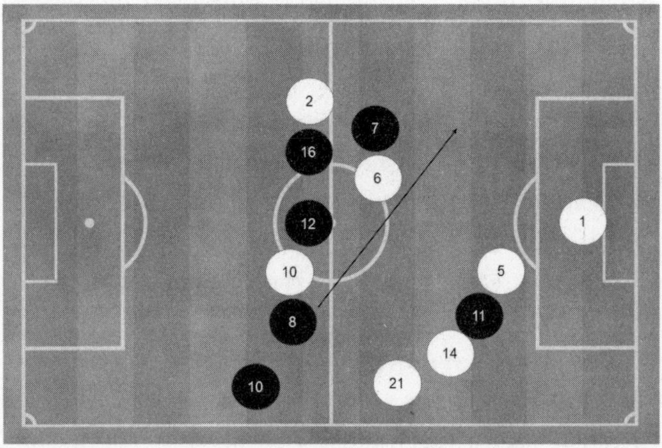

FIGURE 62

After being let off by Fàbregas's miss a few minutes earlier, Chelsea carried out their counter-attacking instructions to perfection and were rewarded with the lead. Lampard's pass for Ramires (shown by *Figure 62*) was perfectly weighted. Ramires successfully won the race to the ball and Drogba – the side's star striker of eight years – supplied the finish. Di Matteo's men had to wait until the very end of the opening half for their first key attacking moment of the semi-final, but they capitalised on it and gave themselves something to defend in the second 45 minutes.

Half-time – Chelsea 1 Barcelona 0

There were no substitutions at the interval and neither side made any significant changes to their approach. Barcelona rotated with fluidity to get Messi on the ball in a variety of areas on the pitch, but their general approach remained the same. Alves now stayed deeper when his team had the ball, though, to protect the space that Chelsea wanted to exploit on transition. This was reactive and too late from Barça – Chelsea had already scored with this tactic. Furthermore, it left Sánchez isolated wide on the right by himself, with nobody exploiting the half-space inside of him because Messi was coming deep and central instead.

The home side knew that they had to win the first leg to stand a chance of going through and protecting a 1-0 lead was safer than pursuing a second goal – they could not adopt any tactic that would leave gaps for Barcelona to exploit. A one-goal victory at Stamford Bridge would keep them in the tie, and that was what they wanted – to be in it for as long as possible.

The Catalans controlled the opening stages of the second half, dominating possession and winning some corners. Disciplined and focused, Chelsea stood firm – Čech palmed away a long-range Adriano shot in the 51st minute but was otherwise well protected.

Sánchez then spurned a chance in the 57th minute after Fàbregas lobbed the ball over Chelsea's back four and into the path of the in-moving Chilean, who could not finish under pressure from Cole. Adriano began to push forward more from left-back, allowing Iniesta to move inside and occupy the left half-space alongside Fàbregas. This heaped even more defensive responsibility on Ivanović, Mata and Lampard, who had to work extremely hard to stay compact and difficult to beat.

After an hour's play, the possession stats favoured Barcelona by 70 per cent to 30 per cent. It may seem strange to describe such a ball-dominant performance as 'conservative', but that had indeed been the approach from Guardiola's men. Obsessed with retaining possession, keeping the ball in midfield with extreme patience was their version of a conservative game plan. Whereas many teams play defensively by conceding space in front of their defensive block and letting the opponent have the ball, Barça did the opposite. They wanted to keep the ball and, upon losing it, restrict the space in which Chelsea could perform long passes. This would consequently force Chelsea errors and see the Catalans regain possession as soon as possible, continuing the cycle. They believed that the goals would come for them eventually, whether in this leg or the next, because at some point they would create and exploit some useful space – the space that Chelsea sat deep to protect at all costs. This match produced a clash between two completely different ways of playing defensively, and Chelsea's first shot on goal had given their style the all-important advantage.

Messi managed to dribble dangerously on a couple of occasions, but Cahill and Terry were defending magnificently. In the 66th minute, Barcelona replaced Sánchez with Pedro, a direct winger who had scored against United in the 2010/11 final. Ramires was then booked in the 69th minute for a foul on Messi.

With Alves deeper to limit space against Ramires, Drogba's role became even more important. His movement improved in the second half and he was caught offside less often, allowing him to get hold of the ball, protect it from the Barça defenders and buy his team valuable seconds of rest. He even managed to win some free kicks, which temporarily forced the Catalans back into their own half.

Di Matteo made his first substitution of the night in the 74th minute, taking off the exhausted Mata and bringing on Kalou, who was faster than Mata and could hope to force Adriano back with direct attacking runs. Now, Barcelona were faced with a quick Chelsea outlet on both wings, one of whom was fresh. Busquets was yellow-carded for fouling Ramires in the 76th minute, with the Brazilian's subsequent time on the ground wasting more valuable seconds. Guardiola took Fàbregas off two minutes later, replacing him with young midfielder Thiago. Thiago's role was to try and create space for Messi. If Messi was in one half-space, Thiago would occupy the other to try and stretch the Chelsea midfield. If Chelsea were vertically compact and there was limited space between their defence and midfield lines, Thiago would move in front of Chelsea's midfield so that Messi did not have to.

Guardiola did not want Messi coming as deep as he had been – even he found it difficult to dribble through the entire core of a team. The home fans willed their team on, desperate for the clean sheet that would provide hope for the second leg.

The introduction of Thiago helped Barcelona to maintain pressure on their hosts, but the Blues continued to hold out and edge their way to full time. The Catalans still circulated possession via regular short passes, hoping that their tiring opponents would eventually make a fatal mistake as they moved from side to side. Young winger Isaac Cuenca came on for Xavi after 86 minutes, meaning that Barcelona now had two wingers either side of Messi for the first time in the match, with Cuenca on the right and Pedro on the left. The Catalans now adopted a more generic 1-4-3-3, with Busquets behind Thiago and Iniesta in midfield. Barça wanted to be more direct for the last few minutes and see if they could force an away goal. After Puyol nearly scored with a glancing header from a Messi free kick, the yellow-carded Ramires was replaced by Bosingwa after putting in a fantastic shift. Bosingwa played on the right of midfield, with Kalou moving over to the left.

When Barcelona knocked Chelsea out of the Champions League in 2009, their crucial away goal came in stoppage time at the end of the second half. Chelsea, knew, therefore, that they needed to stay strong right up to the final whistle. Regardless, the Catalans still created a huge opportunity to equalise in stoppage time, but they somehow failed to score. Terry tackled Messi on the edge of the Chelsea box and the ball rolled out to Pedro, whose deflected shot hit the post. The rebound bounced back out to Busquets, ten yards from goal. The midfielder – normally so technically sound – got under the ball and skied his effort over the crossbar. Barcelona had created several big chances in this game, but they failed to take any of them. Chelsea made it to the final whistle with their 1-0 lead intact and the Stamford Bridge crowd rejoiced.

Full time – Chelsea 1 Barcelona 0

Once again, Di Matteo proved his ability to achieve positive results on the biggest stage in European club football. Luck was on his side in relation to Barcelona's missed chances, but we have seen previously in this book that failing to take goalscoring chances warrants punishment and Barça's finishing had been below its normal level. Terry, Lampard and Drogba were all immense, making a mockery of the fact that the club hierarchy had wanted them phasing out at the beginning of the season. It remained to be seen whether Chelsea had enough to progress to the final, but at least they had given themselves a chance.

Second leg: Barcelona 2 Chelsea 2, 24 April 2012

Focused on their pursuit of European glory, Chelsea made eight changes for their London derby with Arsenal and drew 0-0. On the other hand, Guardiola had gone full strength for a do-or-die clash with rivals Real Madrid and lost 2-1 at home, effectively securing Real's place at the top of the table and ending Barcelona's run of three straight league titles. Though Barça were devastated, they still had the chance to retain their European crown and the odds were in their favour ahead of the return leg. Chelsea could take hope, however, from both the manner of Barça's weekend defeat to Real and their 2009/2010 Champions League semi-final exit at the hands of Inter Milan, both of which had been against sides managed by José Mourinho. Real beat Barcelona with just 28 per cent possession and in 2010 Inter successfully defended their first leg advantage despite playing most of the second leg with ten players. The *Blaugrana* were indeed human – sometimes they did lose.

The team selections for the second leg are shown by *Figure 63*:

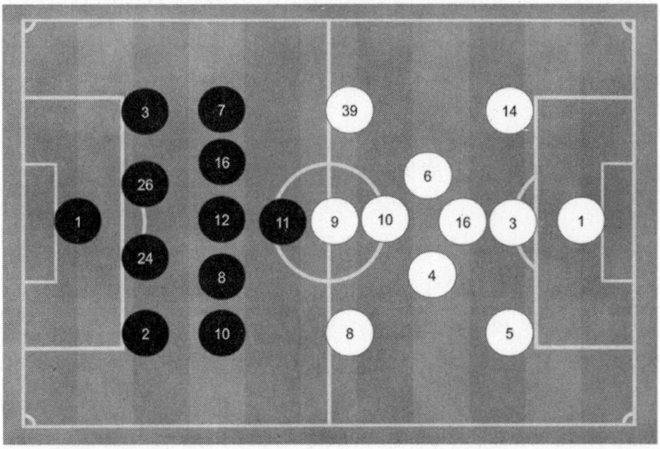

FIGURE 63

Chelsea (1-4-5-1): 1. Čech; 2. Ivanović, 24. Cahill, 26. Terry (captain), 3. Cole; 10. Mata, 8. Lampard, 12. Mikel, 16. Meireles, 7. Ramires; 11. Drogba.

Substitutes: 22. Turnbull, 5. Essien, 9. Torres, 15. Malouda, 17. Bosingwa, 21. Kalou, 23. Sturridge.

Head coach: Roberto Di Matteo.

Barcelona (1-3-3-1-3): 1. Valdés; 14. Mascherano, 3. Piqué, 5. Puyol (captain); 16. Busquets, 6. Xavi, 4. Fàbregas; 10. Messi; 39. Cuenca, 8. Iniesta, 9. Sánchez.

Substitutes: 13. Pinto, 2. Alves, 11. Thiago, 15. Keita, 17. Pedro, 21. Adriano, 37. Tello.

Head coach: Josep Guardiola.

Chelsea managed to stick to Plan A throughout the first leg, only making changes when players were tired. They went with the exact same team for the second leg, where four of the starting 11 were one yellow card away from missing the final, but it would take an almighty effort to get there first. Guardiola made changes for Barcelona, changing to 1-3-3-1-3 – a shape that he usually reserved for teams that would sit back and defend deep, but elected not to use at Stamford Bridge in the name of conservatism. It is an extremely attacking formation that requires near total domination of the ball, which the Catalans wanted to achieve, of course.

The players were greeted by an imposing Camp Nou atmosphere, like United had experienced in Part 3. The Blues were the first team to reach their opponent's penalty area, bursting down the left via Cole and Ramires in the first minute of the match. Although nothing came of the opportunity, it was cause for optimism – Barça were leaving a lot of space in wide areas. Despite this early fragility, Barcelona soon settled into their attacking rhythm and Messi hit the side-netting from close range in the third minute.

Using Sánchez as a central striker who could make runs in behind Chelsea's defence allowed Xavi, Messi and Iniesta or Fàbregas, who rotated positions, to try and overload the midfield in the knowledge that someone was occupying Cahill and Terry. Meanwhile, Cuenca stayed wide on the Barcelona right to maintain width.

Chelsea's game plan was identical to the first leg – defend deep, then look to use Drogba or Ramires on transitions. They had a problem after five minutes when Cahill tracked Sánchez and went down injured. Chelsea survived with ten men as Mikel filled in alongside Terry until Cahill tried to play on, only to be replaced by Bosingwa in the 12th minute. The Portuguese defender came on at right-back, with Ivanović moving inside to centre-back.

Like at Stamford Bridge, Chelsea's central trio of Lampard, Mikel and Meireles had a very important role. Their defensive decision-making revolved around two ideas – closing passing lanes and passively pressing. Firstly, if the ball was in front of them and a Barça player was exploring space behind them, the Chelsea midfielders needed to close the passing lane to the player behind. If a *Blaugrana* player received the ball in front of them – particularly with his back to Chelsea's goal and no Barça player behind the Blues' midfield – then the closest midfielder to the ball could passively press the receiving player to force them into passing backwards or sideways. They wanted to direct Barcelona's play into wide areas, where proceedings were easier to cope with than if Barça were cutting through the central or half-spaces. This was not always possible, shown in the 19th minute when Messi and Fàbregas played a brilliant one-two to get behind Chelsea's defence, but Čech managed to save Messi's shot. The probability of Chelsea keeping another clean sheet appeared rather low.

Barcelona were then forced into an early substitution themselves when Valdés rushed out to clear a long Čech goal kick and clattered both Piqué and Drogba. Piqué was unable to recover, so both teams had lost a centre-back inside the first 30 minutes. Like Cahill, Piqué initially tried to continue playing before being substituted – Alves was his replacement in the 26th minute, playing on the right of the back three, with Mascherano central.

Drogba was defending deep, positioning himself just in front of his midfielders with the hope of preventing passes to Busquets. This prompted Xavi to play alongside Busquets when the Catalans built up from the back, creating a two v one overload against Drogba. This gave Chelsea a decision to make – passively press Xavi or let him have the ball and protect passing lanes instead? They decided to continue to sit in their deep shape, let Xavi have possession and work as hard as they could to prevent him passing through them.

With Chelsea blocking through passes so well, Barça looked to use the 'third man' concept to play around the Blues' midfield before passing into a player positioned behind

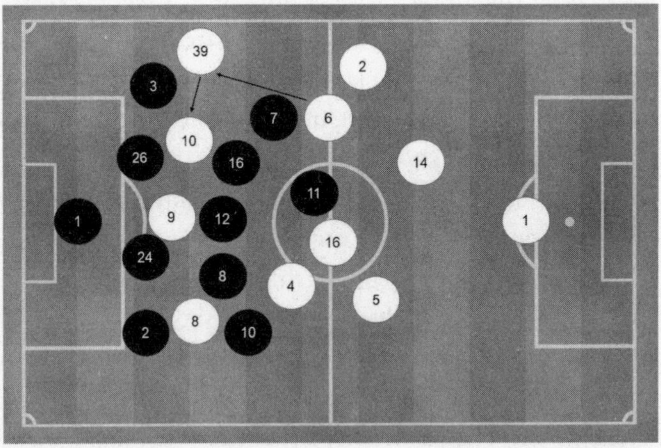

FIGURE 64

it. *Figure 64* shows a combination that Guardiola's men attempted regularly – Xavi would pass wide to Cuenca, who would look to find Messi as the third player behind Chelsea's midfield. However, this move often came unstuck because Cole was dominating Cuenca, winning the ball off the young winger and clearing it away.

All of Chelsea's hard work was undone in the 35th minute when they conceded on the second phase of a corner. Xavi took the set piece from the Barça right, but Drogba headed the cross away. Alves picked up the loose ball, dribbled forward and passed to Cuenca, who had temporarily found himself on the left because of the corner. Cuenca was unmarked, able to receive the ball in the Chelsea box and square it to Busquets, himself unmarked at the back post. Unlike in stoppage time at the end of the first leg, Busquets made no mistake and equalised for Barcelona. After all their hard work, Chelsea failed to effectively defend a set piece ten minutes from the end of the first half and they were duly punished.

Things went from bad to worse for Chelsea less than two minutes later as Terry kneed Sánchez in the back and was red-carded. Despite their clash in the first match, this incident appeared to be totally unprovoked. Chelsea now had neither of their starting centre-backs on the pitch. Surviving until half-time without suffering further damage suddenly felt impossible, let alone winning the tie. Chelsea switched to 1-4-4-1, with Ramires at right-back, Bosingwa at centre-back and Meireles on the left side of a very narrow midfield.

Ramires's inexperience as a right-back was quickly exploited as, in the 43rd minute, Messi played a pass inside the Brazilian for Iniesta to run on to and score past Čech. In the space of eight minutes, Chelsea had conceded twice and lost their captain. They now needed another goal in regulation time if they were to stand a chance of going through. Ramires was yellow-carded in the aftermath of the goal, suspending him from the final if Chelsea were to somehow progress.

Out of position and on a booking, Ramires threw caution to the wind in stoppage time at the end of the first half and managed to score one of the most important goals in the history of Chelsea Football Club. He received the ball in the right-back position after the Blues escaped an initial Barça press. Next, he passed to Lampard and continued his run forward and beyond the ball – what did he have to lose? Mata was wide on the touchline, occupying Puyol. Mascherano stepped out to press Lampard because Barcelona's midfield had been left disorganised by the initial press. This left a gap for Ramires to keep running into and, like he did for Drogba's goal at Stamford Bridge, Lampard found the marauding Brazilian with a brilliantly timed pass. Valdés found himself in no-man's-land – he had come off his line, but not far enough to either beat Ramires to the ball or put him off his shot. With time to look up and pick his spot, Ramires chipped the ball over the stranded goalkeeper and into the net. Having looked dead and buried seconds earlier, Chelsea now led the tie on away goals.

Half-time – Barcelona 2 Chelsea 1

Neither side made a substitution at the interval, but Chelsea changed shape to 1-4-5-0, with Drogba on the left side of midfield. They wanted to maintain their away goals lead for as long as possible in the hope that the Catalans would panic. In the circumstances, it was pretty much all that Chelsea could do. When Inter held out with ten men against Barcelona in 2010, their back four lasted the whole match – two of Chelsea's failed to last for 40 minutes here. Keeping the hosts at bay was going to take a truly monumental effort.

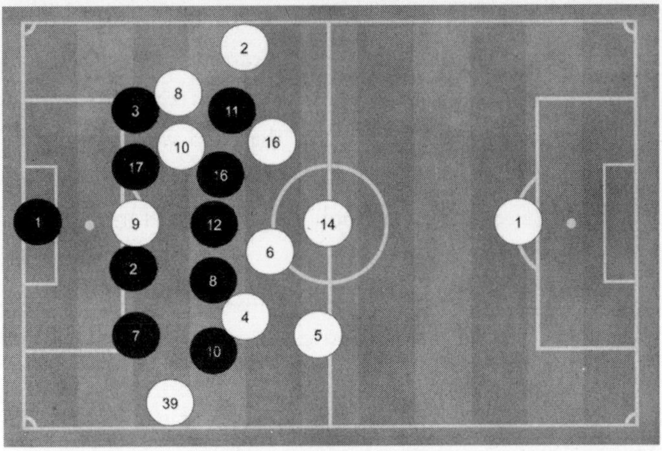

Figure 65

Barcelona moved Cuenca over to the left against Ramires, leaving the wide right area for Alves to explore from right-sided centre-back. Inside of him, Messi, Iniesta and Sánchez rotated occupancy of the right half-space, looking to be as fluid as possible. *Figure 65* shows the two shapes at the start of the second period, with Barça on the ball in Chelsea's half. When Di Matteo's side won the ball, they simply looked to kick it leftward and hope that Drogba could hold on to it for a few seconds before the next Barcelona attack inevitably came.

Drogba was selfless enough to play on the left, but he was defensively vulnerable and it took the hosts less than three minutes to exploit him. He lost sight of Fàbregas in the corner of the Chelsea area as the ex-Arsenal captain played a one-two with Messi. The Ivorian stretched for the ball without checking who was behind him and tripped Fàbregas – penalty. Messi – the most prolific footballer on the planet – was to take, having already scored 63 times that season. Incredibly, he crashed his spot kick against the crossbar and it bounced clear. Though the Camp Nou crowd chanted the name of their hero in the aftermath of his miss, the feeling in the ground changed. Mata was waving his arms around, screaming encouragement to his team-mates, begging them to believe. Amongst the carnage, Ivanović received a yellow card that would rule him out of the final were Chelsea to get there.

Iniesta went into the book for a foul on Drogba, who managed to buy his team a breather and the chance to boot the ball deep into Barcelona's half. Sánchez then headed wide from close range as Barça heaped the pressure on again. The multi-ball system was used repeatedly as the Catalans tried to maintain a fast pace, hoping to tire out the visitors. Di Matteo made a substitution in the 58th minute, bringing Kalou on for Mata. As noted in the first leg, Kalou was a more direct counter-attacking option than his Spanish team-mate. Čech was then booked for time-wasting as he fetched the ball to take a goal kick, with the referee seemingly caving to pressure from the home fans.

Chelsea managed to win a rare corner in the 54th minute and Ivanović rose above the opposition to meet the cross, only to make poor contact on the ball and send his effort wide. Truthfully, it felt like Chelsea needed to take that chance – an aggregate lead with 25 minutes left would have been enormous. Instead, they had to rush back to start defending on the edge of their own box again.

Guardiola made his second substitution of the night in the 67th minute, replacing Cuenca with another homegrown young winger in the shape of Cristian Tello. Tello had been widely criticised for his disappointing display against Real Madrid that weekend, so he was determined to prove a point here. He was deployed on the right, with Iniesta moving to the left. Messi was uncharacteristically booked in the 71st minute. Frustration was growing among the home side as Chelsea edged closer and closer to the final whistle.

This frustration grew when Lampard, a long-term nemesis of Fàbregas, venomously slide-tackled the Barça man and received a booking of his own. Fàbregas was then replaced by Seydou Keita – an energetic box-to-box midfielder – in the 74th minute.

Tello then moved to the left, with Alves on the right, as Barcelona changed to a back two. This mattered very little as every single player bar Valdés was camped in the Chelsea half each time Barcelona attacked. Alves and Tello stayed high and wide, forcing Kalou and Drogba deep to the point that Chelsea's shape practically became 1-6-3-0, with the Ivorian pair acting as wing-backs. Ramires and Cole stayed narrow as full-backs, preventing passes being made through the half-spaces. Both Manchester United and Liverpool had periods of defending deep in the previous segments of this book, but neither of them had ever been forced as deep and as compact as this, especially not for such extensive periods of time. Torres replaced Drogba in the 80th minute and assumed the left-midfield/wing-back role.

Barça had a goal correctly disallowed for offside in the 82nd minute as a winning effort began to feel more and more elusive for them. They were passing from side to side with an air of predictability, failing to create and penetrate gaps in Chelsea's shape. Meireles was then booked in the 89th minute, ruling him out of the final.

As stoppage time began, the ball fell to Torres on the edge of the Chelsea box and he tried to dribble to safety, only to be tackled and the ball sent back into the Blues' area. Chelsea dealt with the cross and Cole booted the ball clear – and Torres was all alone on the halfway line because Mascherano and Puyol had pushed forward. With fresh legs and a 15-yard head start on the nearest Barça outfielder, nobody was catching Torres as he ate up the ground, rounded Valdés and scored the goal that confirmed Chelsea's place in the Champions League Final. Di Matteo ran down the line. Drogba said a prayer. The away end went ballistic. Chelsea had done it.

Full time – Barcelona 2 Chelsea 2; Chelsea win 3-2 on aggregate

The Champions League Final had felt very far away from Chelsea at half-time in Naples, but Di Matteo had restored belief in a team that simply failed to give in. Barcelona used all their technical and theoretical might in pursuit of victory but Chelsea stood firm and, over the course of that second half, produced one of the greatest defensive displays in Champions League history. Of course, there was an element of luck involved regarding Messi's missed penalty, but ultimately Chelsea deserved to go through. Their excellent work across the two legs was sufficiently rewarded. Next up were Bayern Munich. In Munich.

Chapter 12

Final – Bayern Munich 1 Chelsea 1; Chelsea win 4-3 on penalties, 19 May 2012

Despite finishing sixth in the Premier League, Di Matteo guided Chelsea to FA Cup Final glory with a 2-1 victory over Liverpool, thanks to goals from Ramires and Drogba. They had been favourites to win that final but were huge underdogs for the clash with Bayern Munich, who were determined to win the trophy in their own stadium. After topping Napoli's group, they battered FC Basel 7-1 on aggregate in the round of 16 and swept Marseille aside 4-0 in the quarter-final. In the semi-final, they drew 3-3 with Real Madrid before winning 3-1 on penalties at the Santiago Bernabéu. The Bavarians had lost the 2009/10 final against Inter Milan and were expected to put that disappointment behind them with a victory against Chelsea. They needed European glory to salvage an otherwise disappointing campaign, having been beaten to both the Bundesliga title and the DFB-Pokal (German Cup) by Jürgen Klopp's Borussia Dortmund.

Like with Liverpool in Part 2, Chelsea needed to win the Champions League to qualify for the tournament's next edition. Not only would victory make them the champions of Europe for the first time, but Chelsea would also become the first European Cup/Champions League winners from London if they were to come out on top. This was far and away the biggest game in the club's history.

The teams chosen to start the final are shown by *Figure 66*:

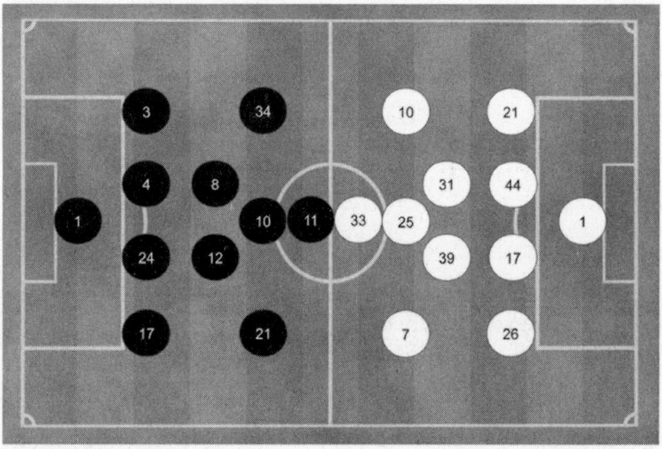

FIGURE 66

Chelsea (1-4-2-3-1): 1. Čech; 17. Bosingwa, 24. Cahill, 4. Luiz, 3. Cole; 12. Mikel, 8. Lampard (captain); 21. Kalou, 10. Mata, 34. Bertrand; 11. Drogba.

Substitutes: 22. Turnbull, 5. Essien, 6. Romeu, 9. Torres, 15. Malouda, 19. Ferreira, 23. Sturridge.

Head coach: Roberto Di Matteo.

Bayern Munich (1-4-2-3-1): 1. Neuer; 21. Lahm (captain), 44. Tymoshchuk, 17. Boateng, 26. Contento; 31. Schweinsteiger, 39. Kroos; 10. Robben, 25. Müller, 7. Ribéry; 33. Gómez.

Substitutes: 22. Butt, 5. Van Buyten, 9. Petersen, 11. Olić, 13. Rafinha, 14. Usami, 23. Pranjić.

Head coach: Jupp Heynckes.

Both sides were weakened by suspensions – Ivanović, Meireles, Ramires and Terry were unavailable for Chelsea, while Bayern were without David Alaba, Holger Badstuber and Luis Gustavo. In the absence of Ramires, Di Matteo handed a first European start to young left-back Ryan Bertrand, starting him on the left wing. This was a brave move from the Italian, but he had faith in Bertrand to provide energy and discipline, with Kalou acting as a more natural winger on the other side. Whereas 1-4-5-1 had been used to nullify Barcelona, the Blues reverted to their preferred 1-4-2-3-1 here, with Mata behind Drogba.

Although thousands of Chelsea supporters had made the trip to Germany, the stadium was unsurprisingly dominated by Bayern fans and it was as close to a home match as a modern-day final can be. The German faithful created an incredible atmosphere, having been promised a fast start by their idols on the pitch. Chelsea survived the initial Bavarian burst forward and Bastian Schweinsteiger was booked for a handball, but by the five-minute mark Bayern had already had two shots and one corner.

Jupp Heynckes's side were a dynamic outfit, combining power and athleticism with skill and precision. Manuel Neuer was not just a very good shot-stopper, he was famous for his ability to use his feet and act as a 'sweeper-keeper', both in retaining possession and defending against opposition through balls.

Captain Philipp Lahm enjoyed a reputation as one of the world's best full-backs, although left-back Diego Contento was less celebrated and started in the absence of David Alaba. At centre-back, the experienced and technically adept Anatoliy Tymoshchuk partnered ex-Manchester City man Jérôme Boateng, who was physically strong in addition to also being composed on the ball. Schweinsteiger was an intelligent and technically strong central midfielder, as was his young partner, Toni Kroos.

Bayern's star players were their inverted wingers – Arjen Robben and Franck Ribéry. Whereas he was a touchline-hugging winger for Chelsea in Part 2, by now Robben was renowned for cutting in from the right wing and shooting dangerously with his favoured left foot. On the left, Frenchman Ribéry liked to cut in on his favoured right foot, often dribbling for longer than Robben before passing or shooting. Thomas Müller loved drifting into pockets of space behind the opposition's midfield line, while occasionally moving wide so that Robben or Ribéry could explore space centrally. Mario Gómez was the side's target man. Known for being both an aerial threat and a clever finisher, he was enjoying his most prolific season in a Bayern shirt.

As expected, Bayern dominated possession and looked to seize the initiative. They would often begin moves with Kroos in a false full-back position outside of Boateng, giving the midfielder room away from Mata and Drogba in which he could safely receive the ball. The Bavarians would wait for Chelsea to shuffle across to shut off Kroos' options down the Bayern left, before quickly distributing the ball to

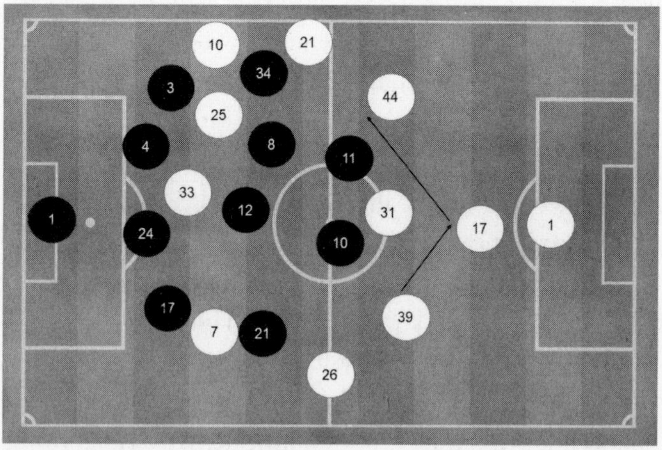

FIGURE 67

Tymoshchuk via Boateng, as shown by *Figure 67*. From there, Tymoshchuk drove forward with the ball, hoping to attract Lampard or Bertrand into pressing him, which would either leave space for Müller behind Lampard or Lahm outside of Bertrand. Chelsea allowed the Ukrainian to dribble forward – Bertrand diligently tracked Lahm and simultaneously closed off the more progressive passing lane to Robben, showing the defensive awareness that Di Matteo wanted to see from him. Lampard worked hard to shut off passing lanes to Müller, before moving forward to press Tymoshchuk once Mata had retreated into a position between Lampard and Mikel, covering the central area. Chelsea, therefore, had two primary defensive shapes at the beginning of this match – 1-4-4-2 when Bayern had deep possession, and 1-4-5-1 once Bayern were advancing in Chelsea's half. Ribéry would wander inside as Tymoshchuk advanced forward but would drift wide when Bayern switched play back across to the left. Contento did not support attacks as much as Lahm, preferring to stay deep and protect the space that Chelsea wanted to counter-attack into via Kalou.

After establishing early dominance of possession, Munich began to build some periods of pressure that Chelsea struggled to escape from. Unforced errors from Lampard and Bosingwa gifted the Germans a corner, one of several in a spell that resulted in Čech having to save a Robben strike with some help from the goalpost. The Blues dealt with the corners, though, showing the same willingness to defend their 18-yard box that was seen in both legs against Barcelona. After 24 minutes, Bayern had enjoyed 64 per cent of possession.

Figure 68 shows how Chelsea adapted their defensive shape to try and counter Bayern's use of Tymoshchuk, but the Bavarians bypassed this change with ease. Chelsea's more advanced defensive shape changed from 1-4-4-2 to 1-4-4-1-

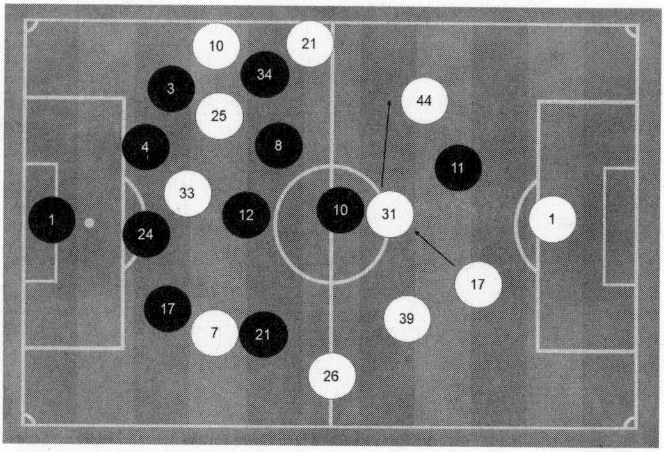

FIGURE 68

1, with Drogba ahead of Mata. Drogba positioned himself between the Bayern centre-backs, preventing Boateng from passing across to Tymoshchuk. It was easy for Bayern to adapt, though, by passing centrally to Schweinsteiger, who could resist pressure from Mata and pass square for Tymoshchuk to move forward and receive the ball. Fortunately for Chelsea, Bertrand, Cole and Lampard were defending their areas well. Müller and Robben consequently began rotating with each other to try and find space, but the pair still found it difficult to create clear-cut opportunities on a regular basis.

Chelsea had two big let-offs in the last 15 minutes of the first half. Firstly, Bosingwa committed a bad tackle on Ribéry in the 31st minute but he inexplicably escaped a yellow card. Bayern were yet to really target Bosingwa's side of the pitch, and if he had been on a booking before they switched attention to him then he would have been in for an even harder evening. Secondly, Robben created a big chance for Gómez in the Chelsea penalty area in the 42nd minute. The Dutchman had successfully moved inside from the right and found his German target man but luckily for the Blues, Gómez skied his shot over the bar. Cahill had been a doubt for the final due to the injury that he suffered at the Camp Nou but, with Terry absent, his presence in the side was necessary. He suffered a slight reoccurrence of this groin problem as he attempted to block Gómez's shot, and it remained to be seen if he would be able to continue.

Di Matteo's men finally managed to establish some possession in the dying stages of the first half, safely taking them to the break with the score still goalless.

Half-time – Chelsea 0 Bayern Munich 0

The players were greeted with flares from the Bayern fans as they entered the pitch for the second half – Chelsea still felt like the away side despite the efforts of their own supporters behind one goal. Cahill was still on, but he was limping. With no natural centre-backs on the bench, Di Matteo desperately needed Cahill to go the distance if possible. The Blues started the second half well, with Mata deeper to help his side retain the ball better in midfield. Bayern changed their game plan and began to attack down their left more, getting Ribéry on the ball against Bosingwa, who had shown his ability to make rash challenges, and the injured Cahill. This left Robben in reserve on the other side should the Bavarians win the ball and look to counter quickly, or if Chelsea blocked off the Bayern left but allowed them to switch play to the right. Chelsea failed to create anything meaningful with their time on the ball and Bayern were the first team to create chances in the second period, with Cole and Luiz making good blocks to keep Bayern at bay.

It was easier for the Blues to sit back and defend rather than try to get on the ball and leave themselves open to dynamic Bayern counter-attacks, so they looked to use Mata and Lampard to play quick diagonal balls forward. The left-footed Mata positioned himself to Lampard's right, from where he could play direct diagonal passes across for Bertrand to chase. The right-footed Lampard looked to play similar passes across to Kalou on the other wing. This did not stop Bayern showing their counter-attacking abilities again in the 54th minute, when Ribéry had a goal disallowed. Cole then made yet another block, this time covering his centre-backs and denying Robben in a central position.

Like against Barcelona, Chelsea were now defending deep on the edge of their own area without offering a consistent offensive threat themselves. In fact, Bayern looked more prepared to deal with Chelsea on transition than Barcelona had been, aided by the fact that Kalou was struggling and Bertrand was not as powerful as Ramires. Čech kept kicking long to Drogba, but he was finding it difficult to protect the ball from Tymoshchuk and Boateng.

Whereas he rotated with Robben in the first half, Müller began to interchange with Ribéry instead, allowing Ribéry to explore central areas. Robben stayed wide on the right, looking to receive the ball with space to perform his signature move – dribbling inside and unleashing a curling shot towards the far corner. Chelsea needed to remain wary of Bayern moving down Ribéry's side before switching to Robben, isolated against Cole. Robben managed to get a few shots off, but he failed to find the target. Di Matteo made his first substitution in the 73rd minute, replacing Bertrand with Malouda. Bertrand had performed commendably on his European debut, but as he tired he found protecting Cole more difficult. Malouda – who suffered from fitness issues in the lead-up to the match – was an intelligent footballer also capable of offering a more attacking threat than Bertrand. Bayern's bench was not as strong as Chelsea's, so Heynckes opted against making any substitutions at this stage.

Cole was booked in the 81st minute, before Chelsea suffered an enormous setback two minutes later. Robben had drifted over to the Bayern left to receive in space, which he did before passing the ball forward to Ribéry. The Frenchman dribbled forward against Bosingwa and Kalou retreated to help his full-back, creating a two v one in Chelsea's favour. Instead of trying to dribble into the box against this overload, Ribéry passed backwards to Kroos, who was in space thanks to Kalou's deep positioning and Contento staying in defence. Kroos crossed towards Gómez at the back post, the big target man attracting Cole inside, leaving Müller free outside of him. The ball sailed over Gómez and Cole, and Müller headed the ball into the ground with such power that it bounced over Čech and into the goal. The German majority inside the stadium celebrated wildly, convinced that they were now European champions-elect.

Chelsea responded with their second substitution, bringing off Kalou and introducing Torres. The shape remained 1-4-2-3-1, with Torres on the right. Defending deep had kept Chelsea level for 83 minutes, but now the onus was on them to push forward in search of a goal.

Luiz was yellow-carded in the 86th minute, before Heynckes made his first substitution of the night. Looking to see the game out, he swapped goalscorer Müller for veteran centre-back Daniel Van Buyten – a back-up who had hardly played in months. Kroos moved forward into the central attacking midfield role, with Tymoshchuk replacing him next to Schweinsteiger. Heynckes seemingly expected Chelsea to play long, central passes, because Van Buyten was taller than Tymoshchuk. Bayern wanted to sit back, see the game out and win 1-0. As he left the field of play, Müller looked up at the crowd and pumped his fists in celebration. The formations at this stage of the game are shown by *Figure 69*.

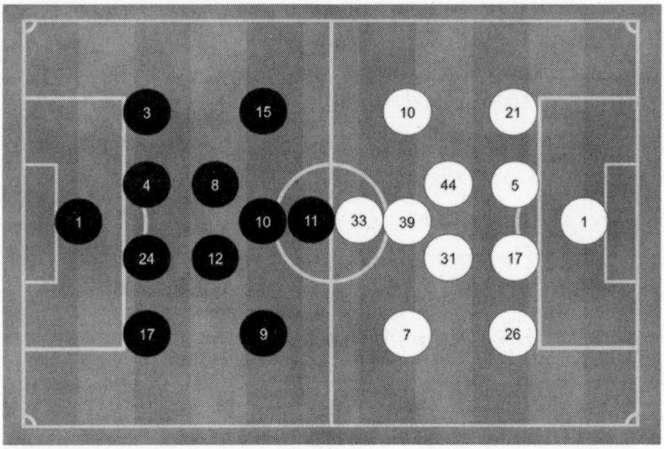

FIGURE 69

With Bayern sitting deeper, Mata was able to receive the ball from Mikel in the 88th minute, turn and pass to Torres on the Chelsea right. Torres dribbled menacingly down the line against Contento and won his side a corner. Instead of taking it himself, Lampard positioned himself in the Bayern box so that Mata could take the set piece with his left foot. Boateng was marking Drogba in the middle of the penalty area, but he was flat-footed as Mata ran up to the ball, allowing Drogba to get in front of him and meet the cross. From the front corner of the six-yard box, the Ivorian powered an incredible header past Neuer and sent the Chelsea fans behind the goal into absolute ecstasy. The player for the big occasion, this was Drogba's seventh goal in a final for Chelsea. After being on the ropes for prolonged periods of the match, Chelsea were back on level terms thanks to one fantastic set piece.

Bayern came forward from the restart, with Kroos and Robben rotating so that Kroos was in crossing positions on the Germans' right-hand side. Chelsea survived though and, willed on by their fans, finished regulation time on top.

They kept the ball better than they had done all night and built pressure well, winning a free kick in the dying seconds. Unfortunately for the Blues, there was no repeat of United's comeback against Bayern in Part 1 – Drogba overhit the free kick and the referee blew for full time.

Full time – Chelsea 1 Bayern Munich 1

As Müller's header found its way above Čech and into the goal, it seemed as though Chelsea's extraordinary Champions League run was finally coming to an end. Their European curse appeared to have struck once more. However, they had survived adversity once again and at the end of the 90 minutes they looked more excited and ready for extra time than their shellshocked Bavarian opponents.

There were no changes at the start of extra time, as both sides waited to see if the other would blink and make a gamble. The Blues started positively, continuing to harness their new-found positive momentum. Torres's directness was troubling Contento as he burst forward with the ball, helping his team to advance up the pitch and establish possession in Bayern's half. Mata still dropped into midfield to ensure safe retention of the ball – it would be a nightmare were Chelsea to lose the ball centrally and be counter-attacked against, so Mata's positioning ensured that they matched Munich three v three in the middle. When Chelsea did eventually lose the ball and this move ended, Drogba tracked back to act as the right-winger because Torres was high and central when possession was conceded.

While this was selfless and intelligent from Drogba, his next defensive action was not as wise. Contento found Ribéry on the corner of the Chelsea penalty area, with Drogba failing to shut the pass off into the Frenchman. Ribéry turned to take on Cahill and Drogba desperately tried to make up for his error by making a tackle. Like in Barcelona, he made contact with the player instead of the ball and gave away a penalty, receiving a booking for his misdemeanour. After being sent off in extra time against United four years earlier, he had now given away a penalty this time around. Ribéry was injured by the tackle and required treatment, delaying the taking of the penalty. Robben was to take the spot kick against his former side, despite missing an important penalty against title rivals Borussia Dortmund earlier in that season. Incredibly, he missed again – Čech dived the right way, blocked the shot and pounced on the loose ball. Chelsea's survival story saw yet another amazing twist. Ribéry never recovered from Drogba's tackle and had to be replaced by Ivica Olić, a powerful Croatian striker now tasked with operating as a left-winger.

In spite of Robben's miss, Bayern improved and pushed forward, forcing Chelsea back into defending deep. The Blues defended their box well, but they still had a problem on their right-hand side. Drogba and Torres rotated the responsibility of being the right-winger but regularly got exposed, leaving Bosingwa to defend against the fresh Olić. Again, Chelsea survived a period of pressure and eventually improved themselves. Torres crossed dangerously towards Drogba at the back post and Lahm was forced to make a good clearance.

Mikel and Lampard were defensively solid when Bayern looked to advance forward through the centre, though their job had become easier now that Bayern were beginning to tire. They made one mistake on the stroke of half-time of extra time, when Lampard gave a soft free kick away. Luckily for the Londoners, Bayern wasted the chance and the scores remained level at the break.

Half-time of extra time – Chelsea 1 Bayern Munich 1

Bayern squandered an enormous chance in the 108th minute when Bosingwa was caught out of position and Olić was free to meet a Lahm cross from the Bayern right. Caught between shooting and passing square to Van Buyten, Olić's volley rolled wide of the Chelsea goal. It should have been 2-1 and it should have been game over. But Chelsea survived another let-off – they were still in it. Olić then fouled Cahill but the referee failed to give Chelsea a free kick, allowing Bayern to attack again when the Blues should have been given a chance to regain their breath. Again, though, Bayern failed to capitalise on the situation. Under growing pressure, Chelsea deployed Torres permanently on the right wing, with Drogba as the central striker as an option for Čech to kick long to.

With Chelsea maintaining vertical compactness and limiting space between their defence and midfield lines, Kroos began dropping deeper to receive the ball in front of the Blues' midfield. This was straightforward for Chelsea to defend – they were able to guide Bayern play into wide areas. Their key task was to defend crosses well, which they did. Robben managed to cut in from the right a few times to perform his trademark move, but his shots were consistently wayward and harmless. The referee made a controversial call when he forced Cahill off the pitch to receive treatment when the Englishman wanted to help his side defend a Munich corner. Fortunately for Chelsea, and indeed for the referee, Torres headed the ball clear of danger.

The last few minutes of extra time felt like a game of 'Defence v Attack', but the attacking side had lost their energy and verve, making the defending Londoners feel more comfortable. Di Matteo was going to make his third substitution in the dying stages and bring on right-back Paulo Ferreira, possibly for Cahill. He changed his mind, though, keeping faith in those on the pitch to survive until the end. Heynckes did not make a final substitution either. Chelsea had one final chance to spring a rare attack in the 120th minute, but Torres was booked for a pull-back on Contento, ending the move.

Full time of extra time – Chelsea 1 Bayern Munich 1

Bayern won their shoot-out in Madrid 3-1 thanks to successful penalties from Alaba, Gómez and Schweinsteiger, while Kroos and Lahm missed. Neuer saved the kicks of Cristiano Ronaldo and Kaká before seeing Sergio Ramos blast his effort over the crossbar. Lampard and Cole were the two surviving scorers from Chelsea's 2008 final shoot-out loss to Manchester United. Of course, Terry was now unavailable and, crucially, Drogba had stayed on the pitch and would be able to take a penalty this time around. The kicks were to be taken at the end housing the Bayern Munich fans, adding to the Bavarian sense of fate – they had the chance to win the Champions League with a penalty in front of their own supporters.

Bayern were to take first, and Lahm stepped forward despite his miss in Madrid. He had taken the fourth penalty in the semi-final but assumed the responsibility of replacing the suspended Alaba here. Although he dived the right way and got a hand to the ball, Čech could not prevent Lahm's shot from hitting the back of the net. Mata, who had missed two penalties earlier in the season, saw his strike saved by Neuer – advantage Bayern. The angle of Mata's run-up was too narrow, preventing him from wrapping his foot around the ball enough to guide it into the bottom corner. Gómez then scored for Bayern with his first good shot of a disappointing evening. Luiz scored for Chelsea, placing the ball brilliantly into the top corner and then, amazingly,

Neuer was selected to be Bayern's third taker. Čech dived the right way but the ball went under him and into the goal. Lampard – Chelsea's usual penalty-taker – scored, blasting the ball into the roof of the net, but it was still 3-2 to Bayern.

Although Čech failed to save any of Bayern's first three penalties, he had shown his ability to dive both ways and, importantly, dive the right way. Olić took Munich's fourth attempt. Destined to leave in the summer, this was to be his last competitive kick in a Bayern shirt. Like with Mata, Olić's run-up was too straight, so he was unable to wrap his left foot around the ball enough to guide it into the bottom corner to the goalkeeper's left. And, like Neuer had done with Mata, Čech punished the run-up and made a crucial save. Cole took Chelsea's fourth strike, showing Mata and Olić how it is done by hooking the ball into the corner that the pair had unsuccessfully aimed for. Chelsea were now level at 3-3.

Schweinsteiger, who scored the winning penalty in Madrid, walked forward to take his side's fifth effort. Robben had not been chosen to take another spot kick after his miss in extra time. Schweinsteiger paused as he approached the ball, seeing if Čech would react and move to one side. Unfortunately for Schweinsteiger, Čech managed to stay still like he did against Ronaldo in Part 3. Unnerved, Schweinsteiger hit the post and Chelsea were one shot away from glory.

The Blues were in the same situation that they had experienced in Moscow when Terry took the fifth penalty in Drogba's place and missed. Now, the Ivorian had his chance to make amends and deliver the Champions League trophy for his team with his last kick of a ball before leaving the club for a new challenge. Of course, he had also given away two penalties in two consecutive European matches but had seen both go unpunished. He took three steps back from the ball as Neuer bounced up and down on the line – the whistles and jeers raining down from the Bayern fans behind the goal. Drogba remained unfazed, sending Neuer the wrong way and tucking his penalty into the bottom corner. Chelsea had done it – they had finally won the Champions League.

Chelsea win 4-3 on penalties

Di Matteo deserved enormous credit for instilling belief and discipline into a side that appeared to have lost both just three months before the final. He managed the second leg of the round-of-16 clash well and overcame a stern quarter-final test from Benfica. He was already adored by the Stamford Bridge faithful for his exploits as a player, but his managerial performance against Barcelona took the supporters' admiration to new heights. Some outsiders bemoaned Chelsea's ultra-defensive performance, but how else were they supposed to set up? The two sides that managed to knock Guardiola's Barcelona out of the Champions League were Inter Milan and Chelsea. They did so by defending deep and making the most of the precious few goalscoring opportunities that they were presented with. In the other two years of Guardiola's reign, Barça faced an excellent United team that tried to stand toe-to-toe against them and they swept the Mancunians aside with aplomb. The Catalans missed the directness of David Villa, but still possessed the world's most dangerous player and some of the greatest midfielders of the modern era.

The brave decision to start Bertrand in the final paid off, limiting Bayern's progression down that side of the pitch. As much as Chelsea rode their luck at times regarding some of Munich's missed chances, that luck was earned – just like with United and Liverpool in the previous sections. Chelsea's heroic defending built pressure on Bayern to score whenever a clear-cut opportunity presented itself. This intensity, in addition to being overwhelming favourites in their home stadium, was too much for Bayern to cope with. The introduction of Torres led to the corner that Drogba equalised from. The Blues then got the better of their opponents in the penalty shoot-out, making up for the hurt of the 2007 semi-final defeat to Liverpool and the 2008 defeat against United.

Di Matteo was given the Chelsea job full-time but was sacked six months later. He won the 2012 Swiss Sports Award Coach of the Year, as well as the LMA FA Cup Manager of the Year for guiding Chelsea to glory in the competition. The FIFA World Player of the Year and the Ballon d'Or merged in 2012 to offer one singular award – Drogba was Chelsea's only nominee, finishing eighth.

Part 5

Liverpool 2018/19

Chelsea's 2011/12 victory did not just mark the end of an era for the London club, it was the dramatic finale of a period in which the Premier League dominated the Champions League. There was at least one Premier League team in the final of Europe's premier club competition in all but one of the seasons from 2004/05 to 2011/12 and it took legendary AC Milan and Barcelona sides to take the trophy away from English soil.

The 2012/13 Champions League belonged to the Bundesliga – there were no Premier League quarter-finalists and Bayern Munich buried the demons of their defeat to Chelsea, defeating Borussia Dortmund in an all-German final held at Wembley. It was a season that opened the eyes of the world to the power of dynamic, structured pressing – something that will be relevant throughout the remaining chapters. Chelsea reached the last four in 2013/14 but were stunned by Atlético Madrid, who then lost to Real Madrid in an all-Spanish affair. Like in 2012/13, the English sides all failed to make the quarter-final stage in 2014/15. Barcelona swept Juventus aside in the final, with Luis

Enrique employing a more direct possession strategy than that seen under Guardiola, notably using midfield players to create space for Alves and Messi in key areas. La Liga's dominance continued the next season as Real Madrid beat Manchester City in the semi-final before overcoming Atlético Madrid again, this time on penalties. This was Real's first of three consecutive titles, beating Juventus in 2017 and then Liverpool – the Premier League's first finalists in six years – in 2018.

After Rafael Benítez's departure in 2010, Liverpool struggled for consistency and only managed one Champions League campaign in five years, coming in 2014/15 under Brendan Rodgers. The Reds finished third in their group behind Real Madrid and FC Basel. Rodgers was replaced by Jürgen Klopp in October 2015, with Liverpool mid-table and in the Europa League, struggling to come to terms with the loss of club captain Steven Gerrard and the mercurial Luis Suárez – the latter of whom had starred in Barcelona's triumphant 2014/15 team.

As Klopp came to terms with the week-to-week demands of English football, it was unsurprising that the club's resuscitation came in continental competition. Dramatic wins against Manchester United, Borussia Dortmund and Villarreal in the 2015/16 Europa League reminded Liverpool and its fans of what the club did best – defying the odds on the European stage. Despite losing the final to Sevilla, experiencing pulsating Anfield nights for himself gave Klopp a taste of what was possible on Merseyside. The club returned to the Champions League in 2017/18 and, as previously mentioned, made it all the way to the final. The highlight of their journey was a 5-1 aggregate victory over Josep Guardiola's Manchester City, who had steamrollered the Premier League, in the quarter-final. Roma were then beaten 7-6 on aggregate before two goalkeeping errors from Loris Karius and a sensational overhead kick from Gareth Bale saw the Reds lose 3-1 in the final.

Liverpool had sold Philippe Coutinho to Barcelona in January 2018 for an initial £105m, potentially rising to up to £142m. They immediately reinvested £75m and recruited Virgil van Dijk from Southampton. After reaching the final against Real Madrid, the Reds looked to build on their progress by bringing in Naby Keïta, Fabinho, Xherdan Shaqiri and goalkeeper Alisson Becker (Alisson).

By February 2019, Liverpool were not just enjoying one of their strongest ever seasons, but one of the most impressive performances in the history of English football, having only lost one league match. They were sustaining a serious title challenge for the first time in several seasons in addition to making it through a strong Champions League group that consisted of Paris Saint-Germain, Napoli and Red Star Belgrade, despite losing all three away matches. The feelgood factor was back at Anfield and Klopp was determined to end the club's seven-year wait for a trophy.

Chapter 13

Round of 16 – Liverpool 3 Bayern Munich 1 (aggregate)

First leg: Liverpool 0 Bayern Munich 0, 19 February 2019

For the third time in this book, Bayern Munich stood between a Premier League side and European glory. Not only did they enjoy hegemony in the Bundesliga (winning every title since 2012/13), but they had reached the quarter-final stage of the Champions League in every season since 2010/11. Despite losing to Chelsea in the 2011/12 final, they had an excellent recent record against Premier League opposition that included three consecutive 5-1 wins against Arsenal.

Of course, they were also an old nemesis of Liverpool manager Klopp because of his successful time at Borussia Dortmund. Although Klopp's former side were offering a significant threat to Bayern's Bundesliga crown in the 2018/19 campaign, the Bavarians still looked solid in Europe. They topped their group unbeaten against Ajax, Benfica and AEK Athens. They travelled to Merseyside off the back of a 3-2 win away at Augsburg, while Liverpool's most recent fixture was a 3-0 win against Bournemouth.

The team selections for the first leg are shown by *Figure 70*:

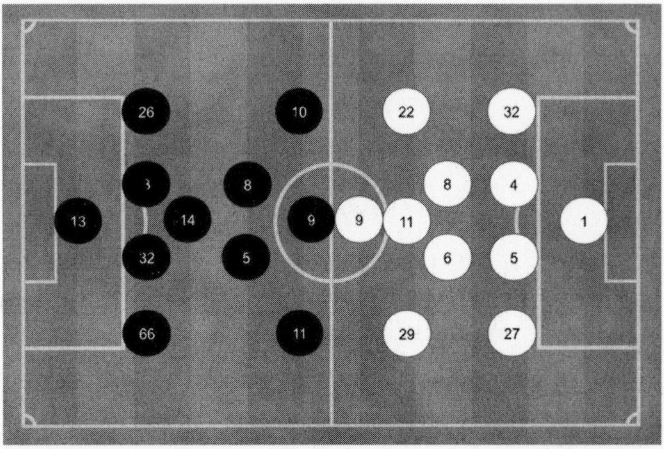

FIGURE 70

Liverpool (1-4-3-3): 13. Alisson; 66. Alexander-Arnold, 32. Matip, 3. Fabinho, 26. Robertson; 14. Henderson (captain), 5. Wijnaldum, 8. Keïta; 11. Salah, 10. Mané, 9. Firmino.

Substitutes: 22. Mignolet, 7. Milner, 15. Sturridge, 18. Moreno, 20. Lallana, 23. Shaqiri, 27. Origi.

Head coach: Jürgen Klopp.

Bayern Munich (1-4-2-3-1): 1. Neuer (captain); 32. Kimmich, 4. Süle, 5. Hummels, 27. Alaba; 8. Martínez, 6. Thiago; 22. Gnabry, 11. Rodríguez, 29. Coman; 9. Lewandowski.

Substitutes: 26. Ulreich, 7. Ribéry, 13. Rafinha, 19. Davies, 33. Mai, 35. Sanches, 39. Shabani.

Head coach: Niko Kovač.

Virgil van Dijk was suspended while Joe Gomez and Dejan Lovren were both injured, so midfielder Fabinho partnered Joël Matip at centre-back for Liverpool. Roberto Firmino had missed training with a virus but was well enough to start in attack. Thomas Müller, Jerome Boateng and Leon Goretzka were unavailable for the visitors.

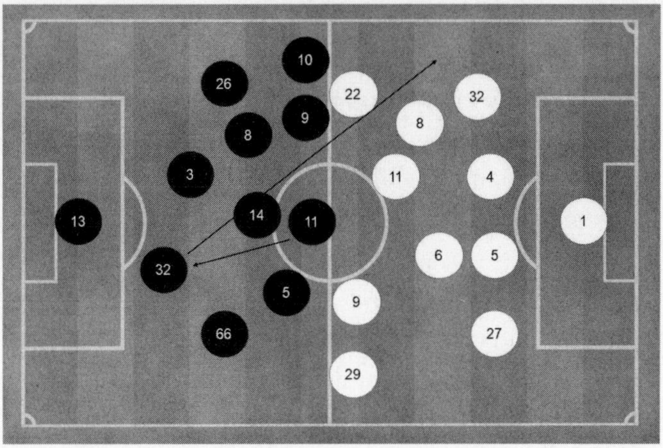

FIGURE 71

The players were greeted by a wonderful rendition of 'You'll Never Walk Alone' that drowned out the official Champions League music pre-match. *Figure 71* shows how Liverpool set themselves up for their kick-off – Mohamed Salah passed backwards to Matip, who was deep to give himself space to play a long diagonal pass across to Firmino and Sadio Mané on the left, with Keïta and Andrew Robertson behind them in support. The Reds battled well for the loose balls after the initial aerial battles, forcing Joshua Kimmich into rushing a clearance that was swept up by Wijnaldum and Jordan Henderson in midfield.

Klopp's side were strong from back to front, even in the absence of their star centre-back. Alisson combined excellent positioning and shot-stopping with an ability to distribute the ball superbly. Young right-back Trent Alexander-Arnold was exceptional in possession, passing and crossing from deep areas to great effect. Left-back Robertson tended to overlap more often than Alexander-Arnold, crossing from more advanced positions. The tall, fast centre-back Matip was partnered by the versatile Fabinho in the absence of van Dijk.

The energetic captain, Henderson, loved to press opponents in partnership with the technically excellent Wijnaldum and Keïta. Liverpool's front three received widespread acclaim for their performances in the 2017/18 Champions League and were now one of the most feared attacks in Europe. Salah and Mané were extremely fast and powerful, cutting inside from wide positions while Firmino looked to drop deep and link midfield with attack.

Now managed by ex-player Niko Kovać, Bayern remained a powerful outfit despite their questionable form. Neuer now captained the team, with adventurous full-backs Joshua Kimmich and David Alaba flanking Niklas Süle and Mats Hummels, both of whom were strong but vulnerable to pace. Javi Martínez was an industrious Spanish international team-mate of Thiago – Bayern's main dictator of play. On-loan attacking midfielder James Rodríguez explored spaces between and behind members of Liverpool's midfield, while Serge Gnabry and Kingsley Coman provided width to attacks. Bayern's star striker, Robert Lewandowski, had a reputation for being a very clinical goalscorer but was enduring a difficult season by his own extremely high standards.

Liverpool pressed Bayern in a compact 1-4-3-3 shape that fell back into a 1-4-5-1 when the visitors managed to progress into the Liverpool half. Bayern played out from the back and initially used Martínez as a single deep-lying midfielder, with Thiago further forward to occupy Keïta. When Neuer or the Bayern centre-backs had possession, Firmino blocked the passing lane to Martínez, while Salah and Mané blocked the passing lanes from the centre-backs to the full-backs. If Bayern managed to play around or over Salah and Mané and reach their full-backs, then the ball-side central midfielder – Wijnaldum on the right and Keïta on the left – would move across and press the receiving player. If Wijnaldum or Keïta did have to move wide and press, then Henderson moved forward to cover the space that they vacated in the middle, making sure that no ball-side Bayern midfielder was free and unmarked. If the Bavarians bypassed Liverpool's press and advanced forward, Salah and Mané would try to retreat and support their full-backs against the dangerous Gnabry and Coman.

Liverpool's high press was terrifyingly effective, convincing Bayern to adapt by dropping Thiago alongside Martínez in deep build-up, trying to attract a Reds midfielder forward and create space for passes through to Rodríguez. Rather than always playing short to his centre-backs, Neuer began to also look long to Lewandowski, avoiding the Liverpool high press altogether.

Bayern defended in a 1-4-4-1-1 shape, with Rodríguez marking Henderson when Liverpool played out from the back. Martínez and Thiago marked Wijnaldum and Keïta in central areas but would pass marking responsibility on to their ball-side winger if the Reds midfielders drifted deep or wide. With this central three v three, Firmino moved away from Bayern's last line into space behind Martínez and Thiago to create a 4v3 overload – initially, he was not followed by either Süle or Hummels because they did not want to leave space for Salah or Mané to run into. When Firmino dropped deep, either centrally or in the right half-space, then Wijnaldum had permission to make a forward run on to Bayern's last line, further discouraging Süle and Hummels from tracking Firmino into midfield.

Kovač's men soon settled into the game, though, and began to retain possession in deep areas once more. Their game plan was clear – they wanted to maintain careful, methodical possession of the ball before attacking via one v ones in wide areas (Gnabry v Robertson and Coman v Alexander-Arnold). They believed in their collective technical ability to execute this plan – keeping the ball in deep areas meant that there was no space for Liverpool to play direct passes into on counter-attacks, but it also meant that the Reds were closer to Bayern's goal if they did win the ball back. Attacking in wide areas was less risky than attacking centrally, allowing the wingers to dribble and look for crosses to Lewandoswki, Rodríguez and their fellow wide man while the midfield and defence stayed back in case of counter-attacks. The Bavarians successfully established control of possession, in no small part thanks to Thiago's excellent ball retention and passing range. The Spanish international switched play to Gnabry in the 13th minute, taking Mané out of the game and isolating Gnabry one v one against Robertson. Gnabry beat the Liverpool left-back and whipped a dangerous cross into the box that Matip almost put into his own net. The Merseysiders needed to be wary of these situations.

There was a chance for Salah in the 24th minute on the second phase of a Liverpool free kick, but he headed wide of the far post. This chance aside, Bayern had settled well and successfully negotiated the first 25 minutes of the match – the first visiting team to do so at Anfield in this book. However, Kimmich was booked in the 27th minute, ruling him out of the second leg.

As expected, Alexander-Arnold operated deeper in possession than Robertson. This helped him to protect the space that Coman wanted to attack, but it also gave him space to showcase his passing range, whereas Robertson was more suited to bursting forward and performing crosses from further forward. In line with this positioning, Salah stayed high and wide so that Alexander-Arnold could only overlap on rare occasions, but also so that he occupied Alaba and prevented him from attacking Alexander-Arnold in support of Coman. Alaba liked to support attacks and was very good at doing so, but he needed to be more restricted here. On the other side, Mané looked to either drift into the left half-space or make forward runs into more central areas so that Robertson could overlap him.

Mané missed a good opportunity in the 33rd minute after Firmino won the second ball following a direct Matip pass. The ball found Mané via Firmino and Keïta, but he struck wide. Neuer should have been forced into making a save, but it was still a warning to Bayern of Liverpool's strengths on transition – they were excellent at winning loose balls and bursting forward at speed. Alisson then made a good save from Gnabry, who shot from outside of the Reds' penalty area after Liverpool had given the ball away cheaply.

The home side lifted the pace of proceedings by getting Keïta on the ball so that he could dribble forward menacingly, with Mané making direct runs that pinned back the Bayern defence. Unfortunately for Klopp's side, their final ball was lacking in quality and Bayern came through this period unscathed, winning some corners themselves. The Bavarians were clearly up for it, shown by Kimmich screaming in Mané's face after he successfully tackled the Senegalese star. To regain control, Bayern swapped Thiago and Martínez, using Thiago to retain possession amid the Liverpool press. Munich reached half-time without conceding – their plan was working thus far.

Half-time – Liverpool 0 Bayern Munich 0

The tie was well poised, with both sides feeling each other out in the opening stages before conceding some goalscoring opportunities towards the end of the half. For Liverpool, Henderson had a good 45 minutes from a defensive perspective, effectively covering the press of his team-mates ahead of him. Both sides had another level in them, but the question was whether or not they would gamble more in the second period.

After playing in light rain in the first half, the players re-emerged from the tunnel to be greeted by a much stronger downpour. Liverpool started the half by pressing aggressively, trying to prevent their visitors from settling. Munich reverted to using Thiago and Martínez as a deep-lying pair to help them re-establish control of possession, while Neuer still sometimes went long from goal kicks to avoid the press entirely. When Bayern did beat the Liverpool press and create chances to play progressively, they opted to either pass wide or to a nearby team-mate, rather than performing riskier passes that could be intercepted.

Their approach was similar to Barcelona's against Chelsea in 2012 – they wanted to defend by retaining possession. Of course, their interpretation of this tactic was less extreme than Barça's and they had two wingers on the pitch to offer a directness that the Catalans had lacked. Bayern were content to play deep and limit the space behind their back line, even with a sweeper-keeper as adept as Neuer. They wanted to tempt Liverpool into pushing their full-backs higher, which would potentially leave space for direct counter-attacking passes for Gnabry and Coman. Liverpool resisted the temptation, wary of the damage that an away goal could cause.

Keïta continued to look positive for the Reds, providing a dynamism that both Thiago and Martínez struggled to match. Therefore, Kimmich tucked in narrower when Munich had the ball, occupying the space that Keïta wanted to run into during potential transitions. Henderson was then booked in the 55th minute for a cynical foul on Martínez.

Filling in well for van Dijk, Fabinho was rarely passing to his left, limiting Liverpool's build-up play down that side of the pitch. So when the Reds played out from their back four, Keïta began to drop in as a false full-back outside of Fabinho, providing a safe and easy passing option that also allowed Robertson to push slightly higher. On the right, Alexander-Arnold and Salah both remained wide so that Wijnaldum could occupy the right half-space and rotate with Firmino.

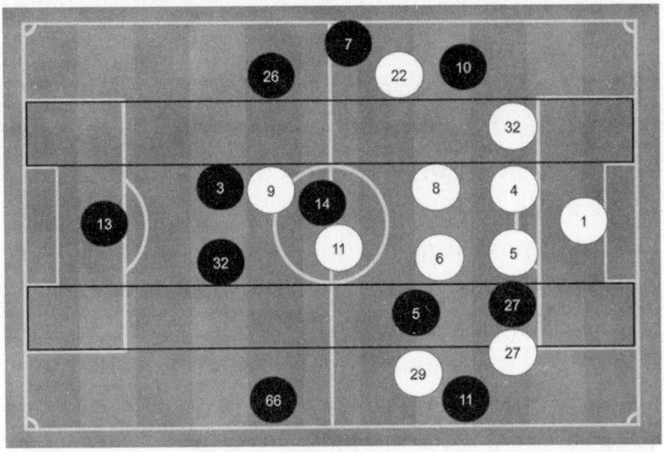

FIGURE 72

Klopp made a double substitution in the 76th minute, swapping Keïta and Firmino for James Milner and Divock Origi. This gave Liverpool a slightly different look in possession, as shown by *Figure 72*. If Liverpool played down their right, Origi would make forward runs to try and create space in front of Bayern's back four for Wijnaldum in the right half-space, with Alexander-Arnold and Salah both still wide. If they played down their left, Milner would move touchline wide and Robertson would stay deeper, leaving the left half-space open so that Mané could look to move into it from wide starting positions. *Figure* 72 provides a general overview of Liverpool's positioning in possession; the aforementioned positions would only be taken up when the relevant players were ball-side. For example, if Liverpool were playing down their right then Milner would stay central so that he was not leaving open space for Bayern to exploit on transition.

Ribéry did not start the match because he had been absent from training for personal reasons, but he was introduced in the 81st minute in place of Coman. Having clearly come for a goalless draw, Bayern were content with the direction of the match and used their final two substitutions to replace tired legs in the dying stages, wasting valuable seconds. Former Swansea loanee Renato Sanches replaced Rodríguez in the 88th minute, before Brazilian full-back Rafinha came on for Gnabry in the first minute of stoppage time, acting as protection in front of the yellow-carded Kimmich. Klopp decided against using his third substitution and his side stayed calm, looking for a goal without overcommitting and leaving themselves open. The two managers settled for a goalless scoreline at the halfway point of the tie, as Bayern became just the second team since 2015 to come to Anfield and keep a clean sheet in a European match.

Full time – Liverpool 0 Bayern Munich 0

Bayern survived their trip to Anfield and gave Liverpool a problem – the Germans had only lost two of their last 26 home games in European competition. A score draw would take Liverpool through, however, and the chances of both sides keeping another clean sheet were small considering the attacking potential on show. As soon as it became clear to Liverpool that they would not win the tie in the first leg, they focused on not losing it. The 0-0 scoreline drew derision from some neutrals and sections of the media who had hoped to witness another fiery European night at Anfield. But keeping a clean sheet in the absence of van Dijk was an important achievement for the Reds, who knew that they had not fully unleashed Salah in the first leg and would hope for better quality with the final ball in Munich. However, Liverpool had not avoided a 90-minute defeat in a European away match since their 2-1 victory against Manchester City in 2018 and Bayern would back themselves to go through on home turf.

Second leg: Bayern Munich 1 Liverpool 3, 13 March 2019

Liverpool endured another goalless draw in their next fixture – away at rivals Manchester United – before battering Watford 5-0. The Reds then surrendered their lead at the top of the table by drawing 0-0 with local rivals Everton, before coming from behind to secure a nervy 4-2 win over Burnley. With the Premier League title race out of their hands, the visit to Munich became even more important to a Liverpool side desperate to win a trophy. Bayern had three league matches to contend with between the two legs and won all of them, scoring 12 goals in the process.

The team selections are shown by *Figure 73*:

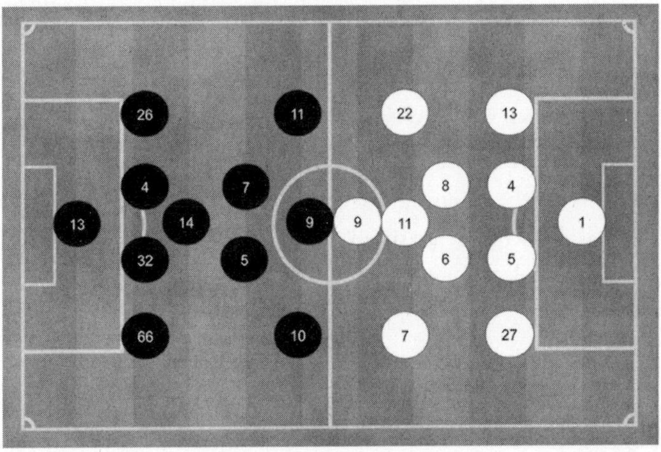

FIGURE 73

Liverpool (1-4-3-3): 13. Alisson; 66. Alexander-Arnold, 32. Matip, 4. van Dijk, 26. Robertson; 14. Henderson (captain), 5. Wijnaldum, 7. Milner; 10. Mané, 11. Salah, 9. Firmino.

Substitutes: 22. Mignolet, 3. Fabinho, 6. Lovren, 15. Sturridge, 20. Lallana, 23. Shaqiri, 27. Origi.

Head coach: Jürgen Klopp.

Bayern Munich (1-4-2-3-1): 1. Neuer (captain); 13. Rafinha, 4. Süle, 5. Hummels, 27. Alaba; 8. Martínez, 6. Thiago; 22. Gnabry, 11. Rodríguez, 7. Ribéry; 9. Lewandowski.

Substitutes: 26. Ulreich, 17. Boateng, 18. Goretzka, 19. Davies, 20. Jeong Woo-yeong, 29. Coman, 35. Sanches.

Head coach: Niko Kovač.

Virgil van Dijk returned from suspension for Liverpool and Milner came in from the start in place of Keïta, who dropped to the bench alongside Fabinho. Bayern also made two changes from the side that started at Anfield, with Rafinha and Ribéry replacing Kimmich and Coman. Müller was still unavailable, but Boateng and Goretzka were able to make the substitutes' bench.

The atmosphere at the Allianz Arena was fantastic, with the Bayern fans creating a mosaic that stretched across most of the stadium. Interestingly, Liverpool kicked off with Salah on the left and Mané on the right. They probably expected Alaba to push forward for Bayern more than Rafinha and wanted Mané's exceptional work rate to curtail Alaba's progress in the opening stages. Like at Anfield, they began the match by using Matip to play a long diagonal pass to the left wing and, once again, Liverpool engaged in a battle for loose balls and won – establishing possession in Bayern's half.

Both sides pressed their opponent's deep build-up, with Bayern pressing with much more aggression and purpose than they had done on Merseyside. Bayern again began the match by safely retaining possession, ruling out Liverpool's chances of a fast start (which they were capable of achieving, even as the away side). Thiago played alongside Martínez to help keep the ball in deep areas. Henderson went down injured in the fifth minute after clashing with Rodríguez. This caused Liverpool to briefly drop into a 1-4-4-1 ten-man shape and defend deeper, retaining vertical compactness until Henderson was fit to continue. Firmino acted as the left-sided midfielder with Salah up front, so that the Reds had a fast striker to deter Bayern from pushing too far forward. This did not stop the Bavarians looking to raise the tempo and exploit their numerical advantage, using Thiago to quickly switch play from side to side, most often to Ribéry so that he could attack Alexander-Arnold one v one. The Reds stood tall and survived until Henderson returned to the field, but he was clearly inhibited by his injury. Salah and Mané swapped wings so that they assumed their normal positions and in the 13th minute Fabinho replaced Henderson.

Liverpool's movements when in possession were similar to those used at Anfield, with Firmino dropping into midfield to facilitate forward runs from Wijnaldum. Milner moved wide when Liverpool had the ball on the left side of their defence, opening the left half-space for potential direct passes to inward runs from Mané. The width of Salah and Mané's starting positions meant that the full-backs stayed deep, protecting space rather than looking to support attacks down the flanks. This width could also explain why Salah and Mané started on different wings to usual, with the left-footer on the left and the right-footer on the right. Regardless, they were now back in their normal positions and looking to pin the Bayern full-backs. Firmino's role was also extremely important on transition if Liverpool played a forward pass but lost the ball, because it was his job to cover for Wijnaldum and block the passing lane between the Bayern player who regained possession and the team-mate that Wijnaldum would have covered otherwise. This prevented Bayern from exploiting what would have been a central overload if not for Firmino's intelligence.

Milner was covering a lot of ground and pressed Rafinha whenever Bayern played over or around Mané. His inclusion also facilitated the in-possession positioning of Robertson and Mané because he liked to either drift wide or act as a false full-back if Robertson was caught in a higher position, whereas Keïta liked to make forward runs himself. He also tracked back to help Robertson defend against Gnabry, which took some defensive responsibility off Mané.

There were no shots on target for either side in the opening 20 minutes – the tie was still a chess match being contested by two teams determined not to blink first. It was evidently going to take a goal of quality to break the stalemate, and it came in the 26th minute as Liverpool took a crucial lead. Van Dijk played a long ball down the left half-space as Mané made a fast diagonal run from the left-hand side. He beat Rafinha to the ball and Neuer rushed out to help his full-back. Mané expertly hooked the ball with the outside of his right foot – sending Neuer to the floor – before chipping it over Rafinha and into the goal with his left. Van Dijk's pass was good, but Mané's turn and finish were superb. Liverpool had their crucial away goal and Bayern needed to score twice.

Having seen his side take the lead, Wijnaldum began to be more conservative with his movement and became a false full-back outside Matip once or twice, rather than bursting forward. Bayern were also looking to play direct passes into space behind Alexander-Arnold and Matip for Ribéry to chase, but the pair had the pace to deal with these passes. Munich would have been better served trying to pass to Ribéry's feet in front of Alexander-Arnold, even though Wijnaldum's positioning now made this more difficult because he could cover his right-back.

Bayern forced an equaliser in the 39th minute and, unsurprisingly, it was assisted by a cross from a winger. Süle played a long pass into space behind Robertson, who was initially attracted forward by Gnabry's good movement – he dropped backwards before turning quickly and sprinting beyond the Scottish left-back. Robertson could not stop Gnabry from crossing into the box and, with Lewandowski waiting behind him, Matip's attempted clearance found its way into the net.

Liverpool still led on away goals, but Bayern had their tails up. Salah and Mané swapped wings again before the restart, for which Liverpool played backwards and retained possession rather than performing their usual routine. The Reds were trying to keep the ball and get to half-time, but they were sloppy and gave possession away several times. Fabinho was yellow-carded in the 43rd minute after losing the ball and taking Rodríguez down to prevent a dangerous counter-attack. Sensing that they had the momentum, Bayern looked to play quickly in search of a second goal before half-time, but Liverpool were saved by the whistle.

Half-time – Bayern Munich 1 Liverpool 1

Bayern finished the half the stronger of the two sides, but Liverpool's away goals lead was intact and they had the half-time break to regroup. Both sides had shown how dangerous their wingers were if given the opportunity to run on to direct passes while the chess match continued all around them. As the rain poured like it had done in the first leg, the players took to the field again knowing that their seasons would largely be defined by the next 45 minutes of action.

At the start of the second period, Lewandowski began positioning himself further to the left, hoping to overload Alexander-Arnold alongside Ribéry and potentially pull Matip away from the centre. Bayern could then build down their left and, if there was no way through, look to switch play to Gnabry on the other side with the similar passes to the one that found him in the build-up to the equaliser. Liverpool's midfield worked hard to shut off the passing lanes into Lewandowski, retaining their compactness well. The Reds were still struggling to retain possession themselves, but for as long as they frustrated the home side then they were in the driving seat. Salah and Mané had swapped wings again, so Salah was on the right and Mané was on the left. Munich made their first substitution in the 61st minute, bringing off Ribéry (who was not fully fit) and introducing Coman. Matip was cautioned in the 63rd minute for a foul on Lewandowski, who had resorted to trying to receive direct passes, hold the ball up and win free kicks because he was feeding off scraps.

Thiago was booked two minutes later as Liverpool began to improve, giving Milner the confidence to make a direct run through the left half-space to receive a pass from Robertson, with both Thiago and Martínez caught on the other side of the pitch. Milner blasted the ball against Süle to win a corner – Liverpool's first real attacking situation of the half. Alexander-Arnold came across to deliver an in-swinger that Neuer punched out for a corner on the other side. Milner took an out-swinger from the right towards the centre of the penalty area, where van Dijk rose highest to head past Neuer. Liverpool had gained a reputation for being a good set piece team (it used to be a significant area of weakness) and this was one of their most important set piece goals yet.

Now in need of two more goals, Bayern removed the defensive-minded Martínez and brought on Goretzka. The Germans began to push higher, but Liverpool were in control of the tie, pressing well and watching as Bayern left more and more space for potential Liverpudlian counter-attacks. Kovać made his final substitution of the tie in the 79th minute, replacing Rodríguez with Sanches as he searched for fresh impetus. His side looked lost, though – their methodical and careful approach to the tie worked initially, but his team found it too difficult to switch through the gears after conceding van Dijk's goal. Coman had some decent dribbles against Alexander-Arnold but they came to nothing, and on the other wing Gnabry was ineffective in the second half because Liverpool restricted Bayern's ability to switch the ball to him. The Reds' midfield had been superb.

Origi replaced Firmino in the 83rd minute, adding more pace to Liverpool's front three as Bayern continued to push forward. Origi played on the left, with Mané central. Sanches was booked in the 83rd minute before Liverpool secured their place in the quarter-final with a third goal. Liverpool played a free kick long to Origi, who received with his back to goal, dribbled infield and then switched play to Salah. The Egyptian dribbled infield before crossing delightfully with the outside of his left foot towards Mané, who snuck behind Hummels and headed past Neuer to send Liverpool into the last eight. Alaba should have done better against Salah – he gave him far too much time to pick out his cross.

The Allianz began to empty and pockets of Liverpool fans began celebrating in the home end. Adam Lallana provided fresh legs in the 87th minute by coming on for Milner, who had put in a very good shift. Robertson committed a needless foul on Goretzka in stoppage time and received a yellow card, ruling him out of the first leg of the quarter-final. Bayern were disjointed and well beaten, waiting for the final whistle to put them out of their misery.

Full time – Bayern Munich 1 Liverpool 3; Liverpool win 3-1 on aggregate

Liverpool went to Munich and made a massive statement. In a battle of wingers, Gnabry and Coman threatened at Anfield without creating a goal before Salah and Mané came out on top at the Allianz. The importance of quality set pieces was made clear once again, with van Dijk's goal taking the belief away from Bayern and all but sealing his side's place in the quarter-final. Liverpool also deserved credit for keeping Lewandowski – one of Europe's most potent strikers – quiet for the entire tie. Going to Munich and winning was a great achievement, but it illustrated that drawing 0-0 in a first leg at home need not be the end of the world. Preventing the concession of away goals is an enormous factor in European success and this tie proves it.

Three Premier League teams knocked out three Bundesliga teams in the 2018/19 Champions League round of 16 and all four English sides were in the pot for the quarter-final draw. After a difficult few years, the Premier League was showing signs that it was capable of reaching the top of the European game once more, but the toughest tests of the season were still to come.

Chapter 14

Semi-final – Liverpool 4 Barcelona 3 (aggregate)

First leg: Barcelona 3 Liverpool 0, 1 May 2019

After defeating Bayern at the Allianz, Liverpool won three consecutive league matches against Fulham, Tottenham Hotspur and Southampton, continuing their quest for a first title in 29 years. Porto – who the Reds beat 5-0 on aggregate in the 2017/18 round of 16 – were then swept aside 6-1 in the quarter-final thanks to a 2-0 win at Anfield and a comfortable 4-1 victory in Portugal. With Robertson suspended for the quarter-final first leg, Milner had successfully filled in at left-back, showing his versatility and reprising a role that he had played for Liverpool in the 2016/17 season. Chelsea, Cardiff City and Huddersfield Town were all well beaten before Klopp's side then travelled to Catalonia to face Barcelona in the last four of the Champions League.

Barça – managed by Ernesto Valverde – had already secured a second consecutive La Liga title and qualified for the final of the Copa del Rey. In Europe, they won their group ahead of Tottenham Hotspur, Inter Milan and PSV Eindhoven before knocking out Lyon and Manchester United with aggregate scores of 5-1 and 4-0 respectively. At the start of the season, Lionel Messi, by now the club captain, had promised Barça's fans that the Champions League trophy would be brought back to the Camp Nou, and the team were expected to deliver.

Figure 74 shows the starting line-ups for the first leg:

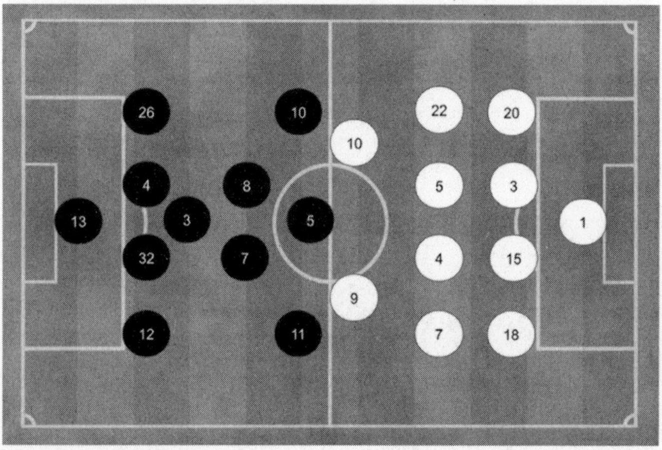

FIGURE 74

Liverpool (1-4-3-3): 13. Alisson; 12. Gomez, 32. Matip, 4. van Dijk, 26. Robertson; 3. Fabinho, 7. Milner (captain), 8. Keïta; 11. Salah, 10. Mané, 5. Wijnaldum.

Substitutes: 22. Mignolet, 6. Lovren, 9. Firmino, 14. Henderson, 23. Shaqiri, 27. Origi, 66. Alexander-Arnold.

Head coach: Jürgen Klopp.

Barcelona (1-4-4-2): 1. ter Stegen; 20. Roberto, 3. Piqué, 15. Lenglet, 18. Alba; 22. Vidal, 5. Busquets, 4. Rakitić, 7. Coutinho; 10. Messi (captain), 9. Suárez.

Substitutes: 13. Cillessen, 2. Semedo, 8. Arthur, 11. Dembélé, 14. Malcom, 23. Umtiti, 26. Aleñá.

Head coach: Ernesto Valverde.

Firmino was suffering from a groin problem and was not risked from the start. Interestingly, Klopp selected Wijnaldum up front instead of Origi or Daniel Sturridge, placing the

Dutchman in an unfamiliar role. Milner captained the side, selected ahead of Henderson in midfield. Keïta also started, despite being benched for the away legs in the last two rounds. In defence, Joe Gomez – who had missed extended periods of the season through injury – started at right-back instead of Alexander-Arnold.

Despite no longer boasting the likes of Xavi and Iniesta, Barcelona were still a star-studded outfit. Like Alisson, Marc-André ter Stegen was an excellent sweeper-keeper, well suited to the demands of the modern game. Versatile academy product Sergi Roberto – capable of playing in defence or midfield – was at right-back, with the attack-minded Jordi Alba on the left. Piqué was partnered by Frenchman Clément Lenglet, who was playing ahead of his compatriot, Samuel Umtiti. The aggressive and physical Arturo Vidal provided energy next to the technically gifted Busquets, Ivan Rakitić and former Red Philippe Coutinho – a talented and creative attacking midfielder enduring a difficult campaign. Messi was still operating at the top of world football and partnered Luis Suárez, who combined intelligence with tenacity to be a persistent attacking threat.

Liverpool used their usual kick-off routine to begin the match, using the deep Matip to play an aerial, diagonal pass across to the left. This time his pass was overhit and the ball went out for a Barça throw-in.

The Reds were brave and pressed high against Barcelona's deep build-up, for which Busquets dropped into defence to form a 1-3-4-3 build-up shape as Vidal tucked inside and Coutinho pushed up alongside Messi and Suárez. This is shown by *Figure 75*, where ter Stegen has passed to Piqué, who then passes inside to Busquets. Wijnaldum has closed the passing lane to the ball-side central midfielder (Vidal), and Liverpool's far-side winger (Salah) has shut off the

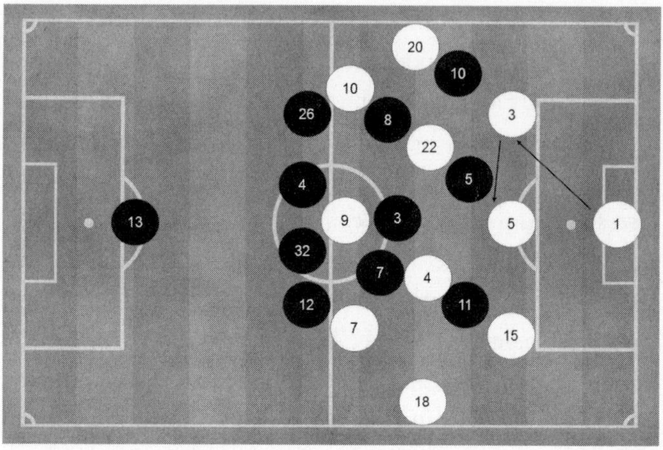

FIGURE 75

pass to Barça's far-side central midfielder (Rakitić), ready to press Lenglet if he is passed to. The Liverpool midfield pushed up right behind Barcelona's, deterring the Catalans from passing into midfield and inviting pressure. Liverpool restricted Barcelona's early possession well, which allowed them to grow into the game.

By making things difficult for Barcelona, Klopp's side were able to enjoy some decent periods of possession themselves, seeking to attract the *Blaugrana* forward before playing aerial, diagonal passes over Alba towards Salah. The Egyptian started the game well, winning duels against Alba, cutting inside and running at Lenglet. The Reds adopted an initial 1-4-3-1-2 shape for their own goal kicks, with Salah and Mané moving central in front of the deeper Wijnaldum. Gomez stayed deep at right-back and Liverpool moved the ball to his side, attracting Barcelona over before switching the ball back inside. As the ball came back inside, Keïta dropped deeper to offer as a shorter passing option. When he did so, Milner would move into a central position behind Barça's midfield, and Wijnaldum would push forward, creating more of a 1-4-2-1-3 shape that forced Barcelona deeper to protect the space behind their back four.

The Merseysiders managed to advance the ball forward with this set-up in the fifth minute before releasing Mané, who attacked Piqué in the Barcelona penalty area and went down, but nothing was given. Right from the start, Liverpool showed a willingness to use possession well themselves, rather than being overawed by the technical ability of their hosts.

As Barcelona settled and began to establish some better possession, they looked to push Alba higher on their left-hand side and occupy Gomez with Coutinho, aiming to form a two v one against the Liverpool right-back. In response to this, Milner dropped back so that Liverpool formed a 1-5-2-3 defensive shape (shown by *Figure 76*) that did not leave Alba unmarked. This appeared pre-planned, considering that

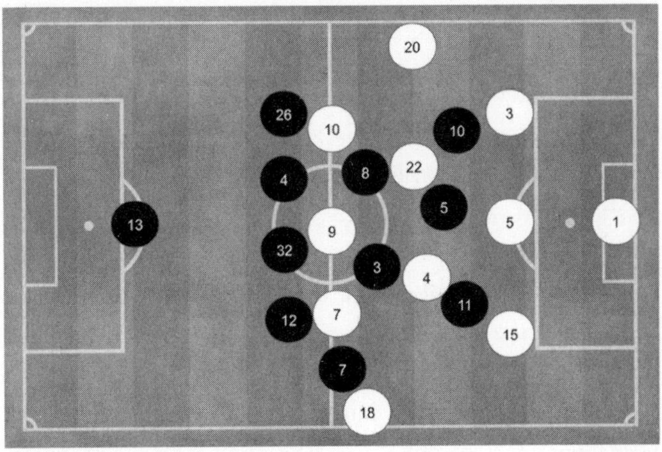

FIGURE 76

Gomez is a natural centre-back and suited a temporary role as a right-sided centre-back more than Alexander-Arnold would have done. While this shape shut off early passes to Alba, it encouraged Messi to move centrally into space behind Fabinho and Keïta, giving Barcelona a central overload over the Liverpool pair if the front three failed to prevent an initial pass into midfield. Concentration and discipline were vital for the Reds, and Wijnaldum occasionally found his defensive role difficult as he tried to operate in unfamiliar territory.

With seven minutes gone, Suárez committed a bad tackle on Milner that surprisingly did not lead to a yellow card. Rakitić then fouled Keïta as the Liverpool man looked to dribble forward with the ball, and he also escaped a booking. Keïta tried to play on but eventually required treatment, forcing Liverpool to temporarily play with ten players and form a 1-4-5-0, with Wijnaldum dropping into central midfield. Keïta was replaced in the 24th minute by Henderson, who came on as the right-sided central midfielder, with Milner moving across to assume Keïta's role. Firmino's lack of fitness was clear, otherwise he would have surely come on so that Wijnaldum could replace Keïta in midfield.

Barcelona took the lead two minutes later as Suárez struck to haunt his old club. The Catalans won possession on their left and quickly switched play across to Vidal and Roberto on their right, who overloaded Mané two v one. Vidal played wide to Roberto, who then returned the ball inside to his team-mate, taking Mané out of the game. Despite moving across after the switch of play, Milner was still too far away from Vidal to close him down and prevent the Chilean from playing a diagonal pass back across to Coutinho on the Barcelona left. Coutinho was positioned outside of Gomez, who was occupied by Messi (he had rotated with Suárez). The original switch of play to the Barça right had forced Henderson inside so that he retained horizontal compactness alongside Fabinho and Milner, which left Alba free to receive from Coutinho when Vidal switched play again. Alba crossed towards the centre of the Liverpool penalty area, where

Suárez had a made a run inside and between Matip and van Dijk to guide the ball past Alisson.

It was a tremendously worked goal, consisting of two quality switches of play, a great cross and a clever finish. Barcelona clearly wanted to overload and target Gomez, while Suárez's rotation with Messi had given him the freedom to drift into the box unnoticed, ready for Alba's cross. Liverpool had settled into the game well but succumbed to their hosts' first quality move of the night.

The goal lifted both the home players and their supporters, so Liverpool had to endure a difficult few minutes. Messi looked in the mood and had some good touches, despite only being used as a distraction for his team's opening goal. The Reds soon settled down and began to establish some periods of possession again. In their build-up, Milner dropped level with Fabinho, and Henderson advanced forward in the right half-space. Gomez stayed deep and Salah remained high and wide to pin Alba, leaving the half-space free for Henderson to occupy as the Reds looked to play into and through midfield. Henderson could look to rotate with Wijnaldum if the opportunity arose, like the Dutchman had done himself with Firmino against Bayern. By staying deep, Gomez could also tuck inside and form a back three with Matip and van Dijk if Robertson advanced forward in support of possession, creating a three v two against Messi and Suárez and providing further proof of why he started over Alexander-Arnold.

If Liverpool progressed the ball down their right, Henderson would move wide and Salah would make inward runs against Lenglet. As this happened, Mané would look to burst forward between Roberto and Piqué, with Wijnaldum dropping deeper. This rotation created a chance for Liverpool in the 35th minute when Henderson drifted wide and curled a wonderful pass around the back of Barcelona's defence for

Mané to latch on to. Unfortunately for the Merseysiders, Mané's attempted lob of ter Stegen went over the bar, but it showed Liverpool's ability to threaten the space behind Barça's back line.

Both sides resorted to playing more direct in the last ten minutes of the half, wary of making any costly mistakes on the ball before the interval. Liverpool now looked to play down their left before making long switches across to the right for Salah to continue his battle against Alba and Lenglet, the latter of whom was booked in the 39th minute for pulling Salah's shirt as the Egyptian threatened to sprint away from him. In the 43rd minute, Messi dribbled against Robertson and was tackled. As the ball ran out of play for a Barça throw-in, Milner performed a well-disguised late tackle and shoulder-barged Messi, provoking an angry reaction from the Argentine, Suárez and the 90,000-plus Barcelona fans inside the stadium. To the fury of his opposition, Milner escaped a booking. The referee got proceedings back under control and both sides settled for 1-0 at the break.

Half-time – Barcelona 1 Liverpool 0

Liverpool performed admirably in the first period and were undone by the half's best move. Barcelona showed what they were capable of, but the Reds had also shown an ability to use possession and create chances for themselves. They looked capable of scoring an away goal, which would change the feeling of the tie completely and panic a Barcelona side that experienced heartache against Roma in 2017/18 after that scenario gave the Italians hope of an improbable comeback.

That away goal should have come early in the second half, when Liverpool won the ball in midfield and worked it to Henderson wide on the right. He crossed inside to Salah, who excellently laid the ball off to Wijnaldum, who in turn squared it to Milner as the Englishman made an untracked run into the box, with Mané occupying Roberto and Vidal getting attracted to the ball centrally. Milner shot well, only for ter Stegen to dive and palm the ball away for a corner. It was a big chance to squander but Liverpool could take heart from how easily they had created it.

The Merseysiders continued to enjoy spells of possession, aided by a lack of defensive effort from Barcelona's front pairing – Messi and Suárez – who were absolved of defensive responsibility while Barça's two banks of four worked behind them. Messi and Suárez particularly allowed Matip to have the ball when Liverpool had deep possession and he took the opportunity to carry the ball into midfield before looking to make a progressive pass. However, he found line-breaking passes hard to come by. Whereas he could normally look forward and see Firmino expertly timing his movement away from the opposition defenders, natural midfielder Wijnaldum was dropping too deep, too early, which restricted the space that he could receive in. Consequently, Matip often had to pass wide rather than through the lines, limiting the potential danger of his passing.

Coutinho was having a poor half against his former club and was coming under increasing pressure from sections of the home fans, who began to whistle him every time he lost the ball. He was not the only Barcelona player struggling, though – Liverpool were on top and looking positive. Milner missed another big chance in the 59th minute, when van Dijk launched a long diagonal pass over Alba for Salah to chase. Salah controlled the ball, dribbled inwards and passed towards Wijnaldum, who left the ball after receiving a call from Milner behind him. He could not fully steady himself before shooting and could only guide the ball straight at ter Stegen, allowing Barça to survive again. They could not cope with direct balls to Salah and were losing the midfield battle too. Valverde had seen enough, so he replaced Coutinho with Semedo – an energetic Portuguese right-back – a minute later. Semedo played on the right of Barcelona's defence, with Roberto moving into midfield and Vidal switching to the left. This was a defensive change from Valverde, who was looking to slow down Liverpool's momentum rather than push for a second goal. The two teams at this stage of the game are shown by *Figure 77*.

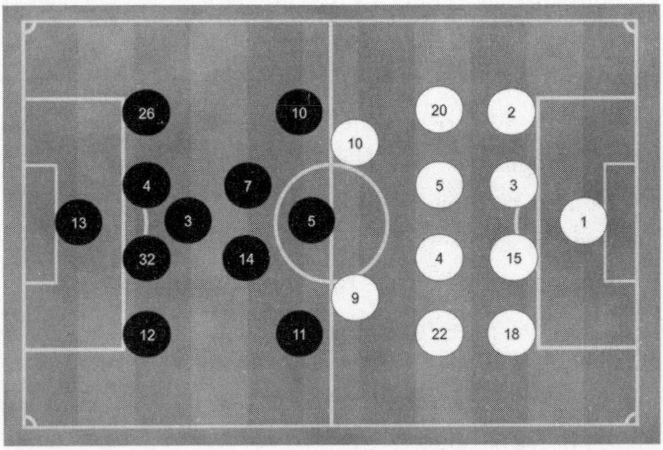

FIGURE 77

Barcelona's build-up shape changed too, moving from 1-3-4-3 to a 1-4-4-2 diamond, with Busquets deep, Roberto to the right and Rakitić and Vidal interchanging centrally and on the left. A distinction needs to be made between this diamond shape and other shapes in this book that have been described as 1-4-3-1-2. Here, Barcelona were utilising a midfield diamond where the four members were able to rotate with each other more freely – particularly Vidal and Rakitić – as well as Roberto at times. In contrast, the shapes described as 1-4-3-1-2 had a single central attacking midfielder with three central midfielders behind them, for example when Kaká operated ahead of Gattuso, Pirlo and Seedorf in Part 2.

This new shape gave Barcelona an overload in midfield, which they exploited once to good effect. Liverpool then dropped Wijnaldum back to man-mark Busquets when Barça had deep possession, creating a four v four. Henderson could no longer move wide to track Alba (remember, he assumed Milner's original role when Keïta came off) because it would leave his midfield partners outnumbered, which created more space for Alba on Barça's left. If the *Blaugrana* lost possession, Vidal had the energy and discipline to move across and cover for his left-back.

Liverpool kept faith with their in-possession system, though Barcelona worked hard to guide the Reds' initial build-up down their right by letting Matip and Gomez have the ball and blocking the central passing lanes. Barça were content to see Salah involved in deeper possession – where he could be pressed by both Alba and Vidal – rather than him being a target for quick switches of play that had already exposed Alba several times. The rotation of Henderson and Wijnaldum became more important, as they tried to rotate and make space to combine with Salah in the hope that the Egyptian could remain dangerous by moving inwards from wide starting positions.

Messi had been quiet in the second half until he capitalised on a moment of good fortune to double his side's lead in the 75th minute. Liverpool had missed three big chances to equalise and been punished. Milner had dropped deep as a false full-back outside of Matip after finding himself on the right-hand side. He attempted a long ball forward, but Barcelona won possession in midfield. Henderson was caught in front of the ball after making an attacking run and rotating with Wijnaldum. Liverpool were consequently outnumbered in midfield and Busquets played through to Messi, who turned and dribbled at the Liverpool defence. Fabinho slide-tackled him from behind and the loose ball ran to Roberto, who had made a run inside, causing Alisson to rush off his line as the ball entered his penalty area. Robertson prevented Roberto from controlling the ball, causing it to trickle to Suárez. The Uruguayan half-volleyed against the crossbar and the rebound fell to Messi, who could shoot into the empty net for 2-0. This Liverpool side were not caught out on transition very often, but they were here.

Klopp then made his second substitution of the night, risking Firmino in place of Wijnaldum, who had tried his best but failed to impact the game up front. Two minutes later, Fabinho was penalised for a very soft foul on Messi, who appeared to simply run into the midfielder. Nevertheless, Fabinho was yellow-carded (as was Suárez for his reaction to the foul) and Messi scored one of the goals of the season, curling in a free kick from 35 yards. It was a moment of pure quality and Messi appeared to have taken a huge step towards fulfilling his promise of Champions League glory.

From the restart, Liverpool went long to their left once again and Barcelona failed to deal with the situation, allowing Mané to win the ball in the Barça area before Firmino had a shot that was cleared off the line by Busquets. Liverpool's kick-off routine, which gives them a platform to show their strengths on second balls, almost led to an away goal that would have transformed the mood in the stadium. It was Liverpool's fourth big chance of the evening and it was incredible that they were still goalless in the tie.

Klopp gambled and made an attacking substitution, replacing Milner with Origi in the 84th minute. He wanted to push for an away goal and hope that his side could turn around a 3-1 deficit in the second leg, which was understandable considering that his side had actually played quite well in this game. This substitution caused a formation change – the Reds switched to 1-4-2-3-1, with Mané and Origi on the wings and Firmino central behind Salah, as shown by *Figure 78*.

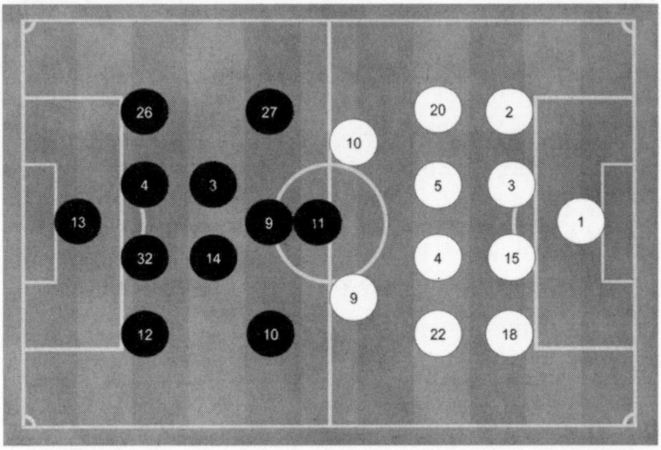

FIGURE 78

Alba was booked in the 86th minute for taking his time over a throw-in – Barcelona were satisfied with a 3-0 lead and were now desperate for a clean sheet. They did, however, have a threatening counter-attack after a Liverpool corner in the 92nd minute, but Robertson – aided by recovery runs from van Dijk and Fabinho – stopped Barça from scoring a fourth. Sensing a chance to keep counter-attacking as Liverpool threw players forward for their corners, Valverde substituted Suárez and Roberto, replacing them with the young and pacy Ousmane Dembélé and Carles Aleñá. The Catalans launched another counter-attack in the 95th minute, with Rakitić bursting forward before finding Dembélé inside the penalty area. Under pressure from

Robertson and van Dijk, the young French winger blasted his shot over the bar.

Incredibly, Barcelona had a third stoppage-time counter-attack two minutes later. Liverpool piled players forward for another corner – Klopp wanted Alisson to go up, but the Brazilian keeper decided to stay back. This turned out to be a wise decision as Dembélé dribbled the ball up the pitch and played a one-two with Messi that took the recovering Henderson, Robertson and Mané out of the game. With just Alisson to beat, Dembélé amazingly shot straight at the Liverpool stopper. After seeing Liverpool miss four big chances across the course of the match, Barcelona went on to miss three in five minutes. They should have made it at least 4-0 and put the tie well and truly to bed. Dembélé should have scored twice in this match despite only playing for five minutes.

Full time – Barcelona 3 Liverpool 0

It is rare that a team plays well in the process of losing by three goals, but the reality is that Liverpool caused Barcelona problems and more than matched their hosts for large spells of the game. The criticism, of course, is that the Reds did not take the goalscoring opportunities that came their way – they should have had at least one away goal to take back to Anfield. At this level, missing several significant chances will often prove costly, as has been shown by some other matches in this book already. Instead of having an away goal or two, they trailed 3-0 thanks to two fantastic Barça goals and one lethal transition that resulted in a lucky rebound. Messi had proven his worth on the biggest stage once again and his free kick sent the football world into a frenzy, as fans across the globe had no choice but to celebrate the greatness that they were witnessing.

Second leg: Liverpool 4 Barcelona 0, 7 May 2019

After losing the first leg, many people began to speculate over whether Liverpool's incredible season would end without a single trophy to show for it. These fears increased across the course of a pulsating weekend that saw Liverpool snatch a late victory away at Newcastle United, before a thunderbolt from Vincent Kompany put the title race back in Manchester City's hands in a nail-biting clash against Leicester City.

The Citizens' dramatic win – which left them three points from the title – took place the night before Liverpool's second leg against Barcelona. Rather than show their devastation, the Liverpool fans gathered outside of Anfield early on the evening of the match to welcome the team to the stadium. Barcelona arrived on Merseyside fresh and ready for action after Valverde had changed his entire starting line-up for their dead-rubber weekend clash against Celta de Vigo.

The two starting line-ups are shown by *Figure 79*:

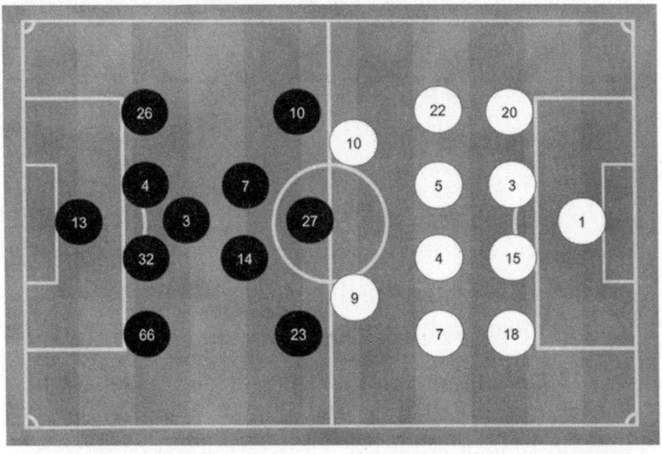

FIGURE 79

Liverpool (1-4-3-3): 13. Alisson; 66. Alexander-Arnold, 32. Matip, 4. van Dijk, 26. Robertson; 3. Fabinho, 14. Henderson (captain), 7. Milner; 23. Shaqiri, 10. Mané, 27. Origi.

Substitutes: 22. Mignolet, 5. Wijnaldum, 6. Lovren, 12. Gomez, 15. Sturridge, 24. Brewster, 58. B. Woodburn.

Head coach: Jürgen Klopp.

Barcelona (1-4-4-2): 1. ter Stegen; 20. Roberto, 3. Piqué, 15. Lenglet, 18. Alba; 22. Vidal, 5. Busquets, 4. Rakitić, 7. Coutinho; 10. Messi (captain), 9. Suárez.

Substitutes: 13. Cillessen, 2. Semedo, 8. Arthur, 14. Malcom, 23. Umtiti, 24. Vermaelen, 26. Aleñá.

Head coach: Ernesto Valverde.

Liverpool's situation had been made even worse over the weekend – Firmino had exacerbated his groin problem by coming on at the Camp Nou and then Salah suffered a head injury against Newcastle. Klopp was consequently without two of his famous front three on a night when Liverpool needed to score at least three times to stand a chance of progressing to the final. Shaqiri started on the right instead of Salah, with Origi chosen up front and Wijnaldum dropping to the bench. With Keïta out for the season because of the injury sustained in the first leg, Henderson started in midfield. Alexander-Arnold replaced Gomez at right-back. Barcelona, on the other hand, were unchanged.

The players were greeted by an extremely intense Anfield atmosphere. The famous stadium had seen some wonderful European nights, but if Liverpool were to overturn this deficit and go through then it would surely top the lot. A positive start was imperative for the Reds, who needed to find chinks in the Barça armour early and prevent the Catalans from settling for as long as possible. Therefore, it was not surprising to see Liverpool press high and aggressively from the off, matching the intensity being shown in the stands. There was a frantic pace to the opening stages, though Messi managed an early dribble that reminded the hosts of his ability to beat players and create attacking situations on his own. He was tackled excellently by Fabinho, though, and Liverpool burst forward on the counter-attack and won a corner after Shaqiri's shot was deflected wide. Robertson shoved Messi's head as Liverpool broke forward on the counter and was lucky to escape with a warning.

As had been the case last week, Messi and Suárez did not work hard defensively, allowing the Liverpool centre-backs time on the ball. This helped the Reds to establish early possession and settle into their system. When the Merseysiders had deep possession, Robertson initially stayed deep, allowing Milner to occupy the wide left space, with Mané occupying Roberto ahead of him. If van Dijk passed across to Matip, his action served as a trigger for Liverpool's movement on their right-hand side, where Henderson would become a false full-back (allowing Alexander-Arnold to go wide) and Shaqiri would move behind Barça's midfield line and into the right half-space, while Origi stayed high to occupy the Catalan defence. The Reds were looking to create a three v two on their right-hand side (Henderson, Alexander-Arnold and Shaqiri versus Coutinho and Rakitić) that they hoped would attract Alba forward to help, sacrificing space behind him for direct passes like the ones that gave him so much trouble in the Camp Nou.

Valverde's side adopted the same 1-4-4-2 defensive shape that they used in the first leg but soon began to suffer because Matip was being allowed so much time on the ball. When the centre-back was able to move forward with possession, Henderson could push higher and occupy the right half-space alongside Shaqiri, doubling Liverpool's presence in the space behind Barça's midfield line. Once again, the Reds were showing a confidence on the ball that would inevitably create chances at some point.

The early goal that Liverpool wanted came in the seventh minute and, unsurprisingly, it was a direct ball targeting Alba that caused it. Liverpool had an unsuccessful corner and played back to Alisson. Due to his positioning on the corner, Mané drifted over to the right-hand side rather than returning to the left. Matip received the ball in a deep area that van Dijk would usually occupy as the left-sided centre-back, finding himself in this position while van Dijk came back from the corner. Once again allowed time on the ball, Matip looked up and played a long pass across towards Mané. His pass was underhit and dropped to Alba, who tried to head the ball back to Lenglet. Little did Alba know that Mané had been lurking behind him, ready to pounce on a backward header. The Senegalese star intercepted the ball and passed inside to Henderson, who had charged through the right half-space. He breezed past Lenglet and into the penalty area before shooting straight at ter Stegen, but the German goalkeeper could only palm the ball back into danger, where Origi was on hand to score. Anfield had lift-off and Liverpool were on the board.

In 2017/18, Barcelona beat Roma 4-1 in the first leg of the Champions League quarter-final before losing 3-0 in Rome and going out on away goals. Their loss from such a commanding position shocked the continent, and while losing to another dramatic comeback was unlikely, this match at Anfield gave them an opportunity to show that they had learned from their mistakes. Roma were helped by their away goal, but their comeback was kickstarted in the second leg by a goal in the sixth minute. A season later, Barcelona had come to Anfield and conceded in the seventh minute, again giving early hope to their opponents. It was clear that lessons had not been learned.

Barça could not settle under the pressure of Liverpool's intense press. The Reds pressed high in their 1-4-3-3 shape,

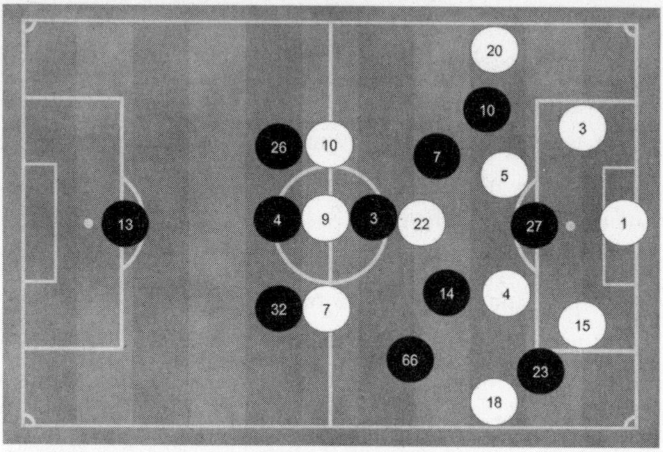

FIGURE 80

as shown by *Figure* 80. Instead of using a 1-3-4-3 shape for their deep build-up, Barcelona utilised a 1-4-2-1-3 shape, with Rakitić alongside Busquets, and Vidal moving centrally behind Messi, Suárez and Coutinho. In *Figure 80*, Lenglet has the ball, so Shaqiri has shut the passing lane to Alba, and the ball-side Liverpool full-back – Alexander-Arnold – is ready to push forward and press should the Spanish left-back receive. This was high-risk play from Liverpool, as Alexander-Arnold left a lot of space behind him and his defensive partners were left in a three v three. Origi blocked the pass to Busquets, encouraging a pass to Rakitić, who had Henderson lurking behind him, ready to pounce. The Catalans noticed this and rarely used Rakitić in deep build-up as a consequence. Klopp wanted his men to suffocate their visitors and make it extremely difficult for them to beat the press and play forward. He got what he wanted – it took 15 minutes for Barça to finally enjoy a period of controlled possession.

Fabinho was yellow-carded in the 11th minute for a strong challenge on Suárez, which was problematic as it removed his margin for error when tackling. Alisson saved well from

Messi four minutes later as the Reds survived Barça's first attack of the night.

Liverpool continued to target Alba with regular diagonal passes, using Henderson to support Shaqiri and battle for second balls, which he did well. If Liverpool worked the ball down their right more patiently, Mané made inward runs between Roberto and Piqué in case the Reds could switch play and thread passes between Barcelona's defence, threatening the space behind them. The Merseysiders rotated responsibility for taking corner kicks at every opportunity, swapping between the right-footed Alexander-Arnold and the left-footed Shaqiri, not allowing Barça to settle and know what to expect.

The Reds could not maintain the frenzied pace at which they began the game so their press became slightly more reserved after about 20 minutes. This allowed Barcelona to improve, but there was no rush for Liverpool – a one-goal lead at half-time gave them a good platform from which to attack the second period, so they needed to defend well and avoid the concession of an away goal before the break. Of course, Barça had been 1-0 up at the halfway point of the first leg, just like Roma had been when they beat the Catalans last season. There was no point in overcommitting at this stage; the Reds just needed to remain in contention for as long as they could.

Henderson fell awkwardly in the 31st minute and injured his knee, triggering widespread concern on the Liverpool bench. Wijnaldum was ready to take his place, but the Liverpool captain recovered to avoid adding his name to the growing injury list.

Messi began to remain central, targeting the yellow-carded Fabinho by receiving deep and dribbling against the Brazilian. Unfortunately for the Argentine, Fabinho was playing very well and he avoided the trap of committing another bookable tackle. Suárez kicked Robertson in the 39th minute and the Scottish full-back was clearly in pain, but he managed to play on until the half-time break. This lessened the threat down Liverpool's left for the remainder of the half, with Vidal using his work rate to protect Roberto well.

Busquets was booked in the first minute of stoppage time for an aggressive challenge on Fabinho before Barcelona missed an enormous chance to score and effectively end the tie. They rapidly counter-attacked from a Liverpool corner before Messi placed an excellent through ball between Henderson and Robertson that left Alba one v one against Alisson. The Brazilian goalkeeper closed down Alba and brilliantly blocked his shot to the relief of the home fans. This was a very significant moment in the context of the tie – a Barça goal on the stroke of half-time would have changed the mood inside Anfield and given the *Blaugrana* players a much-needed boost.

Half-time – Liverpool 1 Barcelona 0

Liverpool got what they needed out of the first period – a route back into the tie. After scoring early, they pressed well throughout the 45 minutes but refused to get lured into overcommitting right up until the end of the half when Alisson rescued his team-mates with some good goalkeeping. The Reds would be attacking towards the Kop end in the second half, which was sure to inspire the players and add to their sense of belief.

Robertson could not fully recover from the injury caused by Suárez, so he was replaced by Wijnaldum at half-time, with Milner moving to left-back. The Reds used the restart to target Alba with another long ball, changing their usual kick-off routine so that they kicked diagonally to their right instead of their left. Once again, their kick-off led to them picking up a loose ball inside the opposition's half and establishing possession.

Milner assumed Robertson's role in possession, meaning that he initially stayed deep but wide as Liverpool looked to attack down their left. This allowed the attacking players to explore the space in front of Milner and look to attack against Roberto.

Alisson made another important save in the 51st minute, this time from Suárez. The Brazilian had proven to be an inspired signing for Liverpool and was enjoying an immense first season at the club. Even though the attention was on his outfield team-mates attacking in this match, his performance was as important as anybody's.

Once they had settled into the half, Liverpool began using their ball boys to exploit the multi-ball system so that they could take throw-ins and corners quickly, maintaining a fast pace. Rakitić was yellow-carded in the 53rd minute for a handball offence, meaning that both of Barcelona's central midfielders had been cautioned.

The Croatian's night went from bad to worse a minute later when his misplaced pass gave Liverpool the opportunity to score their second goal of the night. Liverpool switched play a couple of times after their free kick for Rakitić's handball, moving Barcelona from side to side before finding Alexander-Arnold in space on the right. The Liverpool right-back tried a first-time header inside for Henderson, but he misread the captain's movement and the ball went to Rakitić.

What happens next is a perfect example of Klopp's philosophy and how his side were at the forefront of modern, dynamic defending. Instead of retreating backwards into a more generic defensive shape, the two nearest Liverpool players to the ball – Henderson and Origi– immediately swarmed Rakitić, forcing him to pass sideways to Alba. Meanwhile, Alexander-Arnold edged forward, rather than running backwards. Rakitić's pass was sideways, triggering Alexander-Arnold to sprint forward to pressurise Alba. The pass was also grossly underhit, giving the Reds' full-back an even better chance of reaching the ball. In a 50/50 battle for possession, Alexander-Arnold overcame Alba and then dribbled forward. As Mané, Wijnaldum and Shaqiri advanced into the Barcelona penalty area, Alexander-Arnold performed a low cross that was deflected off the recovering Rakitić. The ball consequently headed straight for Wijnaldum, who got in front of Vidal and fired under ter Stegen.

Not only did this goal typify Liverpool's counter-pressing ability (pressing immediately after losing the ball), but it also rewarded them for encouraging their left-sided central midfielder to make positive runs into the opposition's box. It was this idea that put Milner in the position to have two big chances in the first leg, and it inspired Wijnaldum's run here.

Anfield went crazy as the Liverpool players sprinted back to their own half, ready to restart the match as soon as possible. VAR – being used in the Champions League for the first time that season – decided to check the validity of the goal, granting Barcelona some brief respite. They did not use that time to refocus though, because 31 seconds after restarting the game they conceded again. Their restart was lethargic, playing soft sideways passes and inviting pressure from the rampant Reds. Busquets then found a forward pass through to Messi but the Argentine failed to look behind him before receiving the ball, so he did not notice van Dijk approaching him from behind. The Dutch defender won possession and played the ball forward to Shaqiri, who laid it sideways to Fabinho. Fabinho played a through ball to

Origi, who took hold of possession on the right-hand side of the Barça area. He overhit his cross, but Shaqiri reacted first and passed back to Milner, who had stayed deep and wide instead of overlapping on the Liverpool left. Milner held on to the ball long enough to attract Vidal forward, while Mané moved behind Roberto to occupy the Catalan right-back. This left Shaqiri free to receive a return pass from Milner, with space to look up and cross into the box, where Wijnaldum had been left unmarked between Piqué and Lenglet (the latter of whom was occupied by Origi). Rakitić had left Wijnaldum alone, expecting Piqué to mark the Dutchman and rightly so. Wijnaldum made no mistake with the header, guiding the ball expertly into the net. The left-sided central midfielder had scored again. Liverpool were level and had all the momentum.

Valverde needed to react and repeated his first substitution from the first leg, replacing Coutinho with Semedo. Coutinho had endured a nightmare return to Merseyside and been largely anonymous. Like in the Camp Nou, Semedo came on at right-back, Roberto moved to right-midfield and Vidal switched to the left.

Now level after a crazy two minutes, Liverpool needed to resettle – conceding an away goal now would surely be a terminal blow because the Reds would then have to score two more. Henderson was having a brilliant game, covering across to press Alba, who Barcelona still wanted to use as an outlet on their left-hand side. Matip was yellow-carded in the 66th minute for a foul on Messi, who now had a free kick in a similar position to the one he scored from in the first leg. Fortunately for the Reds, Messi hit the wall this time. Alisson then made another good save in the 68th minute when Messi got in behind Liverpool's defence in the aftermath of a Barça corner.

Messi and Suárez continued to allow Matip to have time on the ball, letting the centre-back dribble forward and force Barcelona's midfield narrow to close passing lanes through the centre. As Matip moved forward, Wijnaldum occupied Roberto and Mané pushed high against Semedo, leaving Milner free out wide to form a three v two overload and receive the ball if Matip was able to switch play. From there, Milner could either look for direct passes to Mané and Origi, or recycle possession back to Wijnaldum, who was having an inspired night. No longer needing to attack as aggressively, Liverpool were content to patiently wait for further goalscoring opportunities to arise.

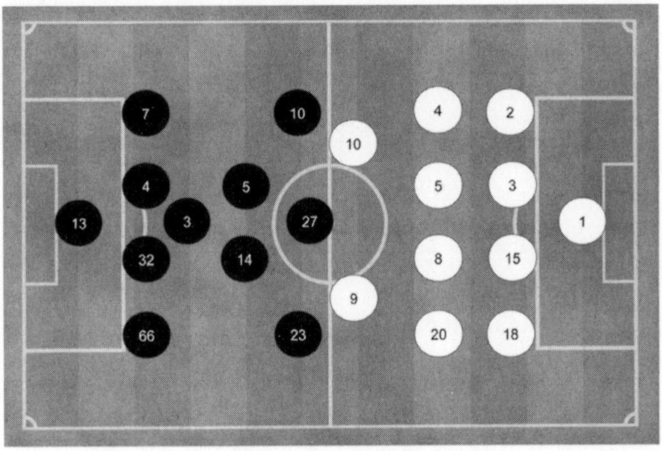

FIGURE 81

Barcelona made their second substitution in the 75th minute, replacing Vidal with Arthur. The teams at this stage of the game are shown by *Figure 81*, with Rakitić on the Barça right, Roberto on the left and Arthur central alongside Busquets.

The *Blaugrana* were set up very defensively, with Rakitić and Vidal out wide to try and counteract Liverpool's wide overloads, and only Messi and Suárez in attacking roles (unless Alba had the chance to burst forward, but he was shellshocked by this stage).

The multi-ball system has been cited several times already for its role in helping sides maintain a fast pace to matches. In the 79th minute of this encounter, it was used to greater effect than at any other point in this book. Alexander-Arnold advanced down the Liverpool right and won his team a corner. The nearest ball boy quickly rolled another ball to the Liverpool full-back before removing the original one from the field of play, which the Barcelona players were clearly not expecting. It was Shaqiri's turn to take the corner, so Alexander-Arnold began to walk away from the ball. The Catalan players in the penalty area took this as permission to temporarily switch off and relax, which Alexander-Arnold noticed. He spotted Origi free in the penalty area, returned to the ball and quickly passed to the Belgian striker, who finished wonderfully into the far corner of the net. The Barcelona players stood horrified, trying to piece together what had actually just happened. Alexander-Arnold's moment of instinctive genius was matched by Origi's fantastic finish, and Liverpool led the tie for the first time.

Liverpool's taking of the lead prompted Barcelona to bring on winger Malcom de Oliveira (Malcom) in place of Rakitić. Liverpool wanted to take off Shaqiri, who had been short on match time before this game and was beginning to tire. However, Origi – who had also put in his biggest shift for a while – had gone down injured and was removed instead. He was replaced by Gomez, who came on at left-back, with Milner moving to the left side of midfield and the tireless Mané going up front as the Reds dropped into a 1-4-5-1 shape. The time taken over this substitution gave the players an opportunity to get their breath back and, in Liverpool's case, focus on the new task of defending their lead. Van Dijk then went down in the 86th minute and required treatment. To the immense relief of his manager, he recovered and played on.

Barcelona began to push forward, though they appeared devoid of fresh attacking ideas. Roberto and Malcom swapped sides, so that Malcom was up against the tired Alexander-Arnold rather than the fresh Gomez. The Reds were content to sit deeper after pressing so diligently for over 80 minutes, placing the onus on the Catalans to break them down. They made their third substitution in the 90th minute, swapping Shaqiri for Sturridge – a technically excellent forward capable of retaining possession well.

Barcelona sent Piqué up front to act as an option for more direct passes forward, with Busquets filling in for him at the back. Liverpool defended well in their deep shape, forcing Barça backwards. Messi ended up dropping deep in the 94th minute – hoping to make something happen himself – but he was dispossessed by Fabinho, who was able to charge forward with the ball and win an invaluable free kick in Barcelona's half. It topped off his magnificent individual performance. Liverpool safely took the ball to the corner on their left-hand side via Milner and Wijnaldum as cries of 'we shall not be moved' rained down the stands. Even the young striker Rhian Brewster, a substitute for the evening, could be seen joining in with the chant from the bench as the clock ticked towards full time.

The final whistle was met by raucous celebrations before the Liverpool players and staff gathered in front of the Kop to sing 'You'll Never Walk Alone' with their adoring fans. Liverpool's love affair with European football had experienced another remarkable chapter.

Full time – Liverpool 4 Barcelona 0; Liverpool win 4-3 on aggregate

Liverpool looked dead and buried at full time in the Camp Nou, but at Anfield they out-ran, out-fought and – with one exceptional corner – out-thought their opponents to complete one of the most sensational comebacks in the history of European football. Messi's promise of Champions League glory went unfulfilled, while the Liverpool fans now believed that their wonderful season would be rewarded with a trophy after all. Defeating Barcelona without Salah and Firmino was particularly commendable, as was the fact that the Reds kept a second-leg clean sheet against such dangerous opposition despite needing goals themselves.

This book has discussed four knockout matches at Anfield – three of which were won by Liverpool when they were not necessarily expected to do so. On each of those occasions, the Reds opened the scoring within the first ten minutes. Anfield is a compact ground compared to a lot of modern football arenas, allowing fans to feel on top of the players and able to impact those on the pitch. Many non-Liverpool fans see the praise that the Anfield atmosphere receives as over the top, but the quality of the atmosphere is less relevant than the fact that it undoubtedly inspires the home players anyway, whether rival spectators think it is uniquely impressive or not.

Of course, Liverpool are not the only football team that likes to start home matches on the front foot, but the club's record when scoring early in European matches at Anfield speaks for itself. The atmosphere was helped by the quality of Liverpool's pressing, which suffocated the Catalans and forced them into mistakes that ultimately resulted in goals for the Reds. Barcelona also appeared to suffer from the same fear of failure that plagued several teams analysed in this book. They had not got over their 2017/18 defeat to Roma and collapsed as soon as another surprising loss looked likely.

Fine margins can often separate winners and losers in elite sport and this was the case here thanks to UEFA's multi-ball system. The Barça players switching off before Alexander-Arnold took *that* corner was unforgivable, but Liverpool were only able to exploit it because they did not have to wait for a single match ball to be redistributed.

Next stop Madrid.

Chapter 15

Final – Liverpool 2 Tottenham Hotspur 0, 1 June 2019

Liverpool won their final match of the Premier League season 2-0 at home to Wolverhampton Wanderers, meaning that they finished one point behind Manchester City and were second in the table. Having only lost one league match all season, Liverpool earned the unfortunate record of achieving the highest points total without actually winning the title – 97 – in the history of English football. Europe now offered their final hope of a trophy.

The 2018/19 Champions League Final was to be the second all-English final in the history of the competition, with the Reds facing Tottenham Hotspur. Spurs' run to the final had been incredible – they survived a group consisting of Barcelona, Inter Milan and PSV Eindhoven despite failing to win their first three matches. Borussia Dortmund were then well beaten in the last 16 by a 4-0 aggregate score, before Spurs overcame Premier League rivals Manchester City in an incredible quarter-final. The north London club beat their Manchester rivals 1-0 at home after City missed a penalty, then progressed by virtue of a 4-3 defeat at the

Etihad Stadium that gave them an away goals victory. City thought that they had won the tie when Raheem Sterling found the back of the net in stoppage time, only for the goal to be ruled out by VAR.

Mauricio Pochettino's side lost the first leg of their semi-final at home to Ajax and conceded twice more in the first half of the second leg before an incredible Lucas Moura hat-trick secured the club's first Champions League Final appearance. Domestically, Tottenham finished fourth in the league, an enormous 26 points behind Liverpool. The Reds had won both league encounters that season by a 2-1 scoreline and they were massive favourites to be victorious in the final.

The teams chosen to start the final are shown by *Figure 82*:

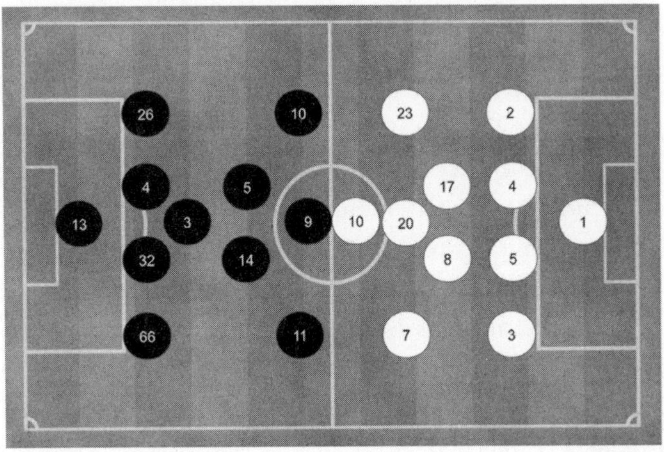

FIGURE 82

Liverpool (1-4-3-3): 13. Alisson; 66. Alexander-Arnold, 32. Matip, 4. van Dijk, 26. Robertson; 3. Fabinho, 14. Henderson (captain), 5. Wijnaldum; 11. Salah, 10. Mané, 9. Firmino.

Substitutes: 22. Mignolet, 62. Kelleher, 6. Lovren, 7. Milner, 12. Gomez, 15. Sturridge, 18. Moreno, 20. Lallana, 21. Oxlade-Chamberlain, 23. Shaqiri, 24. Brewster, 27. Origi.

Head coach: Jürgen Klopp.

Tottenham Hotspur (1-4-2-3-1): 1. Lloris (captain); 2. Trippier, 4. Alderweireld, 5. Vertonghen, 3. Rose; 17. Sissoko, 8. Winks; 23. Eriksen, 20. Dele, 7. Son Heung-Min; 10. Kane.

Substitutes: 13. Vorm, 22. Gazzaniga, 6. Sánchez, 11. Lamela, 12. Wanyama, 15. Dier, 16. Walker-Peters, 18. Llorente, 21. Foyth, 24. Aurier, 27. Moura, 33. Davies.

Head coach: Mauricio Pochettino.

The two sides had three weeks between their last league matches and the final, which gave players carrying injuries a chance of being fit for the showpiece event in Madrid. Salah and Firmino both recovered for Liverpool, and Harry Kane returned from an ankle injury for Tottenham despite lingering debates over his fitness. Harry Winks was also passed fit to start after doubts over his availability. Henderson and Wijnaldum started in midfield for the Reds, with Milner dropping to the bench. This was the first final to allow the selection of 12 substitutes, giving managers more options off the bench. They were still only allowed to make three substitutions in regulation time, however.

Liverpool prepared for the match with a training camp in Marbella, where they played a practice game against a Benfica B team asked to play in the manner that the Reds predicted Spurs to in the final. Tottenham conducted the bulk of their work at their usual training ground before flying to Madrid early.

Atlético Madrid's magnificent Estadio Metropolitano was packed to the rafters on what was a hot, sticky summer evening in the Spanish capital. It remained to be seen how much the temperature and humidity would impact the players and their ability to play free-flowing football, especially as they had not played a competitive match for so long. The atmosphere was fantastic, with both sets of fans belting out their respective club's anthem before kick-off.

Of course, pressure is on both teams to perform in the Champions League Final, but the level of expectancy that had been placed on this Liverpool side was enormous. Including the previous season's defeat to Real Madrid, they had lost their previous four cup finals and Klopp had been beaten in his previous six. The fact that they had already defeated Spurs twice that season added further to the expectation.

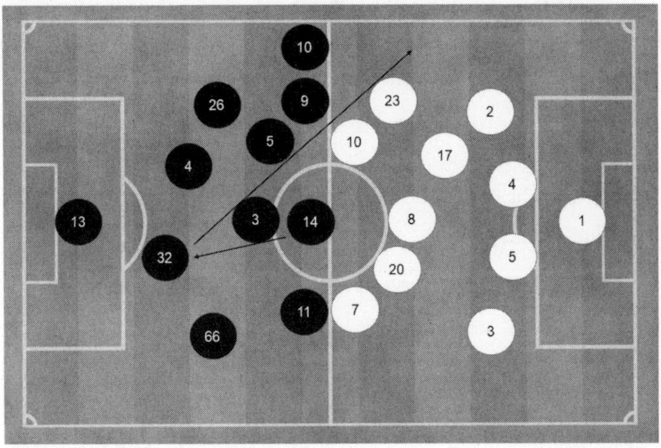

FIGURE 83

Liverpool's setup for their kick-off is shown by *Figure 83*, with Matip deep to receive a pass from Henderson. Matip kicked long and diagonally towards Mané on the left. Although Tottenham right-back Kieran Trippier won the initial header, Liverpool came out on top in a series of battles for loose balls before Henderson played a lofted pass into space behind Trippier, releasing Mané into the Spurs penalty area. The Senegalese star waited for support to arrive, which gave Moussa Sissoko time to retreat and support Trippier. Sissoko raised his arm to communicate with his team-mates, although it was unclear exactly what message he was trying to convey. Only Mané knows if he was attempting a lofted pass across the box towards Salah or if he purposefully kicked the ball at Sissoko's outstretched arm, but regardless, Liverpool were awarded a penalty just 30 seconds in.

It is not uncommon for teams to play diagonal passes to the wing from kick-off, but few teams start matches with sequences more effective than those performed by Liverpool in their 2018/19 campaign. At the start of both matches in Chapter 13, Liverpool used their kick-off to successfully establish possession in Bayern's half. Against Barcelona in Chapter 14, the restart after Messi's free kick almost resulted in an away goal for Klopp's side and their commencement of the second 45 minutes at Anfield saw them win possession in the attacking half once more. Here in Chapter 15, it earned them a penalty and the chance of an early lead. Of course, there is more to it than creating space for a centre-back to perform a diagonal pass. After the initial diagonal pass has been contested for, Liverpool come into their own and show their ability to win loose balls.

When Klopp joined Liverpool in 2015, the Reds were one of the worst teams in the Premier League when it came to battling for and winning these sorts of duels. Klopp – a coach obsessed with work rate and effective transitions – had created a side that was arguably the best in Europe at challenging for the ball after knock-downs and loose passes. The players displayed a hunger to compete strongly in every duel that they contested, showing that effective tactics also require effort and application in order to succeed.

Penalty-taking duty fell on the shoulders of Salah, who had of course suffered controversial injury heartache in the previous season's final. He seemingly put all that hurt behind his strike, blasting the ball past Hugo Lloris and into the net …

This was hardly the first adverse situation that Spurs had faced in the Champions League that season, so they appeared relaxed despite falling behind. They settled well in the aftermath of Salah's goal and dominated possession. Their captain, Lloris, had skippered France to World Cup glory the previous summer and was an excellent leader. Energetic full-backs Trippier and Rose could both support attacks well, while the Belgian centre-back pairing of Toby Alderweireld and Jan Vertonghen were defensively sound and very good on the ball too. The tireless Sissoko partnered Winks in midfield, a clever player with a good passing range. Christian Eriksen began the match on the right-hand side of an attacking three behind star forward Harry Kane, with Dele Alli central and Son Heung-Min on the left.

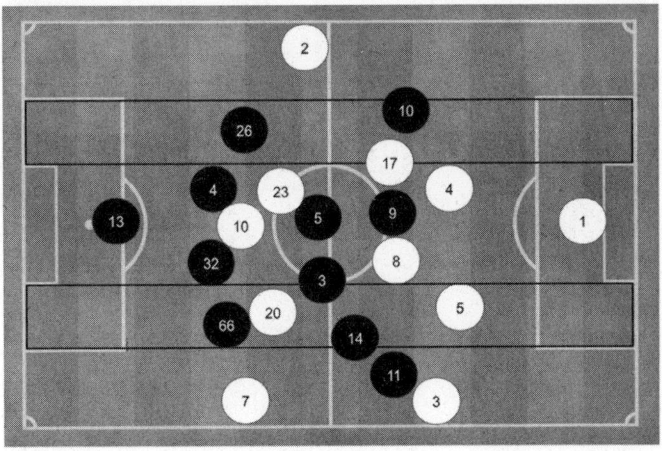

FIGURE 84

Figure 84 shows Spurs' general setup when they had the ball. In this instance, the left-sided centre-back – Alderweireld – has possession, with left-back Rose acting as a short passing option, which Salah allows. Son Heung-Min's initial task was to stay high and wide when his side had the ball, with Dele inside him in the left half-space. Alexander-Arnold stuck tight to Dele, while Henderson blocked the passing lane from Alderweireld to Son Heung-Min. Firmino marked Spurs' ball-side central midfielder (Winks), but positioned himself to Winks's left so that he was also able to intercept passes to Sissoko if necessary. Trippier was touchline wide on the Tottenham right and Eriksen was central while Alderweireld had the ball, vacating the right half-space.

Spurs were happy to build possession on their left-hand side before switching across to their right via Winks, who started well. Eriksen could move into the half-space as the ball moved across, so that Spurs had both him and Trippier in crossing positions. From here, they could look to cross to Kane, Dele and Son Heung-Min, who could attack the centre

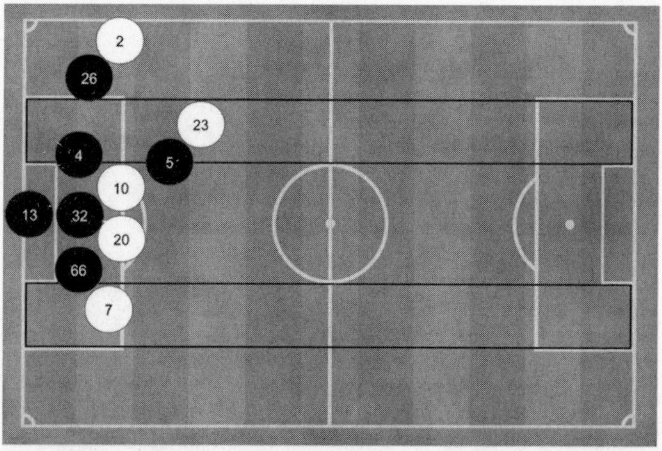

FIGURE 85

of the box as well as towards the far post – as shown by *Figure 85*. Kane was primarily used to occupy van Dijk, who was widely regarded as Liverpool's most dominant defender. This left Son Heung-Min and Dele to attack Alexander-Arnold and Matip two v two.

However, Trippier and Eriksen squandered their side's first important crossing opportunity from the right in the

14th minute. Trippier passed backwards to Eriksen in the half-space, but his pass was too hard and it forced Eriksen to take a touch with his left foot and turn inside instead of whipping a cross in with his favoured right foot. This allowed Wijnaldum to recover and prevent Eriksen from performing a cross, ending Spurs' promising move. The weight of a pass is extremely important at the top level, where overhitting the ball can cost a side valuable split seconds because players may need extra touches to control it, or they may not be able to control it on the foot best suited to helping them perform whatever they want to do next. Quality crossing opportunities are often few and far between in elite football and Spurs needed to be more clinical than this.

Pochettino's side continued to dominate possession and it took Liverpool until the 16th minute to enjoy a decent period on the ball. The Lilywhites then began to build moves down their right, looking to attract Liverpool forward before playing through passes to Son Heung-Min, who made inward runs from the left into space behind the Liverpudlian defence. When the South Korean did manage to break through and latch on to a through pass, he was dealt with by the Reds and the attacking situations petered out. Again, Spurs lacked a clinical edge.

Whereas Spurs wanted Son Heung-Min to make runs away from Alexander-Arnold into space behind the Reds' centre-backs, Liverpool continued trying to get Mané in space behind Trippier – like they did when they won the penalty – by playing direct passes, either in the air or on the ground. Both teams were using their left-wingers to target the opposition right-back, but in slightly different ways. Mané was also giving his opponents a lesson in efficiency. Not only did he win a penalty with his first foray forward, but he won his side two corners in the first 25 minutes by striking the ball against Trippier so that it went out of play.

Why is this significant? Because the subsequent corner kicks were better crossing opportunities than those Mané faced when he initially received the ball. For example, in the 24th minute he had possession on his weaker left foot, with three team-mates in the Spurs penalty area against eight Lilywhites. Instead of trying a hopeful, weak-footed cross towards his outnumbered team-mates or having a speculative shot at goal, he edged closer towards the byline before striking the ball against Trippier to win a corner, from which Liverpool could send players forward and perform a pre-rehearsed set play. Liverpool only had 35 per cent possession in the first 35 minutes, but they had had more shots and more corners than Spurs.

The Reds' first two corners were in-swingers where they crowded Lloris on the Frenchman's goal line. With their third, they appeared set up for another in-swinger before playing short and working the ball to Robertson in a deeper position from which he could perform an outswinging cross. Despite this lack of success, they elected to stick with outswinging deliveries for the remainder of the match.

Spurs' back four began to drop deeper in order to limit the space behind them, which left room in front of them for Alexander-Arnold and Robertson to drive forward themselves. Both full-backs managed a dangerous shot each in the first half without being sufficiently closed down, because the Tottenham defenders were too preoccupied by runs from the Reds' attacking players. Alexander-Arnold and Robertson were vital cogs in Liverpool's system thanks to their excellent passing and crossing ability. Spurs restricted the space for them to cross into, hoping that their shooting would instead be less potent. They were proven correct, but not by much, as Lloris was forced to dive for both shots.

Pochettino changed the configuration of the attacking midfield trio in the 40th minute, putting Son Heung-Min on the right, Eriksen central and Dele on the left. He hoped to use the South Korean's directness to restrict Robertson, while wanting to exploit Dele's aerial ability against Alexander-Arnold. Kane had a quiet half, as did Firmino for Liverpool. Both players appeared affected by the injuries that had plagued them in the build-up to the match. The Reds safely negotiated their way to half-time, putting the club 45 minutes away from its first trophy in seven years.

Half-time – Liverpool 1 Tottenham Hotspur 0

Salah's early penalty separated the two sides after a cagey half of football. Although they were struggling to keep hold of the ball, Liverpool had shown themselves to be far more efficient when it came to manufacturing genuine attacking situations. Both teams looked below their best, which was unsurprising given the gap between this match and the final game of the Premier League season. There was a chance that Liverpool could tire if Spurs continued to dominate possession, but the Merseysiders were a physically fit outfit and their 1-0 lead meant that they could stay patient and invite Tottenham to try and break them down. The Lilywhites had not had a half-time lead in a Champions League match all season, so there was no need for them to panic at this stage.

Firmino had a higher starting position in the second half, looking to place himself next to the Tottenham centre-backs before dropping into the space that he previously occupied earlier in Liverpool moves. He hoped that he would be followed by one of Alderweireld or Vertonghen, creating more space for Mané or Salah to run into. The Spurs centre-backs stayed in position, though, and Firmino struggled to exploit his freedom due to evidently lacking match sharpness.

Tottenham started the second half better than the Reds, pushing Rose higher than in the first half so that he could overlap as Dele moved inside. By playing centrally, Eriksen was able to drop slightly deeper and help Winks to dictate play while Sissoko worked hard to cover them should they lose the ball. They still looked to target Alexander-Arnold with crosses from the right towards Dele and managed to create such a situation in the 47th minute, but Dele's header was a poor one.

Klopp made the first substitution of the night in the 58th minute, replacing Firmino with semi-final hero Origi. Liverpool were creating fewer attacking situations in the second half because their midfield's distribution was extremely poor. Wijnaldum gave the ball away cheaply on the hour mark and was duly replaced by Milner two minutes later. Despite leading, Liverpool were not playing well. Winks was dominating the midfield, showing far more technical proficiency than his opponents. If Spurs could find a cutting edge, they had a chance of turning this final around.

The Tottenham wingers began to play narrower so that they left more space in the wide areas for their full-backs to both get forward on the overlap at the same time. Pochettino then made his first substitution in the 66th minute, bringing on Lucas Moura for Winks, who had put in a good performance but was beginning to tire. Many had expected Moura to start considering his heroics in the semi-final, but he could now act as a pacy alternative against a Liverpool team struggling to perform in the Spanish heat. Moura played centrally behind Kane, with Eriksen dropping back alongside Sissoko so that he could look to dictate Spurs' play in the absence of Winks. Moura looked to drop into midfield also, before receiving the ball and dribbling forward with supporting runs from Son Heung-Min, Dele and Kane.

There was a nervous atmosphere inside the stadium, brought about by the below-par performances of both sides. Liverpool began to look for counter-attacks down their right, where Salah could exploit space left by Rose and cut inside. If he then lost the ball, Origi could use his fresh legs to rush across to the right wing and cover for his Egyptian team-mate. Milner missed a chance to double Liverpool's lead in the 69th minute after an excellent run from Mané, who still looked the most dangerous player on the pitch.

Spurs made their second substitution in the 74th minute, introducing Dier in place of Sissoko, who had pulled up with a muscle problem. Trippier and Rose had also gone down with issues, which was significant because Pochettino had substituted his two full-backs in both legs of the semi-final. Now, at least one of them would have to last the full match.

Liverpool changed formation to 1-4-4-1-1, with Milner on the right and Origi behind Salah as they looked to retain their compactness and protect their lead. Salah was exhausted so he was placed up front to take as much defensive responsibility away from him as possible. The Reds looked to find Origi, who was then tasked with threading through balls through to Salah – similar to the setup of Dwight Yorke and Andy Cole against Juventus in Chapter 2. Origi's passes were wayward, though, gifting possession back to a Spurs side now desperate for an equaliser. Tottenham were still enjoying the lion's share of the ball, but clear-cut chances remained hard to come by. They found Dele with a cross to the back post in the 80th minute, but he headed over the bar. Moura then shot tamely at Alisson from within the penalty area – it was a chance that he should have done better with.

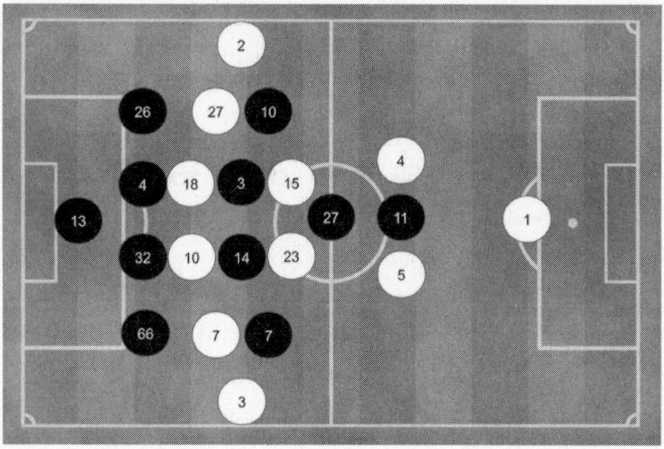

FIGURE 86

The Lilywhites made their third substitution in the 81st minute, replacing Dele with Fernando Llorente – a tall target man who had wreaked havoc on Ajax's defence in the second leg of the semi-final. With this change, Spurs switched to 1-4-4-2 with Moura on the right and Son Heung-Min on the left, as shown by *Figure 86*. Alisson then saved well from an Eriksen free kick in the 83rd minute as the clock began to tick away against Tottenham.

Robertson stormed down the Liverpool left in the 86th minute, aided by Mané making an inward run forward that pinned back the Spurs defence. The Scottish left-back then crossed in search of Salah at the back post, but Rose cleared the ball out for a Liverpool corner. Milner went across to take an out-swinger, with Alexander-Arnold staying deeper, ready for both a potential second phase to the set piece or a Spurs counter-attack. There was indeed a second phase to the corner, but it took place inside the penalty area. After Spurs failed to clear the ball away following the initial delivery, the ball dropped to Matip, who cleverly flicked the ball to Origi on his left. The Belgian took the ball on to his left foot with an excellent first touch before striking across Lloris and into the far bottom corner of the goal.

Throughout this book, we have seen several important goals scored on second phases of set pieces after nothing had come of the initial delivery. It is unsurprising that a team as good at challenging for second balls as Liverpool was also adept at dominating second phases, where players compete for loose balls and ricochets. It is also important for defending sides to track opposition players beyond the initial phase, something that Spurs failed to do here. Origi was unmarked because no Tottenham player was aware of him as they pushed out and tried to clear the ball.

The Liverpool fans inside the stadium went ballistic at the sight of the ball hitting the back of the net – the hurt of the previous season could be forgotten and the disappointment at losing out on the Premier League title by just one point suddenly lost its impact. Origi did not have a Champions League goal to his name before the semi-final against Barcelona, but now he had scored three in two games – three of the most legendary goals in the history of Liverpool Football Club at that. After a poor overall performance, Liverpool had been efficient and clinical when it mattered the most, capitalising on two key attacking moments at different ends of the game.

Determined to stay focused and see the rest of the game out properly, Klopp made his final substitution in the 90th minute, replacing Mané with Gomez. The Senegalese star had been brilliant in both the semi-final and the final despite not scoring in either tie, thoroughly deserving the round of applause that he received as he left the pitch. Gomez came on at right-back, with Alexander-Arnold on the right of midfield and Milner moving to the left.

Alisson saved a stoppage-time shot from Son Heung-Min, but the game was effectively over. Spurs began to play long balls forward, something that Liverpool could deal with easily. Liverpool's substitutes and backroom staff flooded the pitch upon the full-time whistle, celebrating the Reds' return to their beloved European perch.

Full time – Liverpool 2 Tottenham Hotspur 0

Returning Liverpool to the summit of European football was a wonderful achievement for Klopp, who finally had his Champions League winner's medal after two previous final defeats. He had transformed a club that was desperately soul-searching when he entered it less than four years beforehand, creating a winning machine adored by a fanbase that had been starved of major success in recent seasons. The culture that he had instilled at the club is best represented by the semi-final comeback against Barcelona, where the players and fans came together and simply refused to get knocked out by their Catalan opponents. Although they were not great in the final, his players showed how far they had come as a team by getting over the line despite not playing to their full potential.

This win was Liverpool's sixth European Cup/Champions League title. The other 19 clubs in the 2018/19 Premier League had four between them. After seven years without a major European title, the Premier League was back on its throne – a position consolidated further by the fact that the 2018/19 Europa League Final was also an all-Premier League affair, with Chelsea defeating Arsenal. Liverpool embodied how the league had developed technically and tactically, catching up with the continental rivals that dominated European competitions between 2013 and 2018. Although the final was not particularly entertaining for neutrals, Liverpool reached it by defeating the champions of France, Germany and Spain. Overall, their title was certainly well earned.

As much as certain fundamentals have featured in every part of this book, such as compactness when defending and challenging for second balls, the matches played by Liverpool in Part 5 were noticeably different from those involving Manchester United in Part 1. In the 1999 knockout stages, United faced two sides that employed systems deeply embedded in their respective nations' football culture, featuring strict man-marking and a sweeper. United themselves, of course, employed a 1-4-4-2 that was commonplace in England at the time. The Mancunian outfit's European triumph came just a few months after Ralf Rangnick – a young German coach working in his country's second division – was derided in his homeland for promoting a futuristic style of football that consisted of things like zonal marking and more intense, organised pressing (including counter-pressing) in high areas, rather than man-marking across the pitch and using deep-lying sweepers. By 2013 he had generally been proven correct, as two counter-pressing German sides stunned technically gifted La Liga opponents to set up an all-Bundesliga Champions League Final.

By 2019, pressing in elite-level football had become so refined that teams needed to be more wary of how they could be exploited when they actually had the ball themselves. Remember, for example, how Bayern carefully retained possession before playing wide into one v one situations, rather than playing more expansively and risking exposing themselves to both Liverpool's press and their ability to transition effectively. Alternatively, consider Liverpool's use of Firmino away at Bayern, positioning him ready to prevent passes into midfield while his side still had the ball. Teams now must simultaneously create space for what they want to do with the ball *and* prepare themselves for losing it – and in a way, that is more specific than in past eras. *Trequartisti* that can operate with minimal defensive responsibility are now few and far between.

Unsurprisingly, the earliest effective in-possession solutions to the German-inspired pressing and counter-pressing of the early 2010s came from La Liga. For example, when Barcelona won the 2014/15 Champions League, they used the right-sided central midfielder – Rakitić – to form a rotating triangle with right-back Alves and right-winger Messi. Rakitić both created space for his team-mates' attacking movements and protected space that the opposition wanted to counter into. Time progressed, ideas spread and Barcelona then faced a similar structure in 2019, where Henderson's movements were performed in relation to those of Alexander-Arnold and Shaqiri, using the Liverpool captain's energy and tenacity to win loose balls and provide protection on transition. Henderson's movement also allowed Alexander-Arnold to assume positions from which he could show off his immense passing range, rather than simply overlapping and crossing from high areas like a lot of modern full-backs do. Liverpool could therefore play more direct passes when necessary, especially to Mané. In 2018/19, Klopp's Liverpool combined German pressing with elements of Spanish positional play and, when required, stereotypical English directness. His side epitomised many elements of the modern game that his compatriot, Rangnick, had been mocked for promoting two decades beforehand.

Goalkeepers capable of playing outside of their box and taking part in phases of possession had been around, in some form or another, for decades by 2019. However, few have been as adept at the role as Alisson, who played an indispensable role in Liverpool's run to European glory. As methods of playing out from the back have developed, goalkeepers have been forced to evolve *en masse*, while still being capable of performing the goalkeeping basics such as shot-stopping and dealing with crosses. Alisson's distribution was excellent throughout the 2018/19 campaign, while he also made important saves in big moments to keep his side in the competition.

The role of centre-backs has changed dramatically too. They have also become more important in possession, shown by Matip's importance against Barcelona and van Dijk's assist against Bayern. Defensively, the pair displayed the pace and game intelligence required to play in teams that press high, especially against Barcelona. The demands placed on Matip and van Dijk were extremely different to those on the likes of Stam, Hyypiä, Vidić and Cahill in previous parts of this book, who spent more time defending in deeper positions.

Salah and Mané acted as more than mere inverted wingers, but as all-rounders capable of contributing to their side's press and also maintaining excellent levels of offensive efficiency. Mané's performance in the final serves as the perfect example of this – he won a penalty, forced Spurs into conceding corners that created high-quality crossing opportunities, and worked tirelessly for his side off the ball. Although he was not at his best in the final, Firmino also played his part in Liverpool's run and was defensively important away at Bayern.

Klopp won several individual honours in 2019 as a result of his success with Liverpool. He was the German Football Manager of the Year, the Onze d'Or Coach of the Year, the IFFHS World's Best Club Coach, the Best FIFA Men's Coach, the World Soccer Awards World Manager of the Year and the Globe Soccer Awards Best Coach of the Year. He was also inducted into the LMA Hall of Fame.

Van Dijk finished second in both the 2019 Ballon d'Or and Best FIFA Men's Player awards. Mané finished fourth in the Ballon d'Or vote, with Salah fifth and Alisson seventh. Firmino, Alexander-Arnold and Wijnaldum also made the shortlist. Salah was fourth in the Best FIFA Men's Player awards, with Mané fifth. Alisson was named the 2019 Best FIFA Men's Goalkeeper.

So, where will the next two decades take football? Liverpool ended the 2010s as the champions of Europe, but they had needed a German coach to do so. The 2020s began with another German – Hans-Dieter Flick – taking Bayern Munich to the Champions League title after defeating Thomas Tuchel, also of Germany, in the final. None of these three coaches favours a playing style remotely comparable to that used in the German game in the 1990s, showing how their nation's footballing ideology has changed. Of course, the future of football does not belong exclusively to German coaches, nor to those from Spain, Portugal, Italy or the Netherlands, whose styles created the necessity for the more organised and tactically dynamic game that we watch currently. Football's advancement will be a global effort and, as the world's richest domestic competition, the Premier League is well placed to take advantage of future development and innovation.

In this book, we have seen Premier League managers guide their respective teams to European glory despite facing a multitude of interesting tactical challenges. There can be no doubt that the honour of sitting on the throne of European club football is always well earned. I hope that this book has helped you to appreciate those that have managed to reach the summit, as well as inspiring you to study those aiming to replicate their success.